Civil War Voices from York County, Pa.

Remembering the Rebellion and the Gettysburg Campaign

By Scott L. Mingus Sr. and James McClure

Foreword by Dr. Mark A. Snell

©2011 — all rights reserved

Publisher

COLECRAFT INDUSTRIES
970 Mt. Carmel Road
Orrtanna, PA 17353
Website: colecraftbooks.com
e-mail: colecraftbooks@embarqmail.com

Copyright © 2011 by Scott L. Mingus, Sr. and James McClure

The authors wish to thank the York County Heritage Trust and its staff, Pennsylvania Civil War 150, and the *York Daily Record/Sunday News*, coordinators on this project, for their gracious support. We also extend our gratitude to the many people in York County and the surrounding region who freely gave us transcripts, letters, newspaper clippings, and other documents, as well as those who filled out our oral history surveys and questionnaires.

All rights reserved. No part of this publication may be reproduced, stored in a retrieval system, or transmitted, in any form by any means, electronic, mechanical, photocopying, recording or otherwise, without prior permission of the publisher.

ISBN 978-0-9833640-0-9

For regular Civil War posts, visit Scott Mingus' Cannonball blog, yorkblog.com/cannonball, and James McClure's yorktownsquare.com blog.
For more information, please contact the authors at
scottmingus@yahoo.com and jem@ydr.com.

First Edition

PRINTED AND BOUND IN THE UNITED STATES OF AMERICA

Front and back cover design: Samantha Dellinger
Editing: June Lloyd
Copy editing and indexing: Joseph McClure
Reviewers: John T. Krepps, Ed LeFevre, James W. Moss, Sr.

TABLE OF CONTENTS

On the front cover

Nineteenth-century York County artist Lewis Miller captures York's busy North Duke Street area near the Northern Central Railway depot. Many York residents stuck near the railroad station and telegraph office across the street to absorb war news from afar. In this September 1861 scene, the 87th Pennsylvania, a regiment made up mostly of men from York and Adams counties, march to a waiting passenger train for transport to duty in the South. This drawing comes from the York County Heritage Trust collection, which includes several other Miller drawings from the Civil War era.

On the back cover

Private Daniel Roland was away at war, leaving his wife, Ellen, to fend for herself and their five children, when the Confederate army occupied York County in late June 1863. She lived in a remote area, more than a mile from Emigsville. With Rebel invaders in that area, she figured she was safer in Emigsville. She headed there with her children and ran into a band of about 20 Confederates. "Where is your husband?" they asked. "Why are you leaving your home? Do you know we will burn down your house sooner if it was unoccupied than if you lived there?" They moved on, and she walked through Rebel lines to the safety of friends in the Manchester Township village.

Top photo: Charles Roland, left, son of Daniel and Ellen Roland, stands at the Prospect Hill Cemetery gravesite of his wife, Sarah "Sally" King Roland, who died 1906. Ellen Roland, right, (1832-1919) is at the grave of her husband and Civil War veteran, Daniel Roland, (1823-1905). Ellen appears in mourning clothes in this photo, circa 1906. Bottom photo: Private Daniel Roland is pictured in a tintype that has remained in his family and is now in the collection of his great-great-granddaughter, Dianne Gleim Bowders.

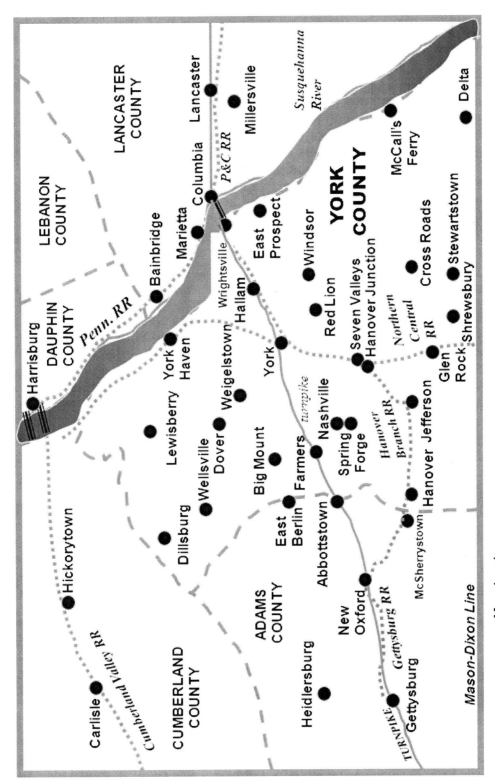

Susquehanna River

LANCASTER COUNTY

LEBANON COUNTY

DAUPHIN COUNTY

CUMBERLAND COUNTY

ADAMS COUNTY

YORK COUNTY

Lancaster
Millersville
Delta
McCall's Ferry
Columbia
Marietta
Bainbridge
Stewartstown
Cross Roads
Shrewsbury
East Prospect
Windsor
Hanover Junction
Seven Valleys
Red Lion
Glen Rock
Harrisburg
York Haven
Lewisberry
Hallam
Wrightsville
York
Weigelstown
Dover
Wellsville
Big Mount
Farmers
Nashville
Spring Forge
Hanover
Jefferson
McSherrystown
Dillsburg
East Berlin
Abbottstown
New Oxford
Hickorytown
Carlisle
Heidlersburg
Gettysburg

P&C RR
Penn. RR
Northern Central RR
Hanover Branch RR
turnpike
Gettysburg RR
TURNPIKE
Cumberland Valley RR
Mason-Dixon Line
Maryland

5

Foreword

Growing up in a middle-class family in York, Pennsylvania, only 30 miles from Gettysburg, I was exposed at an early age to Civil War history. My sister still has a photograph in her family album of my paternal grandfather holding his two-year-old grandson — me — in front of the Virginia Memorial at Gettysburg National Military Park.

As a 5½ year-old when the Civil War Centennial began in 1961, my entire family went to the Strand Theatre (or maybe it was the Capitol Theatre) to watch an encore showing of *Gone with the Wind* — the theater's management even handed out blue or gray paper kepis to the younger crowd.

That same year my family moved from Smith Street, near Farquhar Park, to Salem Square on West Princess Street. From our front window, I could see a statue of a Civil War soldier that had been painted with a blue uniform. It was not until many years later that I discovered that even though the statue was indeed that of a Civil War infantryman, it also memorialized soldiers from York who served in the War of Independence.

At the same time, while other kids on the block were collecting baseball cards of Mickey Mantle, Hank Aaron, Roger Maris and Willie Mays, I collected Topps' Civil War trading cards. We did not reside very long on Salem Square and in 1962 moved into a brand-new home in Fireside Park. After attending Devers Elementary School, named for a World War II four-star general from York, I moved on to Edgar Fahs Smith Junior High School, where I played drums in the school band. Every Memorial Day the band met at Penn Park near the Civil War Memorial before parading through downtown York. In the late 1960s, York's Civil War Memorial was in derelict condition, with pieces broken or missing and its base covered with graffiti.

The parade always terminated at Prospect Hill Cemetery in North York where, at another Civil War memorial — surrounded by the graves of Union soldiers who had died in the General Hospital that had been located in Penn Park — we paid homage to members of the uniformed services who had died in all of America's wars, including the divisive conflict that was raging at that time in Southeast Asia.

In 1969, the family moved again, this time to Board Road, near York Barbell between Emigsville and Manchester. By this time, I was attending Central York High School and was more concerned with sports, band, and girls than the Civil War. Upon graduation, I was accepted at York College, but working 20 hours a week while taking 15 credit hours per semester was too much, so I joined the U.S. Army, primarily to earn G.I. Bill benefits for a free college education.

As it turned out, military service was my calling, and when I returned to college it was courtesy of an Army ROTC scholarship. It was during the last two years at York College of Pennsylvania that I really began to study and appreciate Civil War scholarship. I took courses under Professor James L. Morrison, an esteemed Civil War historian, joined the 87th Pennsylvania Infantry re-enactment unit, volunteered my weekends at the Gettysburg National Military Park Visitors Center, and even bought a metal detector so I could find my own Civil War relics.

I also joined the American Legion. While enjoying a beer one evening at one of the local posts, an elderly gentleman sat next to me and began to tell war stories. He was a World War I veteran who recalled his discharge in 1919 and his subsequent application for membership in York's first American Legion Post. The one thing that still sticks in my mind was his request of me to remember our conversation, just as he fondly recalled the times when as a young man he listened to the tales of Civil War veterans at the American Legion. I will never forget his words. The memory of that discussion with the old doughboy still serves as my personal connection to the Civil War.

My Civil War mania came to an abrupt end when I was commissioned a second lieutenant and returned to active duty. During my career as an army officer, I was selected to teach history at the United States Military Academy. Once again, Uncle Sam sent me to college, this time in the mid-1980s for a graduate degree in U.S. history.

When it came time to write a master's thesis, I chose a Civil War topic: a social history of York County from 1861 to 1865, with an emphasis on recruiting and conscription. I also traced the Civil War soldiers in my family tree and found that two great-great grandfathers served in the 87th Pennsylvania while another was assigned to the 200th Pennsylvania Infantry, both regiments raised primarily from York County.

In addition, I became more familiar with York native William B. Franklin, who rose to the rank of major general during the Civil War and early in the conflict commanded the Sixth Corps of the Army of the Potomac. Several years later, I discovered Franklin's personal papers, which became the basis of my doctoral dissertation and later a book-length biography.

By that time, I had retired from the Army and accepted a position at Shepherd University and considered myself a fairly knowledgeable Civil War historian. I also thought I knew just about everything there was to know about York County during the Civil War. I was wrong.

The research of Scott Mingus and Jim McClure for their earlier works and this volume made me realize that I had only scratched the surface. For example, I had no idea that Confederate troopers of the 17th Virginia Cavalry rode right in front of my home on Board Road. These Rebels were part of a foraging expedition to commandeer horses and mules for Robert E. Lee's army during the Gettysburg Campaign, and they took several beasts of burden from nearby farms.

I furthermore learned that the residents of Princess Street, where I lived for one year as a child, also had horses stolen by Confederates as they passed through the Borough of York. And only a few blocks from my alma mater, the old Central York High School in North York, I discovered, thanks to Scott's and Jim's historical research, that Brigadier General "Extra Billy" Smith's Confederate brigade camped in the vicinity during the last week of June 1863.

Scott and Jim have uncovered these stories and many more interesting anecdotes in their years of searching through the archives and collections of the York County Heritage Trust and other repositories, as well as from family attics. They have come across reminiscences, memoirs, oral histories, newspaper accounts, letters, diaries, and official records relating to life in York during the war years. With this informative, well-written and easy-to-read volume, they have brought York County's role in the Civil War back to life just in time for the sesquicentennial of those tragic times.

Nearly two decades after the end of the fratricide, York's most famous Civil War soldier, Major General William B. Franklin, began writing the story of his life. Unfortunately, he never got past the first four pages.

"I was born in York on Feb. 27, 1823 and my

recollections of the place run back nearly sixty years," he wrote. "I know from fair experience… gained in many places about the world that there is no place one can live with more solid comfort, and with a more appreciation of life than York."

Unlike General Franklin, Scott Mingus and Jim McClure are not York natives, but they have been steeped in its history and culture and have compiled this book of common interest stories that will be read by students of the Civil War for years to come.

Mark A. Snell
The George Tyler Moore Center for the Study of the Civil War
Shepherd University
Shepherdstown, West Virginia

Introduction

York County in the early to mid-19th century was a "border county." Its southern boundary was the Mason-Dixon Line, which separated free-state Pennsylvania from slave-state Maryland.

As such, tensions often rose when bounty hunters and out-of-state law authorities entered this south-central Pennsylvania county to seek runaway slaves under the provisions of the Fugitive Slave Law.

"York was distinctly Northern, but not bitterly anti-Southern," industrialist A.B. Farquhar stated. "The community felt that slavery was wrong in principle. At the same time, being acquainted with many slave owners, we also knew that slavery was better in practice than in theory and that the planter who was cruel to his Negroes was a rare exception."

Some residents were active members of the Underground Railroad movement and assisted the escaped Southern blacks, while others helped the bounty hunters or revealed the locations of hidden refugees for a portion of the reward.

Since its establishment in 1749, York County had grown into a regional center of agriculture, commerce, and industry. With some 68,200 residents in 1860, it was among the more prosperous counties in that part of the state.

Farming was the chief occupation, but the area also had many small industries, including railcar manufacturing, cigar making, leather tanning, carriage making, milling, mining, and farm implement production.

The largest community in the county was the city of York, a borough of 8,605 people. Other major population centers were Hanover (1,630 people) in the southwestern corner of the county and Wrightsville (1,294) along the Susquehanna River to the east.

York and Wrightsville had the highest concentration of black families; the county's black population was 1,204, less than two percent of the total. Most York County people were of Germanic descent.

Other significant ethnic groups included Scots-Irish, Welsh, and English (many of them Quakers). Common religious denominations included the Lutherans, German Reformed, Methodists, United Brethren, Evangelical, Presbyterian, Roman Catholic, and Mennonites and various other Anabaptist groups.

Often, services were conducted in the Pennsylvania German dialect, although most official business, such as court records and land transfers, was conducted in English.

Situated along the western bank of the broad Susquehanna River, York countians enjoyed a multitude of options for trade and commerce. A mile-long wooden covered bridge in Wrightsville offered access to Lancaster and Philadelphia.

The southern part of the county had strong ties to Baltimore and northern Maryland, and residents of northern York County focused more on Harrisburg.

Railroads, turnpikes, and canals were the lifeblood of York County's commerce. The Northern Central Railway ran north-south from Harrisburg to Baltimore. At Hanover Junction, it intersected with the east-west Hanover Branch Railroad, which connected in turn with the Gettysburg Railroad.

A gravel-paved turnpike connected York to Gettysburg and Wrightsville. Other key roads went north and south, including the Susquehanna Trail and the State Road to Carlisle. The Susquehanna and Tidewater Canal stretched 45 miles from Wrightsville down to Havre de Grace, Maryland, and offered farmers and businessmen access to the Chesapeake Bay.

Politically, York County was a Democratic bastion. Abraham Lincoln's three opponents in 1860 outgained him locally by a tally of 6,633 to 5,128. Four years later, York County cast 7,875 votes for Peace Democrat Major General George B. McClellan to only 4,690 for incumbent President Lincoln.

Being close to the Maryland border and maintaining strong ties to the South, the county had a fair number of Southern sympathizers, sometimes called "Copperheads," although army enlistment and recruitment remained strong throughout the war.

More than 13,000 men from York County served in military units during the Civil War, including emergency and short-term militia. In addition, several local men served in units not primarily from York County such as Company K of the 45th Pennsylvania, which was raised in Columbia. A few Yorkers, most notably Brigadier General Johnson K. Duncan, fought in the Confederate army.

It was an area that would experience firsthand the effects of an invading army. More than 11,000 Confederate soldiers tramped on York County soil in late June and early July 1863 during the Gettysburg Campaign. The first incursion came from the west, when Major General Jubal Early's 6,000-man division arrived from Gettysburg. Almost simultaneously, a small battalion of Virginia cavalry rode down from Cumberland County into northwestern York County and raided the area for horses and livestock.

Finally, perhaps the most threatening for the livelihoods and livestock of York countians, Major General J.E.B. "Jeb" Stuart brought almost 5,000 cavalrymen north from Maryland in hopes of rendezvousing with Early, a plan that was thwarted by the June 30 Battle of Hanover. Nearly a thousand residents of York County would later file damage claims with the state or federal governments for losses to the Southerners, ranging from horse blankets to buffalo robes.

Refugees fleeing the Rebels clogged most roads between June 25 and 29, and some York countians didn't return until after the war was clearly decided. They chose to stay in safer locales in case the "Johnny Rebs" returned. A handful, particularly blacks from York and Wrightsville, never came back, having found employment and a better life in Philadelphia or Harrisburg.

This was York County, Pa., during the Civil War. Some of the residents left reminiscences of the war years, mostly through oral tradition and story-telling passed down to their grandchildren. In addition, letters, diaries and other written accounts have surfaced.

It is our goal to present them to you, in context of known historical facts, and allow you to obtain a sense of what it might have been like to live in a border county during the most tumultuous period in America's history. To quote one of York's leading women of the Civil War era, "Aunt Bella... thought it a pity someone shouldn't make an account of all these funny things, that they would make an interesting book." – Cassandra M. Small, York, Pa. July 1863

Most wartime events were far from funny — devastating, in fact. But voices describing them make an interesting book, indeed.
– Scott Mingus, Manchester Township York County, Pennsylvania

Chapter 1

Early Civil War Voices

'It is impossible for one who lived in the sections of the country remote from the seat of war to realize the meaning of life in the Border States in that time that tried the souls of all men and wrung with anguish the hearts of the devoted women both North and South.'
– Mary C. Fisher, York, Pa.

1861

The American Civil War, though rooted in decades of dissention and violence over slavery, westward expansion, and states' rights, erupted in the dark on April 12, 1861. At 4:30 a.m., Secessionist forces in Charleston, South Carolina, fired artillery at Federal-held Fort Sumter.

A succession of heavy shells arced through the pre-dawn coastal sky, and the lengthy political hatred and fiery partisan rhetoric gave way to weaponry.

The masonry bastion in Charleston Harbor capitulated several hours later, sending shock waves through both the North and South.

President Abraham Lincoln and his controversial anti-slavery Republican Party had captured the White House in 1860, sparking several Southern "Cotton States" to secede from the Union and form the Confederate States of America.

It was the CSA's newly formed provisional army that lit the fuse early that fateful morning in Charleston.

No one could have imagined the suffering and pain that was to result.

**

Long before Fort Sumter fell, the seeds of discord had been sown.

Among the many points of contention was the Underground Railroad, with several York County and other south-central Pennsylvania residents playing important roles in trafficking escaped slaves to freedom.

The controversial Fugitive Slave Law of 1850 declared that all runaway slaves must be returned to their owners.

Those who worked in the Underground Railroad now risked fines and imprisonment. For many Northerners, that unpleasant possibility did not outweigh betraying their values and beliefs.

Fugitive William Parker, late of an Anne Arundel County, Maryland, plantation, was in York in the summer of 1839 or 1840.

"Once in York, we thought we would be safe," he believed, "but… our ideas of security were materially lessened when we met a friend during the day, who advised us to proceed further, as we were not out of imminent danger."

He moved farther east to Columbia that night.

Twenty years later another fugitive, Osborne Perry Anderson, escaped Federal forces that quelled his leader John Brown's occupation of

Harpers Ferry, Virginia.

"At night, I set out and reached York," the freedman wrote, "where a good Samaritan gave me oil, wine and raiment."

Neither man named former slave and York merchant William C. Goodridge as their "friend" or "good Samaritan." But scholars believe Goodridge aided both as an agent on the Underground Railroad.[1]

**

In the early 1850s Frances Ellen Watkins Harper taught in the school for black children in York.

School directors found her qualified to instruct in geography, grammar, arithmetic, reading, writing, and orthography. She received $20 per month for assuming the position, formerly held by Glenalvin J. Goodridge, William C. Goodridge's son and a pioneering photographer.

In York, she reflected on whether she should continue teaching or move into the anti-slavery field. She later chose the abolitionist path.

She observed the Underground Railroad in operation in York, which had a lasting impact on her:

"I saw a passenger per the Underground Railroad yesterday; did he arrive safely? Notwithstanding that abomination of the nineteenth century — the Fugitive Slave Law — men still determine to be free. Notwithstanding all the darkness in which they keep the slaves, it seems that somehow light is dawning upon their minds."

Frances Ellen Watkins Harper later became the leading black poet and anti-slavery advocate.[2]

**

Sectional tensions intensified after firebrand abolitionist John Brown's stunning 1859 raid on Harpers Ferry, in which several civilians and raiders died.

U.S. Army officers Robert E. Lee and J.E.B. "Jeb" Stuart were involved in finally bringing Brown to bay.

The uprising immediately became the major news story in the country, sparking significant controversy and debate.

"John Brown was controlled by the noblest motives, the highest sentiments of philanthropy and humanity," York countian Edward W. Spangler later wrote. "However fatuous, unlawful and violent his methods, he represented in his convictions on the great national evil of slavery the sentiment and conscience of the North."

Many Southerners considered Brown a traitorous heretic who rightfully was executed for his heinous crimes. Some in York County agreed.

Others considered him a martyr and later joined in singing the popular refrain, *John Brown's Body Lies A'mouldering in the Grave.*

The lines of contention grew longer.[3]

**

Harry I. Gladfelter was 10 years old when the war began.

"Alongside of my infant and school age days," the resident of Seven Valleys in south-central York County later recalled, "strode the Ghost of the oncoming war between the north and the south, on the question of slavery."

Gladfelter deemed the publication of the controversial book *Uncle Tom's Cabin* "a powerful agitation" that portrayed "the horrors and inhumanities the colored race had to endure at the hands of taskmasters throughout the south."

It was a view shared by many in the North and denounced widely in the Southern states, exacerbating the political divisions between the Republicans and Democrats.

"Wherever men belonging to the two parties existed," wrote Gladfelter, "arguments, disputes, controversies, arose over the fallacy of going to war, and neighbors were not quite as amiable as they used to be."

Democrats referred to Republicans as "Black Republicans," and Republicans derisively called Democrats who opposed the war or sought a negotiated peace "Copperheads."[4]

**

Warrington Township housewife Phebe Angeline Smith also held strong political opinions.

"Father says he don't want to have anything to do with eny that belong to sutch a party," the Quaker woman from northwestern York County said of the Copperheads.

"I don't want you to think that I am so partial to one party. For thare is good democrats as Americans but I do think it is a sin to turn traters to ones own country and wish our country to be destroyed and our men all cut up."[5]

**

Three days after the bombardment of Fort Sumter, Abraham Lincoln called for a massive army of 75,000 volunteers to put down the rebellion.

In response, four more Southern states seceded, bringing the fledgling Confederacy to 11 states. Lincoln struggled to hold Kentucky, Maryland, and other slave-owning states in the Union.

David Small's *York Gazette*, a Democratic newspaper, trumpeted, "The news of the attack upon, and capture of Ft. Sumter, and that the President had called for 75,000 troops, caused a feeling of the most intense excitement, and the pervading topic of the community was, War!! War!! War!!!"

Citizens eager for news crowded the telegraph office.

Residents put up flags, and those with sewing skills made even more.

"At the present writing," the *Gazette* reported, "flags innumerable are floating beautifully and gracefully at various points. They are so numerous that nothing of the kind was seen in York before, and none can look upon the beautiful sight without a feeling of love and admiration for the flag which has so long protected them, and which has been outrageously insulted, not by a foreign foe, but by those who like ourselves, have grown up and prospered beneath its 'bright stars and broad stripes.' "[6]

**

On April 18, York residents assembled in the courthouse "in great numbers, for the purpose of giving a practical expression of their devotion to the Union," according to teenager Ed Spangler.

Borough authorities authorized $1,000 to help raise troops in the county seat, and county commissioners later approved $10,000, stating that "the gallant volunteers and their families will be well taken care of." Other towns followed in contributing money for the new soldiers.

Patriotism was the order of the day for most residents.

The pro-Republican *Hanover Spectator*, owned during the war by a widow named Maria Leader, reported, "Many of our young men evince their patriotism by wearing Union neckties, composed of the red, white, and blue.

Throughout town the ladies "have also taken to wearing the national colors, which to our notion, heightens and adds to their attractions very considerably."

The *York Gazette*, which had pleaded for peace prior to the attack on Fort Sumter, now urged that "the laws of the United States must be enforced, the orders of the government must be obeyed, and the Flag of the Union must be respected at whatever cost."

It was a sentiment shared by many Northerners as the mass rush to arms commenced.[7]

**

W.P. Karr hated the idea of secession.

With a passion.

The 21-year-old wrote a letter to his friend Milton Ruby of Hellam Township expressing his strong feelings.

"I am this much Republican that I think Honest Abe will do right. My motto is to protect the union and make the Southern Rebels come to terms. They are Nabobs and thieves, have stolen government property, and fired on Fort Sumter. They should be slain as traitors."

His patriotic fervor spilled over, "I glory in the spunk of Old Pa. for sending volunteers… And I hope you Old Hellam folks will stand by the

Stars and Stripes."[8]

**

On April 20, Robert E. Lee resigned from the U.S. Army.

He traveled to Richmond, Virginia, where he accepted command of the state's military forces.

That same day, the Rev. Francis F. Hagen of York's Moravian Church sat down to write in a journal, in keeping with the long-held practice of his denomination.

"A day of great excitement. During the week the sad tidings came of civil war begun — thru the bombardment of Fort Sumter near Charleston," he wrote.

He also noted that "a fearful event took place at Baltimore."

An anti-government mob had attacked Massachusetts troops marching through town to the train station. They were en route to the defense of Washington, D.C., "which is sorely threatened by the South."

The news from neighboring Maryland brought swift response in York and other nearby towns.

"Our companies were ordered out this evening & great excitement prevails," the Rev. Hagen penned. "The York companies — two — went down the railroad to guard the bridges."

Confederate saboteurs indeed would cause significant concern for railroad executives and military officials.

The *Gazette* stated, "We deeply regret the severing of the business relationship which so long has existed between York and Baltimore, but the necessity which has been forced upon us, knows no law, and trade, like water, will

14

always find its level."[9]

**

Following the angry riot in Maryland's largest city, fears spread that the Rowdies, a pro-secessionist Baltimore gang, planned to rob banks in Hanover and then burn the southwestern York County town.

Alarmed residents barricaded streets, and some folks armed themselves to protect their property.

Edward Steffy was one of those taking up arms. He sat on his front porch cradling an old, defective musket.

When asked what he planned to do with a useless gun, he uttered, "There is *nothing* wrong with the bayonet."

The feared Rowdies never made an appearance in Hanover, much to the residents' relief.

Ed Steffy put away his weapon.[10]

**

Volunteers in the North stood in line to sign up for the military.

Some were ardent Union men, determined to see the country held together. Others sought adventure or glory, or perhaps just a way out of the drudgery of factory or farm work. Still others came because of peer pressure or family expectations, or they believed it was the right thing to do.

Some prospective soldiers were devoutly anti-slavery and felt this was a chance to put teeth to their abolitionist ardor. For a few men down on their luck, war offered a chance for a steady paycheck. In New York City and other places across the North, persuasive recruiters targeted

newly arrived European immigrants.

The young men of York County echoed most of these reasons for enlisting.

They left their civilian jobs, sweethearts and wives, parents and family members, and rushed off to join the army.

David Givens, a 20-year-old Wrightsville resident, was one of those men. He had worked as a boatman on one of his uncle's barges on the Susquehanna and Tidewater Canal, linking York County to the Chesapeake Bay and then Baltimore.

He enlisted as a private in the 3rd Pennsylvania Artillery.

Givens would be a soldier for more than four years before resuming his career as a boatman, marrying, and raising eight children.

His oldest son would die from pneumonia in an army camp during the Spanish-American War.[11]

**

Joseph W. Ilgenfritz, a 29-year-old blacksmith from York, with a wife and two small children, was among the thousands in the region to respond to Lincoln's proclamation.

Struck with patriotic fever, Ilgenfritz enlisted on April 20 as a private in the 16th Pennsylvania Infantry. His brother David would enroll in the 1st Pennsylvania Cavalry.

Joe traveled by train with his company to Harrisburg, where they mustered into the service and received uniforms and equipment. The regiment guarded railroads in northwestern Virginia, later the state of West Virginia.

Joe wrote a short letter to his brother in July from a camp in Martinsburg, Berkley County.

He recounted the march into Virginia two weeks earlier and described one of the first deadly encounters by York countians with the Confederates:

"We marched over into Virginia on the 2nd and at Falling Waters we had a small skirmish with the rebels whome where from 4 to 5 thousand & there was only 1 rigment of our brigade took part in the battle as the rebels run before we got up to them but they railed 3 times & where drove off again with a heavy loss."

After arriving in Martinsburg, the York boys camped in a field west of town. They seized an abandoned Confederate hospital, a comfortable "long 2 story brick house with a good many rooms in it. It is about 60 by 100 feet."

Two days later, the boys of the 16th Pennsylvania engaged in another firefight. They captured their first prisoners, a regular occurrence in the subsequent two weeks: "Our rigment went to get skirmishing on the 5th & Co. I shot one of the rebels. We captured some of the rebels every day."

It was dangerous work for the newly trained soldiers, who had signed up for three months in the field.

With only two weeks left in his own unit's term, Ilgenfritz closed with a line that revealed the nagging uncertainty of soldiers through the ages, "I hope to see you all again soon if God permits it."

If indeed.[12]

**

Some businesses, their ranks thinned as employees marched off to war, curtailed or suspended operations.

The *Star*, a newspaper in Wrightsville, was one of those to close its doors.

Its competitor across the Susquehanna River, the *Columbia Spy*, later recounted that the suspension of the rival paper lasted "for four years, caused by the whole printing corps going into the Army."

One of them, Lt. Robert W. Smith Jr., of the 5th Pennsylvania Reserves, would be mortally wounded at Second Bull Run. He was the son and namesake of the *Star*'s owner.

"The *Star* corps has done its share towards crushing the rebellion," the *Spy* added.

Not to be outdone, editor/owner Samuel Wright of the *Spy* sold his paper in 1863 and also joined the army.[13]

**

Dillsburg, a bustling village along the old State Road between York and Carlisle, responded well to President Lincoln's requests for troops.

Of its 66 able-bodied men between 21 and 45, all but nine (mostly conscientious objectors) eventually entered the Union army.

In the spring of 1861, Samuel N. Bailey, a former state representative and justice of the peace, led the first group of volunteers to York to enlist. They became part of the 12th Pennsylvania Reserves, and Bailey eventually reached the rank of colonel before illness sidelined him.

Some of the other early responders from the Dillsburg region headed for Mechanicsburg, where they joined the 7th Pennsylvania Reserves. The men, though in different regiments, often fought side by side during the war.

Eight of those Dillsburg soldiers would be

killed in combat or die of disease, including Jacob Koontz, Alexander McKeever, and William W. Arnold. Four other men would suffer serious wounds.

McKeever had moved from Dillsburg to Bird-in-Hand in Lancaster County to become an apprentice carpenter. He was "the only support for his parents thanks to an alcoholic father."

He joined the army and died from a gunshot to the forehead at Fredericksburg in December 1862.[14]

**

It was common early in the war for businessmen in both the North and South to figure out methods of maintaining some semblance of trade, despite government orders that forbade such activities.

York resident Arthur Briggs Farquhar was one such entrepreneurial merchant and industrialist. The young Maryland-raised and Virginia-educated Quaker owned a young business that produced and sold farming implements and machinery.

Farquhar was able to skip being in the army by paying a substitute, a common practice, and kept his business going despite the loss of several Southern clients.

"Having been married on September 26th, 1860," he later related, "I was among those who were simply not expected to enlist. I provided a substitute, however, and joined with other men in a troop of volunteer cavalry — a home guard. The majority of the workmen in our shop were unmarried and most of them enlisted, but with those men remaining we could easily carry on, for there was nothing much just then to do."

An early act of the Confederacy was to cancel debts owed to Northerners by Southerners and made payable into the Confederate Treasury. The North did the same.

"However, this was a gentleman's war," Farquhar recounted, "and men on both sides, who liked to pay their debts, found ways to do so."

Bills were paid through Canada, a mutual clearing house. Farquhar received several such payments, and much of the balance was paid after hostilities ceased.

"There was more bad feeling after the war," he believed, "than during the contest."[15]

**

After the firing on Fort Sumter, the York fairgrounds took on a martial air.

Sabotage of the Northern Central Railway between York and Baltimore and unrest in Baltimore — the work of Southern sympathizers — meant Union troops could travel no farther south.

They settled at the fairgrounds, then southeast of the intersection of King and Queen streets, and were the first of tens of thousands to camp and train there. Soldiers slept on straw in sheds designed for livestock at this newly named Camp Scott.

Local newspapers reported the death of a young infantryman from Hanover from pneumonia, among accounts of several soldiers suffering from illness in camp.

Drills taking place in town squares throughout the country brought wounds and even death.

One of Edward L. Schroeder's comrades cut the Worth Infantry soldier in the back of the head during a bayonet exercise in York's Centre Square.

In southeastern York County's Stewartstown, a fellow solder accidentally blasted Benjamin Ebaugh in the back with his shotgun.

At Camp Scott, a soldier shot a comrade from Pittsburgh in the head after a disagreement. But the bullet did no harm. It glanced off the Pittsburgh man's head.

War had come to York County.[16]

**

So had bad weather.

The spring of 1861 was wet and inclement.

"The soldiers suffered severely from rheumatism, contracted by lying on damp straw, and from colds and intermittent fevers," Mary Cadwell Fisher later wrote.

No military hospital existed at the time, and private homeowners took in the sick solders.

"In many households a meal was rarely eaten," Mrs. Fisher recollected, "without one or more guests from the camp."

The ladies of York formed a committee for the relief of the sick and wounded soldiers, with Cassandra Small Morris, the wife of druggist Charles A. Morris, as the president. She was the sister of prominent merchants P.A. and Samuel Small.

Mrs. Fisher later commented that the society was "perfect in organization and effectiveness, and the attention, sympathy and aid afforded by it have been gratefully appreciated."[17]

**

The intersection of George and Market streets in downtown York was a historic spot.

In 1777, Continental Congress debated and adopted the Articles of Confederation in the courthouse, which stood in Centre Square. By the Civil War, the old building was long gone, but the square was still the heart of York's culture and commerce.

It also bore a visible sign of York's patriotism.

A pine pole was raised in the square between its two market houses. While that pole was hoisted, Judge Robert J. Fisher and the Rev. J.A. Ross addressed a large crowd.

"After the addresses, a beautiful bunting flag was run up, the band meanwhile playing the 'Star-Spangled Banner,' Edward Spangler wrote. "Since then a larger flag, 35 feet in length and of heavier material, has been attached to the pole."

This large flag would later play a prominent role in the Gettysburg Campaign.[18]

**

Horatio Gates Myers, named after the victorious Continental Army general in the American Revolution's Battle of Saratoga, lived a relatively quiet life before the Civil War.

He owned a retail store in downtown Hanover and was married with two children. At the war's onset, the 30-year-old Myers became a Yankee.

On April 25, Myers was appointed captain of the Marion Rifles in the 16th Pennsylvania Infantry, a three-month unit. He suffered from exposure at the regiment's campsite near Hagerstown, Maryland, and was left behind when the 16th returned to York to be mustered out of the service in July.

Myers died from typhoid fever on August 7.[19]

**

In early May, a stray dog wandered into the 13th Pennsylvania's encampment at Camp Scott.

The canine became the regiment's mascot and accompanied it for months. In recognition of the dog's hometown, the stray was named "York."

The Rev. Alexander M. Stewart, regimental chaplain, described York as a "curious-looking specimen of the canine. One must be more skilled in doggery than the writer to define his species. Spaniel, cur, terrier, and water-dog all seem blended into one."

York was clearly a town dog, lacking natural hunting instincts.

"York's reasoning facilities seem to operate slowly," the chaplain wrote, "He is accustomed to bound away, and bring back in his mouth whatever missile any one of the boys may throw from them, whether falling upon land or water. With live game he has but little acquaintance."

He explained York's response after spotting a rabbit on the run: "Thither he bounded with wonderful agility, then he stopped and snuffed and snorted to find the rabbit as he would a block or stone — seeming wholly oblivious, that although the rabbit was actually in that spot when he started in pursuit, it might not perchance be in the same spot when he arrived."

York "re-enlisted" with nearly all of his comrades in the 102nd Pennsylvania after the three-month term of the 13th Pennsylvania expired. Eighteen months after York first wandered into the camp, he perished from injuries, disease, and exposure.

Members of his regiment buried the dog with full military honors.[20]

**

Thousands of soldiers trained at Camp Scott under sub-par conditions.

One member of the 2nd Pennsylvania wrote to a Philadelphia newspaper on May 4, "Our quarters are cattle-sheds and temporary structures hastily thrown together for the purpose. We lie down at night upon nice clean straw, draw our blankets over us, hob-nob the stars a few minutes, and ere we know it, are locked in the arms of Morpheus."

"After drilling all day," he added, "we could sleep soundly on an oak board. At home it is my habit to toss for an hour or two before I subside into the night's slumber; but I know no such dalliance with the treacherous sleep-god here. I just tumble over into the straw and into the deadness of dreamless sleep."[21]

**

In late June, the first hostile shots in the region were fired in southern York County.

Little is known of the incident other than some sketchy newspaper accounts.

"Intelligence has also been received here that the workmen engaged in preparing the ground for a new camp near the Maryland line, at New Freedom, York County, were fired on by a body of Maryland Rebels, and two severely wounded," a Harrisburg correspondent reported.

For the next few years, residents of the border counties of south-central Pennsylvania — specifically York, Adams, and Franklin — would live in fear as reports trickled in that Rebel raiding parties were approaching.

Often these rumors were mere fantasy. But on a few occasions, Confederates would appear in the Keystone State.

York resident Mary C. Fisher noted,

"Unprotected by military force, with no natural barrier between the seceding and the loyal States, the exaggerated rumors and the constant suspense were appalling in the early days of the deadly struggle."

She added, "But soon familiarized to the life we became indifferent to the danger."

The *Philadelphia Press* warned against complacency, "There is a danger that having been so frequently alarmed by reports of previous raids which have proved unfounded, our people may allow themselves to rest in a false sense of security."[22]

**

On July 4, with the original three-month units facing the end of their terms of enlistment, the U.S. Congress authorized a call for 500,000 fresh troops.

Passing soldiers had little doubt of York's outward support for the military. In mid-July, the 12th New York State Militia returned home by train from Baltimore after its three-month term expired.

"The old flag was flying from church, school-house, work-shop and private house," one soldier recounted as the train passed through York, "The men, women and children ran out to meet us and gave us cheer, until we were hoarse and tired in answering them."[23]

**

Northern hopes for a quick end to the war disappeared on July 21 when Confederate forces stunned the Union army at Bull Run and sent the Yankees flying back to Washington, D.C.

Within days, thousands of new recruits headed for the North's capital to bolster the ranks of Major General Irvin McDowell's beaten army. Within a week, Lincoln would replace him with George B. McClellan.

Descendants of two famous early Americans passed through York County on July 26 on their way to fortify the Union ranks.

Fletcher Webster, son of famed orator Daniel Webster, was the colonel of the 12th Massachusetts Infantry. He and his men were traveling southward through the county on the Northern Central toward Baltimore.

They paused at Glen Rock to eat their breakfast and load their muskets. They filled their canteens from a nearby spring.

It took five-and-a-half hours for the train to steam the 25 miles from Glen Rock to Hummelstown, Maryland. That was far longer than expected, so Webster became suspicious that the engineer could not be trusted.

Colonel Webster dismissed him and turned to a soldier in his regiment.

"Can you run this train to Baltimore?" he asked.

The soldier answered in the affirmative. He was Private Nathan L. Revere, grandson of the Boston silversmith who made the legendary midnight ride to warn patriots about the British approach at the start of the American Revolution.

Revere hopped into the locomotive, took the throttle, and safely guided the train through Secessionist territory down to Baltimore.

He made very good time.[24]

**

In August, the Rev. J.T. Bender addressed a gathering at Mount Pleasant Bethel Church of

God near Siddonsburg in Monaghan Township.

His northwestern York County audience was the Independent Rifles of York County, who were awaiting their turn to head into harm's way.

"Today we live in the midst of great events," Bender lamented, "but a few months ago ours was a nation of peace and prosperity. Now the flash of bayonets, the thunder of musketry and cannon, the tread of thousands of Columbia's sons marching to the sound of music, with hearts brave, and minds determined to repel the rebel forces, which have made battle against our institutions, announce in unmistakable language, that we are in the midst of war — a great and terrible war. A war created by the unwise acts of Jeff. Davis and his subordinates."

After presenting arguments as to why the Confederates would be formidable foes, the preacher passionately encouraged the men about their distinct advantages and explained why they would win the war.

Also concerned about the political divisions in the North, Bender twice warned, "We fear a compromising policy more than the enemy."

The Reverend Bender would come to know the anguish of war personally, losing two sons while serving in the Union army.[25]

**

In September, recruiters enlisted enough men primarily from York and Adams counties to form a three-year regiment, the 87th Pennsylvania.

Seventeen-year-old Henry Schultz was among those eager volunteers. He was a hired hand on the Baum farm in Hellam Township.

"I worked on a farm, and they didn't want me to go," he later stated.

One evening, he threw his clothes into the garden and waited for an opportunity to further his getaway.

That came when those in the house tended to a sick girl staying there.

"When they went to take care of her, I sneaked out to the hay loft with my clothes and hid them under the steps," he wrote.

He described his departure: "The next morning, I took the colt out to the pasture and kept looking into the house at the table. When I saw Mr. Baum go to the table, I watched my chance and went to the barn where I changed clothes. I jumped from the barn when no one was looking, into the corn field and came out at Kreutz Creek."

Henry walked to York and enlisted at Penn Common.

Mr. Baum and his father wanted him to come home, and the enlistment officer asked Henry if he really wanted to go to war.

"When I said I did," Henry said, "they left me go."[26]

**

Historian George W. Prowell recounted one of the newly raised 87th Pennsylvania's first "battles" in October.

Several companies were ordered to participate in a battalion drill.

"When the order 'Forward March' was given, a delightful and inspiring sight was afforded the spectator," he wrote. "The men moved down the slope with steady ringing tread in almost perfect alignment."

They seemed invincible. The band playing. The

colors flying. A martial spirit in the air.

Then some of the boys stepped on a bumble bee's nest. Then another.

"They were regular black-headed Maryland buzzers and stingers, and soon began a spirited attack," Prowell noted. "The line was temporarily broken along the left and the amusing antics of some of the men excited the risibilities of the sternest officers."

But the bumble bees lost the fight.

"Camp kettles filled with hot water were hurried to 'the front,' " Prowell related, "and the live bumble bees soon disappeared from the face of the earth."[27]

**

That October, a different kind of battle loomed.

York countians went to the polls to cast their votes in the first general election since the war began. As usual, the region voted heavily Democratic.

But David Small, owner of the *York Gazette*, cautioned his fellow Democrats.

"In our exaltation of the glorious victory achieved by the Democracy of York county on Tuesday last, we must not lose sight of one important truth… It is the incalculable injury that has been done to the course of the Union by the peculiar manner in which the Republican leaders and their allies attempted to defeat the Democratic ticket," his newspaper opined.

He complained that his Republican competitor had held up the entire Democratic Party as nothing more than "secession sympathizers, and hostile to the government."

The newspaper considered this to be a "gross slander," because it did not differentiate between the "loyalty and patriotism of the Democratic candidates" in Pennsylvania and their former political allies now in the rebellious states.

Small bemoaned that Republican "fabrications" would only aid the Rebels.

He made sure his constituents knew that he and other party leaders were most certainly not Copperheads.

"We are proud that the Democratic party of York county, as a unit, followed its old flag, upon which is written, 'Liberty and Union, now and forever, one and inseparable,' " the newspaper reported.

A majority of voters in the county supported the Peace Democrats, the so-called Copperheads, whose mantra was "The Union as it was. The Constitution as it is. The Negroes where they are."

Of course, the Republican leaders renewed their attacks that all Democrats were merely Southern pawns and were plotting disunion.

The opinionated Small, using his popular newspaper as a propaganda organ, would go on to win nine one-year terms as the chief burgess, or mayor, of York.

In November, Small's fellow Democrat, Major General George B. McClellan, would be named as general-in-chief of all Federal forces.

This was despite "Little Mac's" political differences with President Lincoln.[28]

**

In late November, Benjamin Snyder was performing guard duty along the Northern Central Railway, when a train struck and killed

22

this father of two daughters and a teenage son, William.

He was buried in Salem United Brethren Cemetery in York County, and another family, the Shaws, raised William.

Benjamin Snyder is regarded as the first casualty in the 87th Pennsylvania Infantry, but he's remembered for another reason.

A comparison of family records and public documents suggest to descendant Sam Snyder that Ben Snyder had relations with two different women in the same time frame. A month before the two pregnant women were due to deliver, he ran away and joined the 87th.

A month after Snyder signed up, his wife Phoebe's three brothers, the Flinn boys, enlisted. Ben Snyder's stated death date is November 29, which also happens to be his wedding anniversary.

The story takes yet another strange twist. A woman in Ohio contacted Sam Snyder about her own ancestor, a Benjamin Taylor whose life story strongly parallels that of Ben Snyder. That comparison goes down to the William Shaw who had adopted the fatherless William Snyder, son of Ben.

Sam wonders whether his great-grandfather might have been a philanderer with a killer instinct instead of a casualty of war, who actually lived out his life with yet another woman in Brookville, Pennsylvania.

In the days before ID cards, fingerprint sciences, and Social Security numbers, thousands of men used aliases during the Civil War and Reconstruction.

Did Benjamin happen to come across an accidental death of someone along the railroad on his anniversary, and decide to use that as an easy way to escape his dilemma back in York County, or did he calculate the date, find someone of his build, height, and complexion, etc. and murder him to fake his death?

Regardless if Benjamin was a murderer or an opportunist, the question remains — who is actually buried at Salem United Brethren Cemetery with a marker of the 87th PA Inf. and the name Benjamin Snyder?[29]

**

The life of a soldier for the most part was one of routine.

Drills or guard duty marked much of the typical day when a regiment was not on the march. But there was often time in camp for practical jokes.

The 87th Pennsylvania's historian George Prowell recounted, "In the evenings of the early fall, after the sun had given place to the moon, pranks of course were played without being noticed."

Prowell described one such prank: "A wag in one squad gathered all the toads he could find near the company headquarters and tied them in the legs of a comrade's pantaloons.

"The next morning the owner of the trousers, not at all confounded, said with a smile: 'Boys, I didn't think any of you would be guilty of toadying to me in this way.'"[30]

**

Christmas 1861 was a decidedly different holiday for York countians.

Many families had at least one empty chair at their annual Christmas feasts with so many men off in the army. For some, the chair would remain vacant, for the beloved son or husband would never come home again.

The residents of downtown York and the vicinity interacted with another group of young soldiers.

The 6th New York Cavalry had established winter quarters at Camp Scott, and the residents of York were determined to make this holiday away from home pleasant for the boys from the Empire State.

"The citizens of York were very kind to us… on Christmas Day [they] furnished every man of the regiment with a large and succulent Pennsylvania pie," cavalryman James Wheeler marveled. "This was most touching, particularly to our internal anatomy."[31]

1862

Private Hiram E. Bixler of the 76th Pennsylvania had been born and raised in Hellam Township. The 23-year-old soldier was now serving at Port Royal, South Carolina.

He wrote home to his friend Milton Ruby in late January, "I am enjoying serving pretty well. The only fault that I find [is] that uncle Sam has not paid us off yet but nevertheless we expect it before long.

"Some of the boys are complaining very much as they have no tobacco. This is a scarse article here, a five cent plug selling for 25 cts. Some of the boys give as much as 5 cts for one chew."

Bixler turned retrospective: "Milton how did you spend the holidays very pleasantly? It appears you have been at home on Christmas. I would have liked very much to have been with you on that day. I know we would have enjoyed ourselves very well. I often think of the time we had spent together. Do you never expect to see me again? Never let such foolish thoughts cross your mind. I expect to see you again and I hope that we may have some good old times."

His thoughts turned to his stomach: "We get pretty good grub from uncle Sam here, fresh every day pork, coffee, sugar, etc."[32]

**

On January 31, Lincoln issued orders that Union forces should begin a general advance by February 22.

The results were inconsistent, although some territorial gains resulted from the movements, particularly in the Western Theater.

In March, General McClellan began what would prove to be a slow and bloody advance on Richmond in what became known as the Peninsula Campaign. A month later, General Ulysses S. Grant won a hard-fought victory along the Tennessee River at Shiloh.

As fighting and casualty counts escalated, the need for a military conscription arose.

Hundreds of men in York County paid for substitutes to avoid the draft.

"When the draft was resorted to," Seven Valleys Harry Gladfelter recalled, "a large number of men in our surrounding community were drawn and obliged to enter the service or furnish a substitute at their own expense."

His brother, Jesse, was one of those then entering the service. He chose to enlist as a regular after being drafted into the 166th Pennsylvania.[33]

**

Many residents in York and Adams counties belonged to the Mennonite Church or other pacifist groups that considered war immoral.

In 1862, for example, 156 York countians sought exemptions from military service on grounds of conscience. Only five counties had more conscientious objectors. Adams County had 129.

The Dunkard Church in Pennsylvania took steps to help its men of military age. That denomination voted to back the government and its men by paying the commutation fee for every member who was drafted.

Pennsylvania as a whole had the largest number of conscientious objectors of any state (North or South) during the War.[34]

**

The Civil War has been referred to as the War Between the States. Perhaps it could also be deemed as the War Between the Brothers.

Several examples of local brothers split by the wearing of blue or gray were among scores so situated in the war.

The North/South divide separated York County's Hoffman brothers, as one example. Their mother, Rachel Clutter Hoffman, died less than two months after the birth of her youngest child. She left behind seven children, and all of the kids were sent to live with other families.

Thirteen-year-old Charles C. Hoffman lived with his aunt and uncle, Valentine and Elvira Clutter, in Virginia. V.J. Clutter was born and raised in York County but had moved to Virginia as a young man. He was a successful builder in the Richmond area, constructing a number of public buildings there.

When war broke out, Clutter and young Hoffman enrolled in the 1st Virginia Light Artillery. In the Gettysburg Campaign, as part of the Artillery Reserve of A.P. Hill's Corps, Lieutenant Clutter and Sergeant Hoffman traveled northward into their native Pennsylvania.

Charles initially manned his gun on Herr's Ridge west of Gettysburg before redeploying on Seminary Ridge late on July 1. Sometime either that afternoon or July 3, he died.

Hoffman was buried on the battlefield, but his remains were later removed along with thousands of others by Dr. Rufus Weaver. He was reinterred in a mass grave of Confederate dead at Hollywood Cemetery in Richmond.

V.J. Clutter suffered a severe foot wound at Spotsylvania in 1864, and the injury never properly healed. Although he lived until 1886, his health steadily declined after the war and as a result, so did his business. He was forced to sell his home to pay debts.

Clutter was admitted to the Camp Lee Soldiers' Home in August 1886, where he died less than two months later. He, too, is buried in Hollywood Cemetery.

Two other nephews were Yankee soldiers.

John Clutter Hoffman enlisted in the 87th Pennsylvania in September 1861. He fought in the Shenandoah Valley during the Gettysburg Campaign in 1863 and was twice wounded at the Battle of Carter's Woods.

The following year, he served in Ulysses S. Grant's army in the campaign to take Richmond, seeing action at such famous battles in Virginia as the Wilderness, Spotsylvania, and the siege of Petersburg.

Hoffman served as the 87th's postmaster until he mustered out in October 1864. He reenlisted in the regular army for several years. He left in 1870 to become a school teacher in Michigan and Indiana before returning to York to teach.

David N. Hoffman enlisted in September 1861 as a private in the 87th. A Confederate bullet snuffed out his life in November 1863, in the

Mine Run Campaign in Northern Virginia.

Two other Union soldiers in the 87th Pennsylvania also had brothers wearing gray.

William Crosby Waldman convinced his sibling George, a prisoner of war held at Fort Delaware, to sign an oath of allegiance to the United States.

And Pvt. William Culp's brother John Wesley Culp served in a Confederate infantry regiment from Virginia. He died at Gettysburg.[35]

**

Dr. George Conn was one of the leading residents in the Pleasureville area of what became Springettsbury Township.

He helped found the local United Brethren Church and had a burgeoning practice with an office in his Pleasant View Road home. He was widely known for his successful homeopathic treatment for cancer, and people traveled long distances to visit Conn after failing to find relief from eminent big-city doctors.

His younger brother served in the Confederate army. Born on a farm in Manchester Township in March 1824, Jesse W. Conn moved to Obion County, Tennessee, when he was 21.

Three years later, he married a Southern girl, Aneliza Reynolds. After her death he married Louisa Jane Waddell and fathered 10 children.

They owned a farm two miles southeast of Rives, Tennessee, which was a long way from Conn's birthplace.

Jesse enlisted in December 1863, in the 20th (Russell's) Tennessee Cavalry at Camp Bell for three years. The unit was part of Colonel Tyree H. Bell's brigade of famed General Nathan Bedford Forrest's cavalry force.

Like most Rebel cavalrymen, Private Conn had to supply his own horse, in this case a bay he valued at $800.[36]

**

Ovid Pinney "Jerry" Reno served in both the Union and Confederate armies.

Born in western Pennsylvania's Beaver County, he had drifted west in the 1850s to live with an older brother in Kansas. He was a 26-year-old boatman on the Mississippi River at the start of the Civil War.

Like many others of his profession, he was stranded in New Orleans and forced to join the Confederate army.

Reno and others later deserted, going to the Federal forces at Fort Pickens. He returned to the North and settled in Chanceford Township.

He then joined the Union army and was injured in a train wreck between Lynchburg and Danville, Virginia.[37]

**

Captain Jonathan S. Slaymaker was far less fortunate than Reno. The York County native had moved west before the war and now served in the 2nd Iowa Infantry.

He met with an unusual manner of death while serving under U.S. Grant in the campaign against Confederate-held Fort Donaldson in Tennessee.

"A bullet struck his pocket-knife in his left pocket," a newspaper reported, "shivering it to pieces, and drove the blade into his body, so that it, and not the bullet, severed the artery, the rupture of which caused his death. Pieces of the knife were found in his wallet."[38]

**

Company K of the 45th Pennsylvania included men from Wrightsville, Columbia, and other river towns.

In early 1862, the regiment served on Otter Island in coastal South Carolina. There, several soldiers died of typhoid fever. Nineteen-year-old Oscar Keller, a former store clerk from Wrightsville, was one of them.

In April Lieutenant Ephraim Myers noted some unusual meals.

"I ate my first South Carolina blackberries on April 25th," Myers wrote, "They were of the dewberry variety and very plentiful."

"While on Otter Island we made frequent visits to different parts of the island, which was the home of the alligator. Capturing alligators was our delight. One day a squad of the boys was out reconnoitering for them. We found one; he was soon dispatched with an ax and measured in length six feet two inches. This gave us a chance to eat alligator meat. It tasted much like fish, only a little strong."

"A large sea turtle was also caught on the beach. It weighed about 300 pounds, contained 125 eggs ready to lay and innumerable small ones. The turtle made all the soup the boys wished to eat."[39]

**

Hiram E. Bixler, the York countian in the 76th Pennsylvania in South Carolina, wrote to Milton Ruby in Hellam Township complaining that he had not received a letter from his friend for almost three months.

Days earlier he had witnessed his first battle — the Union bombardment of Fort Pulaski, a sturdy brick bastion located between Savannah and Tybee Island in Georgia.

"General Hunter ordered us to embark on board the good ship *Catawba* for Tybee Island, Ga.," he penned. "With the intention of storming the Fort, after a delightful ride of some three hours we arrived at the destined place. No sooner did the boat stop then the rebels raised their infernal flag on the Fort."

After disembarking, the 76th "marched through woods and swamps for about three miles when we again laid down to take a rest but we were called to arms several times during the night expecting the enemy to attack us. But morning at last came with a bright sun and clear sky and all was safe."

After describing more of the action near Fort Pulaski, Bixler concluded, "I suppose that by this time you are at home working on the farm while I am laying under a beautiful Palmetto in S. Carolina. Theas are beautiful State trees... I am beginning to like Soldiering very well. Why should we not? We get plenty to eat, fresh bread once every day. Fresh Beef, pickels, Molasses, Coffee or Tea thrice a day, and for a change bean Soup on Sunday."[40]

**

Back in York, the war threatened unity in the borough's houses of worship. In fact, one dispute ended with the local Presbyterian Church's minister in jail.

The Rev. Thomas Street and a visiting geography book salesman squared off one Saturday in early 1862. The minister had endorsed the visitor's product but later learned of his Southern sympathies.

He bellied up to the salesman, a Lancaster native named Alexander Harris.

"My friend, I'll have to ask you for my

recommendation (back)," Street demanded, "as I cannot endorse anyone who would curse the best government in the world."

Street and another man, a wounded Union officer, ended up in jail, accused of hitting the stranger. Out on bail, Street preached the next day on "The Loyalty of the Citizens," making no reference to the altercation.

Street, indeed, had a combative streak in him.

"It was no doubtful utterance which he made in the name of God for right and liberty and union," someone who knew him said.

Still, his church stuck together during his pastorate, which concluded just before the war's end in April 1865.[41]

**

Charles Baum, son of the minister of York's St. Paul's Lutheran Church, wrote that his father left the pastorate in the Shenandoah Valley because of his Unionist views.

His family left in a hurry with only the "clothing on our backs."

The minister ran into problems in Democratic York County, too. A majority in the county supported the Peace Democrats, the so-called Copperheads.

Several influential members left St. Paul's after guest preacher J.H. Menges proclaimed from the pulpit "all Democrats are rebels." Despite these tensions, Baum went on for a fruitful pastorate at St. Paul's, overseeing construction of a new church.

The family's flight from the Shenandoah Valley settled into family lore.

Years later, his son wrote that his father probably had that journey in mind when he preached his first sermon from the York pulpit, based on Psalm 20:5: "We will rejoice in thy salvation, and in the Name of our God we will set up our banners."[42]

**

The 87th Pennsylvania was among the Union troops assigned to Virginia's Shenandoah Valley, where the unit contested Stonewall Jackson's Confederates in what became famous as the Valley Campaign.

The regiment's Henry Schultz suffered wounds in both legs in the first Battle of Winchester.

"I walked to a house a short distance away for protection, and found I couldn't walk after that," he recalled. "Two others were lying beside me. One died a half hour later, shot through the abdomen."

A seemingly endless column of Rebels marched past the house all day. A young boy paused and gave Schultz a drink of water.

An old man with a red-and-white beard offered less encouragement, snarling 'You should be killed.'

"I didn't say a thing to him," Schultz recalled, "and he finally passed by."

Schultz stayed in a Winchester hospital for six weeks and then was exchanged for a Confederate prisoner, among the last 100 soldiers of the 87th traded in the war.

Coincidentally, the regiment would again fight at Winchester in June 1863 in the Gettysburg Campaign and yet again in 1864.

"I fought in the third battle of Winchester," Henry Schultz noted with satisfaction at the turn of events, "where we captured 2500 prisoners."[43]

**

Meanwhile on the Virginia Peninsula, General McClellan continued his slow advance on Richmond.

At the Battle of Seven Pines, Army of Northern Virginia commander Joseph Johnston suffered a serious wound that forced the Confederate War Department to seek a replacement.

On June 1, after trying another general briefly, they found their man: Robert E. Lee.

Back in York later that month, the U.S. War Department replaced a temporary hospital at the Duke Street schoolhouse with a formal dispensary.

It established a military hospital on the grounds of Penn Common. Several white-washed barracks and wards stood on York's south side.

The first 19 patients arrived on July 1. Eventually, more than 14,000 wounded soldiers would be treated at the facility.

Over time, the hospital became "a miniature world in itself, with post office, printing office, cabinet, carpenter, paint and tin shops." Staff members eventually produced a newspaper, *The Cartridge Box*, starting in March 1864.

Mary Fisher recalled community-wide civilian efforts who helped the soldiers before the army took over. The Ladies Soldiers Aid Society, a group of prominent women, headed the effort.

"Little children left their play to scrape lint and roll bandages. Parties and tea-drinkings were neglected for meetings at the work rooms and at private houses for cutting and sewing garments, and packing the stores contributed by the town folk and the country people," she wrote.

The latter group broke into their stores of linen in large chests packed in Germany. The linen was turned into bandages for the boys.

The generosity of York's women continued even after the army took over caring for its own.[44]

**

Northern war news remained bleak through the late summer.

McClellan's Peninsula Campaign ended in a withdrawal from Richmond; progress in the West and Trans-Mississippi had slowed; and casualties mounted in late August with the bloody defeat at Second Bull Run.

On the Northern home front, York County citizens provided for the soldiers and worked to maintain morale in the community.

The musical Henry and Anna Berger family and their six children moved to York in 1859. They wound up on South George Street and built an organ factory behind their home.

That factory burned in March 1861, taking three finished church organs and all of Henry Berger's equipment with it.

The insurance money didn't cover the loss, perhaps because of rising costs with the advent of the Civil War.

But all this didn't keep the four older children from giving a public concert at Washington Hall, just to the north on George Street.

The reviews were so glowing that the Ladies Aid Society asked the group to perform a benefit concert.

That women's group provided nurses and supplies to the military hospital, due west of the Berger home at Penn Common.

By the end of 1862, the Bergers moved to Ohio. They would later tour nationally, joined by a pioneering female concert saxophonist, Etta (Esther) Morgan.

And the Bergers had a pioneering musician, too. Anna Theresa, whose early career included that Washington Hall billing, played cornet.[45]

**

The 87th Pennsylvania's Private Charles E. Gotwalt, on guard duty near New Creek, Virginia, received a tall order.

He was to arrest a big Irishman from an Illinois regiment. The man, a noted bully, had been drinking with two buddies at a local bar and was creating quite a disturbance.

Gotwalt was to take him from the saloon "dead or alive."

Although nervous at the prospect of arresting such a notorious — and much larger — man, Gotwalt quickly walked up to the bar. He put his hand on the drunk's shoulder and arrested him.

To his surprise, instead of resisting, the Irishman docilely went with Gotwalt. His two equally drunken friends accompanied their pal to the guard house.

The regiment was treated to the remarkable spectacle of watching a scrawny, 16-year-old private arresting the "three bad men" of the brigade.[46]

**

Young Harry Gladfelter could track the war by observing trains — and their human cargo — passing through Hanover Junction.

"As the war progressed," he remembered, "we saw more of its horrors by the passing of train load after train load of soldiers going south over the then Northern Central Rail Road, not in passenger coaches, but in all manner of cars, box cars, coal cars, stock cars, and gondolas."[47]

**

Some of the men in Harry Gladfelter's view had embarked at York's North Duke Street station.

Thousands of Union soldiers paraded from Camp Scott, through downtown York, to the station. Troop trains constantly rolled through town, picking up these fighting men.

But, by the end of summer 1862, no Rebel soldiers had yet appeared in York's streets. That would change during the Maryland Campaign in September.

In the week before the Rebels appeared in force at Harpers Ferry, scattered Confederate patrols, scouts, and advance pickets roamed that region where Maryland met Virginia.

The Loudoun Rangers, a pro-Union Virginia cavalry organization, occasionally picked up these Rebels and took them prisoner.

Four Rangers were on special picket duty with the 87th Ohio at Sandy Hook, Maryland. As Stonewall Jackson's main Confederate force approached Harpers Ferry, this squad became separated from the infantry.

The quartet headed for safer confines, riding northward through Maryland into Pennsylvania. Along the way, they captured three Confederate soldiers.

The Loudoun Rangers escorted their prisoners into downtown York, creating quite a stir.

"These were the first 'Johnnies' the citizens had seen, and, of course, they were a kind of curiosity," the Rangers' historian noted. "The Rangers were lionized for this heroic achievement and escorted to the hotel, where an ovation was given them, and a grand dinner which the boys enjoyed."

No record is left of what became of the Southern prisoners, but it is likely they were locked up in the town jail, while their captors feasted with the jubilant citizenry of York.[48]

**

In early September, York businessman A.B. Farquhar accompanied a patrol of Union cavalry into Maryland.

As they neared the Confederate positions, he pushed ahead alone, against the advice of the cavalry captain.

His goal was to meet with an old schoolmate, now a Rebel cavalry general, and seek information on any military push toward York. If so, he wanted to ensure that his business and other private property, and the lives of women and children, would be spared.

The young industrialist, raised as a Quaker, reasoned he would be safe in his civilian clothing.

"Our Civil War," he reasoned, "was a fight between gentlemen."

He was correct that the enemy pickets would not harm him. Farquhar talked his way into seeing his former acquaintance General Fitzhugh Lee, a nephew of army commander Robert E. Lee.

After receiving news that the Confederates were not heading to York, he departed and rode home to spread the welcome news.[49]

**

Edward Webster Spangler helped with chores on his widowed mother's Paradise Township farm in the planting, cultivating, and harvesting seasons, spending the four winter months attending a local public school.

Hating chores and having no desire to spend his life in agriculture, he enrolled in the York County Academy, a precursor to York College. After a year of study, he secured a job as a clerk in one of York's leading dry-goods merchants.

The Civil War had raged for more than a year when Spangler enlisted in the army. In August, the 16-year-old enrolled in the 130th Pennsylvania.

A recruiting officer measured him at five foot two, two inches shorter than allowed. Spangler immediately stretched on his tiptoes and asked to be measured again.

With a wink, the recruiter casually replied, "That's all right."

Ed now was a soldier.

Scarcely a month later, he "saw the elephant," entering combat for the first time at the Battle of South Mountain in central Maryland.

"The first evidence I saw of the conflict was a dead cavalryman, evidently a courier," he recalled. "He was shot through the head, and his blood-covered face and glassy eyes made a ghastly sight. He was the first dead soldier I saw, and it was by no means a pleasing spectacle."

In pursuit of the enemy, young Spangler's thoughts turned to his stomach: "Late in the afternoon, impelled by an aching void and a desire for a change of diet, I repaired to a spacious farm-house near the highway, in quest of a pie for value. The matron emphatically refused compensation, and stated that as she was Union to the core she would take no pay from a Union soldier. As I had neither time nor inclination to argue my faint protest, I thanked her for her hospitality and returned to the regiment much refreshed."

Spangler escaped unharmed from the fighting at Antietam, Fredericksburg, and Chancellorsville.

When the regiment's term of enlistment expired in May 1863, Spangler and his comrades returned home to York and a rousing reception, parade and dinner.

Spangler was appointed as a deputy U.S. marshal and never expected trouble from the Rebels again.

Trouble, however, came to him in late June.

Thousands of Confederates passed through York County, leaving behind hundreds of played-out horses. As Spangler approached one abandoned horse, the frightened animal lashed out, kicking Spangler in his leg, badly breaking it.

Incapacitated and now unfit for the rigors of duty as a marshal, he reluctantly resigned his peace officer's badge and returned to civilian life.

The Confederates had unknowingly put him out of government service but instead sent him into a life of ease and comfort.

Spangler returned to school, studied law, and became a leading attorney and wealthy newspaper owner, a lucrative career move directed by the kick of an abandoned Rebel horse.[50]

**

The 12th Pennsylvania Reserves Regiment was organized at Camp Curtin in Harrisburg in June 1861, made up of volunteers who answered the governor's call to arms following Abraham Lincoln's proclamation for 100,000 to put down the fledgling rebellion.

Company G of the new regiment was raised in York County, with Samuel N. Bailey of Dillsburg elected as the lieutenant colonel.

Stewartstown's Charles W. Diven, who later would become the colonel of the 200th Pennsylvania Infantry, commanded the company. At the time of his enlistment, the thought that the war would last long enough for the Keystone State to raise more than 200 regiments must have been inconceivable to Captain Diven.

The 12th Reserves fought in several engagements during the 1862 Peninsula Campaign under McClellan.

With little time for rest and recuperation, the undermanned regiment participated in the Maryland Campaign. The 12th was part of the grand assault on Turner's Gap during the Battle of South Mountain.

Anchoring the center of the Union line, the 12th, and its York County boys of Company G, "moved on with the most determined gallantry."

Despite a steady rain of bullets from Confederates at higher elevations, the company suffered remarkably light casualties in the successful attack that eventually carried the National Road and the heights. The entire regiment suffered only 25 casualties — six men killed and 19 wounded.

On the evening of September 16, the York countians were again in action in their division's aborted attack on Rebel positions in the East Woods, an engagement halted by gathering darkness.

The following day at the bloody battle of

Antietam, Company G was part of the Union First Corps assault along the Hagerstown Pike southward toward Sharpsburg.

Then the unit manned a wooden fence at the northern edge of Miller's Cornfield in a firefight with John Bell Hood's Confederates. With "its accustomed gallantry," the 12th Reserves fought hard, as evidenced by the casualty count — 13 killed, along with 47 wounded and four missing.

Sergeant James L. McClure was among the 22,000 who fell on "America's Bloodiest Day." He would die on October 9 from his injuries.

Unusually tall for the period at more than six feet, the 30-year-old veteran was also older than most of his men. Auburn-haired with a light complexion and dark eyes, he had been a prewar laborer in one of York's small factories.

A few months later, at Fredericksburg, his brother David would suffer a serious wound that knocked him out of the war. David and James were buried in adjacent graves in Dillsburg.

The day before James McClure died, Corporal Daniel D. Bailey passed away from wounds at Antietam. He had left school at the age of 18 and enlisted in downtown York.

Compared to McClure, Bailey, a five-foot-seven, blue-eyed, black-haired student, was more typical of the men and boys of Company G.[51]

**

Edward Fisher, a laborer and blacksmith from Peach Bottom in southeastern York County, enlisted in the 130th Pennsylvania.

That regiment boasted many "squirrel hunters and duck shooters," who knew how to handle weapons.

In fierce fighting at Antietam, Fisher watched his friend Richard Smith die in the ill-fated attack on Confederates entrenched in the Sunken Road. Not long afterward, Fisher spotted two young Rebels approaching. Instinctively, he raised his rifle and prepared to fire at the foremost soldier.

"For God's sake," they cried, "do not shoot!"

Fisher refrained, despite his anger and grief over his comrade's death. He took the Southerners prisoner and passed them back to the provosts.

Returning to the front line, he experienced "one thing I would not like to do again. I was loading and firing so fast among the hail of bullets and shell etc. that I did not notice where I was until I saw the Johnnys on the right of me in a corn field loading their guns, could see them ram the cartridges plain. I was between the two lines." His own line was behind him, "up on the side of the hill."

He learned that the 130th had fallen back to the Roulette farm, where he found them late in the evening. The exhausted York County boys slept in an open field for two nights.

On September 19, the regiment drew the grim assignment of burying the dead. The men exchanged their rifles for picks and shovels, and at noon commenced digging long burial trenches to inter dead Confederates.

"They were in an awful condition; all bloated and gurgled like a wash tub full of water," Fisher recalled. "When they were moved the odor was something almost unbearable."

Fisher was relieved when the gruesome task ended, and the 130th Pennsylvania marched back to camp near the Roulette house.

Three days later, the regiment departed

Sharpsburg and marched toward Harpers Ferry. They waded across the Potomac River.

"The water was up to our waists so that we had to hold our cartridge boxes up to keep our powder dry and our hard tack from getting soaked," Fisher remembered.

As the men forded the shallow river, the "splendid" regimental band of the 14th Connecticut serenaded the soldiers with the popular tune *Jordan is a Hard Road to Travel*.

After setting up camp on Bolivar Heights, they found tents left behind by other Union units captured earlier in the month.

With shelter and food, Fisher and his comrades took time to sightsee. They visited the old school house where abolitionist revolutionary John Brown had secreted arms for a planned slave rebellion back in 1859.

It was a welcome change from the horrors of Antietam.[52]

**

Before there was war, John Anthony worked as a tobacconist in northern York County's Fairview Township.

He was also a musician and enlisted in the 7th Pennsylvania Reserves in May 1861 to use those skills.

But the need for soldiers outweighed the demand for musicians. Anthony was reduced in rank and given a musket as a common infantryman.

His father George Anthony would never see him again.

Badly wounded at Antietam, young John was taken to a temporary field hospital in the village

of Smoketown, where he died. He is buried in the National Cemetery at Antietam.[53]

**

Lieutenant Samuel Waring of York was among the soldiers ordered to police the festering battlefield of Antietam and its environs.

His job: Stop pesky relic hunters and recover any military items that "got mysteriously transferred into the hands of sundry citizens."

By mid-October, Waring and his patrols had visited numerous farms and houses throughout central Maryland.

Their efforts netted "four hundred and forty-three muskets, and sundry good horses and mules."[54]

**

Twenty-three-year-old Daniel Hostler hailed from Siddonstown, later Siddonsburg, in northern York County.

The shoemaker had left his father Michael's farm in early August 1862, and things happened fast after that. He enlisted at a recruiting station in York and was mustered into service at Camp Curtin.

Scarcely five weeks later, the private with the 130th Pennsylvania died in action at Antietam and was buried on the battlefield.

On December 22, his remains were brought home. His grieving father buried Daniel on Christmas Day in the graveyard of Christ Lutheran, also known as Filey's Church, in Monaghan Township.

"Eloquent and patriotic orations were delivered on the occasion by Reverends Deshirl of Mt. Pleasant, and Dasher of Lewisberry," the York

Democratic Press reported. "We are told that upwards of five hundred persons attended the funeral."[55]

**

Lydia Jane Larew lived in Portis, Kansas, during the Civil War. The young Quaker was a native of Warrington Township in northwestern York County.

About the time of the Battle of Antietam, she sent a lengthy note to her sister Ruth Anna Walker.

After lamenting about the "troublesome world," Lydia Jane reflected, "there is grate trouble her. But Oh it is ent nothing to compare with what I have sean. We have no caus to complane her yet. We have plenty here."

She felt sorry for the soldiers.

"I feel as though I could go to try and help them," she wrote. "Oh sister what will become of our country whin the union flag is take frum us. I pray that wont be saken."

Ruth received a second letter, this one from another sister, Phebe Angeline Smith, a resident of nearby Washington Township.

Angeline mentioned that 500 Rebels were within 95 miles of her family. Union fighting men got there in time and stopped their advance.

"(T)hey sed thy pour dead soldiers lay in evin rows 8 and 9 men deepe," Angeline noted. "Ken Smith and John ( ) and yong Kunkle was this last weeke to see thy battleground… It was awfull to think of the many lost lives. I wish they could settle this war and not shed any more blud."[56]

**

York County artist Lewis Miller drew a group of black people celebrating the Emancipation Proclamation.

Those portrayed danced and sang to the sound of a fiddle and banjo.
"The Negroes Slavery is Abolished, and the Colored population set free," he wrote beneath his drawing.

President Abraham Lincoln issued the proclamation in late September, freeing slaves in territories at war with the Union. The order went into effect Jan. 1, 1863.

Some in York County's black population did more than celebrate the freedom promised their kinsmen in the South.

They marched off to war, joining what were then called colored troops, to fight the Confederates, contributing to the demise of the Rebel forces.[57]

**

A steam train carrying the 115th New York Volunteers paused at York's depot for a respite in mid-September.

The unit had taken a barge from their base camp in Annapolis up the Chesapeake Bay to Baltimore. There, the men had boarded a special train of the Northern Central Railway.

Telegraph messages flashed at every station along their route, passing along the news that the soldiers' train was approaching. The men rode northward through New Freedom, Hanover Junction, and the Howard Tunnel, and then passed through downtown York in mid-morning to the cheers of the populace.

One York woman recalled that news spread quickly when troop trains, such as the one carrying the New Yorkers, were arriving. She and her neighbors always made it a point to have some extra food and delicacies on hand, both as a treat for the patients in the Penn Common military hospital and for the travel-weary soldiers who stopped at the stationhouse.

The young soldiers were "always so appreciative," and she made it a point to be as motherly as possible to them.

Lieutenant James Clark appreciated such motherly love, describing the tour through Pennsylvania as one long ovation.

"Mothers took their last loaf from the oven, daughters carried jars of jelly and nice preserves from the cellar, and with tearful eyes begged their acceptance," he reminisced. "As the cars moved from each station, the fair sex showered apples, peaches, pears and oranges among the men like rain."

Never again in war would the 115th New York receive such lavish attention. Their future meals while on campaign would often consist of stale hardtack that could crack teeth, salty boiled beef of shoe-leather texture, and coffee that either lacked authority or bit the tongue.

The pleasant memories of the train ride from York to points west must have seemed bittersweet in the trying months to come.[58]

**

During the Civil War, Lamanda (Zeigler) Sweitzer and her husband William lived on a farm near the Northern Central tracks between the villages of Glen Rock and Railroad.

She told her grandsons that she remembered "seeing the trains carrying soldiers to fight in the Civil War going past their home. Because of the steep grade from Glen Rock to New Freedom, the soldiers were required to alight from the train and walk. It took two engines to

pull the train up the steep grade toward the town of New Freedom."

Sometimes wayward soldiers took advantage of the situation.

In the kitchen of Lamanda and William's home was a box used to store firewood. Behind the box, near the chimney, was a secret door. The family often hung their coats over the door, hiding it from view.

Many years later Lamanda recalled, "During the Civil War there was this guy from the area, who tended to go AWOL from the Union Army. One time an officer came looking for him and he said, 'We will take him dead or alive,' in his Pennsylvania Dutch accent. When the officer left, the family left the AWOL soldier out and he would run into the woods."

She added, "This was a common occurrence until the war was over and they never did get him. It was a good hiding place, when the coats were hanging there; you never knew what was there."[59]

**

York's military hospital was among the largest in Pennsylvania, and its record of cleanliness and sanitation was unparalleled.

Dr. Henry Palmer, a Janesville, Wisconsin, native, was the surgeon of the famed Iron Brigade of the West through the summer of 1862, when he took command of the York hospital.

He instituted sanitary measures that resulted in his facility having an enviable record that only 200 men would die out of 14,000 patients that came through the facility in its three years of operation.

Major Palmer required that his patients were

well nourished, slept in clean wards with frequently changed bedding and got lots of fresh air and sunshine. His commissary staff bought fresh eggs, bread, milk, and other staples from the women of York.

Anna Maria (Stallman) Miller lived near the hospital on South George Street, a comfortable neighborhood of scattered two-story brick and wooden houses. She ran the family household while her husband, Henry, was away in the Union army.

Though pregnant, she walked every day to Penn Common and sold eggs and butter to hospital officials. It provided a steady source of income to augment her husband's army pay.

The Millers had married in 1850, and he worked as a laborer in P.A. & S. Small's downtown warehouse. He did not enlist at first, possibly because of family obligations. He was the father of eight children.

The army drafted Miller in October 1862, and he served as a private in the 166th Pennsylvania Drafted Militia. While he was in uniform, Anna Maria gave birth to a daughter, Martha Matilda, on April 15, 1863.

Now he had nine children and would live to see them all.

He received an honorable discharge when the regiment mustered out in July 1863.

Henry Palmer, the skilled surgeon and medical director, saved many lives. But all his training and experience could not save his beloved daughter.

The youngster became ill and died in York despite his efforts.[60]

**

A member of the 5th Connecticut Infantry convalescing in Dr. Palmer's hospital informed his hometown newspaper that there were nearly 1,000 wounded then present.

"They have nothing," he wrote, "to cheer them in their lonely hours of pain except books." The hospital library did not have "half enough to fill the demand."

The editor asked the citizenry of Hartford to drop off books at a particular hat store, from where they would be boxed and shipped down to York.

"Send them in at once," he appealed.[61]

**

The 13th Pennsylvania Reserves, passing through York County in the autumn of 1862, stopped in Shrewsbury awaiting orders.

Woodsmen and lumberjacks from the mountains of western Pennsylvania filled the Union regiment's ranks. The unit was widely known as the "Bucktails" because its men wore the white tails of deer in their caps.

But the unit became widely known in southern York County for another reason. Colonel Thomas L. Kane and his Bucktails were accused of wanton destruction of private property after pitching camp at the Shrewsbury Camp Meeting Grounds.

The Bucktails borrowed a large board tent from Shrewsbury resident Levin Willey. When Kane's men broke camp and moved off to their next destination, several soldiers tore down Willey's tent and destroyed it.

He complained, but to no avail, and even tried legal action years after the war to recover his money, claiming that the Federal government should recompense him $65 for his loss.

Like most York countians who also filed damage claims during the war, Willey never received a dime.[62]

**

In November, President Lincoln again sacked General McClellan as commander of the Army of the Potomac and replaced him this time with Major General Ambrose Burnside, a general who came to be more noted for his flowing sideburns than for military prowess.

That choice drew considerable criticism later in the year when Burnside launched a series of ill-advised frontal assaults on Confederates heavily entrenched on the heights above Fredericksburg, Virginia.

He lost nearly 13,000 men, more than double Robert E. Lee's losses.

George W. Stahl, a Hanover cabinetmaker, survived the Battle of Fredericksburg.

He was a staunch Republican and supporter of Lincoln's policies. Consistent with his politics, he enlisted in the 130th Pennsylvania in August 1862, leaving behind his wife Sarah and children.

Stahl had survived Antietam, too, and gained a distinction along the way. Confederate Colonel John S. Mosby's partisan rangers captured him twice, but he escaped both times.

Those escapes were not easy. Known as the "Gray Ghost of the Confederacy," Mosby and his men had the reputation for stealth and quickness in their raids.

The Hanover soldier managed to rejoin his regiment after each escape from the guerilla band.

The second time was particularly harrowing.

Rebels shot Stahl in the leg as he dashed away.[63]

**

Early in the war, Charles Stewart enlisted in the 5th Virginia Cavalry, which served under Confederate General Jeb Stuart.

He shifted loyalties and later enlisted in the Loudoun Rangers, the pro-Union company from Loudoun County, Virginia. He spent the rest of the war as a sergeant in that unit, often clashing with Mosby's partisan rangers from the same region of Northern Virginia.

When it was over, he settled in southeastern York County's Slate Hill, an area noted for producing scores of fighting men for the Union army.

In that Peach Bottom Township region, he lived peacefully with his fellow Civil War pensioners, a man who fought under both flags.[64]

**

Colonel Matthew Stanley Quay of Dillsburg commanded the 134th Pennsylvania Infantry throughout much of 1862. His regiment mustered out of the army in early December, but he was still in camp on the 13th when the Battle of Fredericksburg erupted.

Quay would receive the Medal of Honor for his bravery that day.

His citation reads: "Although out of service, he voluntarily resumed duty on the eve of battle and took a conspicuous part in the charge on the heights."[65]

**

As Christmas approached, thousands of York County men were away from home serving in the military. For some, frustration and boredom

38

proved wearisome; others struggled with chronic illnesses contracted since joining the service.

Stationed at Camp Curtis near Springfield, Illinois, York native William G. Ruhl wrote to his brother Noah, who had recently returned home ill after serving in the 130th Pennsylvania.

"I received a letter from Brother Sam, he stated that he had been sick some two months with the rhersmatison and thought he would get a discharge, it would be the best thing what he could do, for the service will kill anybody in the course of time. I myself would take a discharge if I could get one but neverless we have a good time. We don't have any scouting to do nothing but our regulars culls to blow.

I think you done well when you went home. I would of have done the same if I had been in the same circumstances and would have stayed home all winter or till I get well. I never have been in the army. We have good tents and blankets and plenty to eat and wear."

It is likely that William, the bandmaster of an Illinois cavalry regiment, never saw his two brothers again. Noah Ruhl returned to his unit soon thereafter died at Falmouth, Virginia, on March 3, 1863. A year later, Samuel B. Ruhl perished at Petersburg.[66]

**

George W. McElroy had enrolled in the army in Harrisburg on December 3, 1861, perhaps out of patriotic fervor or from a sense of adventure.

The 36-year-old became a private in the 1st Pennsylvania Artillery.

Within a year, he was a patient at the military hospital in York. In October 1862, he walked away from the ward and somehow slipped past the Patapsco Guards, the hospital's Maryland-raised security unit.

He evaded capture in downtown York, at least for awhile. Soon, he was again a patient in the hospital, with a new attitude.

That included an agreeable Christmas 1862.

"Everyone seemed to enjoy the usual compliment of good things," he wrote.

Townspeople returned their good fortunes to patients at the hospital.

"The citizens of York," he stated, "are widely known and distinguished for their liberality and benevolence, and they would not entertain the idea, even for a moment, that one family, in their midst should, on this annual festival, suffer for the want of anything to render them cheerful and comfortable."

There was one note of discord in town.

The New Year's custom of firing guns at midnight drew criticism.

"I am told, of a few sleepy-headed old bachelors, petulantly complaining of the noise and confusion, for some days afterwards," he penned. "The married men and their unexceptional companions enjoyed the occasion and the tumult, to its fullest extent."[67]

Early 1863

Race relations remained an issue throughout the war, even in many parts of the North.

On January 18, from camp near Falmouth, Virginia, Corporal Jonathan M. Shenberger of the 187th Pennsylvania penciled a four-page note to his sister Mollie Anna at Wrightsville.

"What does the folks up there think of Old Abe's Emancipation Proclamation?" he wrote about the presidential order that had gone into effect on New Year's Day.

The black population thought it's a big deal, he opined, but he "couldn't see it."

He also commented on the controversial commander of the Army of the Potomac, General Burnside, whose ill-fated assaults at Fredericksburg cost thousands of Union lives:

"Yesterday our corps was out on review by old Burnside. He looked right gay, but was not the man to win. When he rode along the lines some of the troops tried to cheer him, but couldn't raise the wind. The old Hundred and Thirtieth made a splash, but broke down on it. Bully for us or any other man. I think if General McClellan had come along it would have been such cheering that's never been heard of. The Colonel of the 14th Indiana Regiment wanted the men to cheer, but not one man would holler. Bully for them."

Turning to less politically charged subjects, the former canal boatman added, "Well Anna, I must bring my letter to a close, for the beans is pretty near done and we must devour them and commence cooking a big rice soup for supper.

"Anna, I wish you would tell Mother not to trouble herself about them shirts, for I got a couple of Uncle Sam's and think that they will last till I get home, but I wish I had my books, just for fun. Tell old Dad that I only weigh one hundred and sixty six, and when I get back I think I will be man enough to carry a bag of wheat up the steps."

Jonathan Shenberger would survive the Civil War to become a railroad engineer.

However he died when the train he was engineering smashed full speed into a parked caboose at 52nd Street in Philadelphia.[68]

**

Morale sank to new lows throughout much of the North after Burnside's poorly planned maneuver stalled in Virginia's rainy January weather.

The so-called "Mud March" led to Lincoln's dismissal of Burnside and the appointment of yet another in the long line of commanders of the Army of the Potomac, "Fighting Joe" Hooker.

Few new volunteers signed up for the army, and recruiters tried unsuccessfully to rekindle the patriotic spirit that had filled the early war enlistment quotas.

In February, a Lancaster County soldier sent a letter from camp in Fredericksburg to the editor of the *Columbia Spy*.

His colonel had sent a recruiting party to Columbia to sign up more men. That delegation had not returned and was supposed to have deserted.

The writer inquired if anything had been done to enlist the blacks of Columbia under a proposed bill by Congressman Thaddeus Stevens that would authorize raising black troops.

He believed that one hidden benefit of Stevens' controversial bill was to "rid the state of free negroes." The good and brave black men would enlist and be sent to the front.

"The rest, to avoid the draft," he sneered, "will run for Canada or *York county*."

"Hurry up the draft and hurry up the soldiers — black or white: let them come!" he added, "Rebel bullets and bayonets are not respecters of persons."

If the politicians opposed black soldiers, let them come themselves — or hold their peace.

The infantryman added a postscript on a completely different matter. The paymaster had not yet arrived.

"We don't grumble at the government for not paying us promptly — we can do without money ourselves, but our poor families," he wrote. "That our children should suffer for want of food simply because Papa is far away. Makes the stoutest of us shudder."[69]

**

Throughout the cold, rainy Eastern winter, casualty lists grew, though much of the fighting had been suspended until better weather.

Among the scores of York countians who perished in the Civil War was 17-year-old Winfield Scott Hamacher of Monaghan Township, in the county's northern tip.

Named for the popular general and hero of the Mexican War, young Hamacher seemed slated for a military career.

He enrolled in the 7th Pennsylvania Reserves and survived the vicious fighting during the Peninsula Campaign, Second Bull Run, South Mountain, and Antietam.

When the regiment was sent to the entrenchments guarding Washington, D.C., in early February, poor sanitation and disease proved more lethal than Confederate lead. Hamacher contracted typhoid fever and died in the camp hospital on March 3.

The fallen soldier's body was transported to Monaghan Township, where he was interred in Filey's Church Cemetery.

The same day that Winfield Hamacher died, the U.S. Congress authorized a draft covering male citizens aged 25 to 45, but exempting those who paid a $300 commutation fee or provided a substitute.[70]

**

For a week in March, York hosted the annual meeting of the East Baltimore Conference of the Methodist Episcopal Church.

The Rev. John A. Gere of York, a relative by marriage to Confederate General Johnson K. Duncan, was one of three pastors to present a special report.

A year before, delegates had passed a resolution on the state of the country, in which they commended President Lincoln and expressed their support for his policies and the course of the war. A special three-man committee was dispatched to convey a signed copy of the resolutions to the president.

Now at the 1863 York meeting, the Reverend Gere and his colleagues presented a letter from the Executive Mansion in Washington. It was a note from Abraham Lincoln expressing his gratitude for the resolutions.

"These kind words of approval, coming from so numerous a body of intelligent Christian people; and so free from all suspicion of sinister motives, are indeed encouraging," the president penned. "By the help of an All-wise Providence, I shall continue to do my duty, and I shall expect the continuation of your prayers for a right solution of our national difficulties, and the restoration of our country to peace and prosperity."[71]

**

Also that March, York's election results gave the post of chief burgess to *York Gazette* owner

David Small, a longtime leader in the Democratic Party.

"In the contest which has just closed, the indomitable Democracy have gloriously triumphed over the advocates of usurpation and oppression — of the unconstitutional and iniquitous measures of Lincoln's Administration — of domestic strife and mob-violence — over secret cabals and Abolition clubs…," his paper gloated.

The county tended to vote decidedly Democratic, whereas Pennsylvania as a whole in those war years voted with the Republicans. Republican Andrew Curtin won re-election rather handily over his Democratic challengers. York County favored his competitors.[72]

**

In April, an executive committee of patients at York's army hospital drafted a letter to President Lincoln.

They outlined a series of resolutions declaring their allegiance to Lincoln's war policies and general course of the war.

"We congratulate your Excellency and through you the country at large upon the continued and unbroken Union feeling prevailing among our gallant soldiers," the patients resolved, "notwithstanding the exertions made on the North by corrupt and unscrupulous politicians to divide them in sentiment."

Among the trio of representatives to sign the document was George W. McElroy, the Lancaster artilleryman who had briefly walked away from the hospital and was now back in a leadership position.[73]

**

James Edie Gordon, convalescing in a Union army hospital in Stafford County, Virginia, was lonely.

So he wrote "A Soldiers Dream at Home" one night in March to his wife, Malinda, back home in southeastern York County:

"You have put the children to bed, Linda / Cyrus, Gusey, and Mary and Sarah / They have lipsed their sweet, Our Father. /And sunk to their night's repose. / Did they think of me, dear Linda? / Did they think of me and say / God bless him and God keep him / Dear father far away."

He penned four more stanzas before concluding:

"God guard and keep you all, Linda / God guard and keep me too / For if only one were missing / What would the other do? Oh when will the war be over / And when shall I behold / Those whom I love so dearly / Safe in the dear home fold."

James Gordon survived the war and returned to Linda, his four children and his "dear home fold."[74]

**

The idea of combining the profession of preacher with that of military officer — Civil War military chaplains — was not universally accepted.

Among the men of the cloth quietly toiling to provide spiritual guidance and direction to the Union troops was an unnamed chaplain assigned to the military hospital on York's Penn Common. At times discouraged by the naysayers, he was seeing positive results from his labors by the spring of 1863.

"We have been cheered by seeing quite a number turning to the Lord," the chaplain wrote in the April edition of *The National Preacher*. "Each month of this year I have baptized some, and added them to the general Evangelical Christian Church."

The chaplaincy has not been a failure, he wrote, as some have contended. Sure, there were discouragements, but such was the case when he ministered at a church. But he had never admitted as many men to church membership as in the previous three months.

"To God's name be all the glory," he penned. "We are quietly working on, and desire an interest in the prayers of God's people."[75]

**

Robert E. Lee's Army of Northern Virginia and "Fighting Joe" Hooker's Army of the Potomac fought one of the war's fiercest and bloodiest battles from April 20 to May 6 near an estate known as Chancellorsville.

More than 30,000 men fell in the confused fighting, which proved to be one of Lee's finest victories.

Samuel Boll, a 22-year-old farmhand from Lower Windsor Township, was one of many York countians fighting at Chancellorsville.

Before the war he worked on the farm of Joseph Dellinger. In August 1862, he volunteered for the 130th Pennsylvania.

Son. Brother. Farmer. Soldier.

Sam Boll could answer to many titles.

At Chancellorsville, he added another: hero.

During the swirling fighting, another York County soldier, Michael Shenberger, fell wounded. As he lay bleeding, the Union line collapsed and panic-stricken soldiers began trampling the helpless Shenberger.

Boll quickly realized his friend's plight and saved him from being crushed to death by the mob.

Sam Boll made it home from the war, married his sweetheart, and fathered 11 children and countless descendants.[76]

**

On May 10, the South lost one of its greatest heroes when Stonewall Jackson, who had lost an arm from friendly fire at Chancellorsville, died of pneumonia.

He had long advocated an invasion of the North, intending to take the war to the banks of the Susquehanna. He believed that such an aggressive move could end the war in the East.

Months earlier, he had authorized his cartographer, Major Jedediah Hotchkiss, to draw a detailed map of the Shenandoah and Cumberland valleys, all the way to Harrisburg.

It must be kept "a profound secret," Jackson warned.

Now, the famed Stonewall was dead.

His invasion idea, however, lived on in the mind and planning of his superior officer, Robert E. Lee.[77]

**

William B. Barr grew up in Hellam Township and attended the same grade school as Elizabeth Ruby.

He had moved west and later enrolled as a private in the 112th Illinois Infantry.

From Camp Somerset in Kentucky, he wrote a

letter on May 11 to Elizabeth in which he requested her photograph, judging it to be "the best in the world."

Flattery aside, Barr turned to the serious matter of war, "But those old and happy times have gone by. We have some fine times in the army & some disagreeable times. We miss our homes & cherishing mothers…My livestock will keep until I get home if ever I am so lucky — which I think I will be if some rebel bullet does not strike me too hard."

"I witnessed one battle, Barr penned, "& took it as cool as eating a meal of victuals. I expect to get into one again unless the Rebs run faster than we can follow."[78]

**

John B. Wagoner of Hanover was among the thousands of fathers throughout York County with at least one son in the Union army — Wesley was serving down in South Carolina on Folly Island.

John himself had received a draft notice from the U.S. Marshal back in 1862, but he was granted an exemption.

While the war raged, life on the home front continued. Concerned over a spate of recent fires in Hanover, Wagoner purchased a fire insurance policy on May 23 for a term of seven years with premiums of $128.

A list of the covered property is insightful as to typical property values at the height of the Civil War:

House covered for $800; washhouse for $100; pig pen, chicken house for $100; barn for $500; carriage house & shed, $100.[79]

**

Colonel Levi Maish's 130th Pennsylvania was one of dozens of regiments which mustered out of the Union army not long after the Battle of Chancellorsville.

At 2:00 p.m. one spring day, York residents learned that the unit had departed from Harrisburg and was heading toward York.

Bells signaled the close of stores and then started up again when the regiment arrived in York, the *York Gazette* reported on May 26.

The volunteers were received on North George Street and marched over the designated route to the barracks where the Ladies Aid Society furnished light fare for the "war-worn and sun-burned heroes."

The Patapsco Guards and the Hospital Band headed the procession after which followed the returned soldiers, Free Masons, Odd Fellows, Red Men, Laurel Fire Company, with its gallery engine drawn by four horses, and then the citizenry.

"All the flags were thrown to the breeze," the *Gazette* reported, "the town was filled with people, which gave it a lively and animated appearance."

Similar joyous homecoming scenes greeted returning regiments throughout the North.

Still, most Union troops were not yet eligible to be mustered out. For many York County soldiers, the worst fighting was yet to come.[80]

**

In the Suffolk, Virginia, area, however, the fighting had stopped after more than a month of siege warfare. Earlier in the year, Robert E. Lee had dispatched General James Longstreet's soldiers there to protect Richmond from an anticipated attack from the southeast.

When no significant Yankee threat materialized, the Rebels began foraging the countryside for supplies. They eventually marched to Suffolk, where Union General John J. Peck awaited with 25,000 men. Longstreet besieged the Federals, but abandoned the quest in early May when Lee urgently summoned his force back to Northern Virginia.

Union soldiers such as James Nickel breathed a sigh of relief.

He informed his wife Barbara, "I must tell you that we have good times now since the rebels is gon[e] and if they don't take us off after them we are just as safe as if at home."

"At this time," he mentioned, "we have got it good. We can lay down or sit set up or walk about or pitch horse shoes or play ball or anything we choose at this time, but I would be better satisfied if I was at home to you."[81]

**

John Jolly of the 35th New York had survived the fighting, making it through his two-year enlistment.

Looking forward to his own homecoming, he was riding atop a railcar as his train rolled near Hanover Junction in south-central York County in May.

But Jolly would not make it home to Jefferson County, New York, alive. As his train passed under a bridge, he was knocked off and killed instantly.

His comrades put his body into a coffin and shipped it, by express, to his home.[82]

**

Strinestown native Harry Fink soldiered faithfully in the 87th Pennsylvania despite being bowlegged, which must have made marching a chore for the musician in his early 50s.

Along with dozens of men in the regiment, Fink, known as the "Pied Piper of Company A," was taken prisoner at Carter's Woods during the Second Battle of Winchester in mid-June. Confederate guards escorted them from Winchester, Virginia, up the Shenandoah Valley to Staunton.

It was a trying time for the men, many of whom were dispirited from the stunning defeat and their new situation as prisoners of war. Their daily food allowance on the march was only a pint of flour for each man, who had to make and bake his own dough cakes.

About halfway to Staunton, one of the officers of the guard detail inquired, "Where are your musicians?"

Harry Fink stepped forward, along with Lewis Renaut.

"Take the front line," ordered the officer.

Fink and Renaut moved to the head of the long column. Two drummer boys tagged along behind.

The guards distributed fifes and drums to the astonished Yankees.

"What shall we play?' asked Fink.

"Anything," replied Colonel Francis H. Board of the 58th Virginia.

The blue-coated musicians led off with *Yankee Doodle*, receiving the applause of their captors. They followed with *When Johnny Comes Marching Home* and then *The Girl I Left Behind*.

"Very good, give us another tune," remarked the

Rebel commanding officer.

Regimental historian George Prowell recorded what came next: "After making big eyes toward the Colonel, riding near him, and holding his fife up to his mouth with one hand, Musician Fink struck up *The Star-Spangled Banner*. Some of the boys joined in the chorus, others cheered. To their astonishment the Confederates applauded and the Colonel laughed, for they all enjoyed the fun. The musical instruments were then returned to their owners, and the men trod along till they reached Staunton, tired and footsore."

As the prisoners entered the town, a guard asked the Pied Piper to play. Fink plucked a leaf from a tree, placed it between the palms of his hands and played *Yankee Doodle*.

That amused soldiers in the ranks and the crowds along the sidewalks.

"I thought the Yanks were wild men, but they are just like the rest of us," said an old man who had just eyed a Union soldier for the first time.

Yankees were rare in that part of Virginia.

Within a week, Rebels would not be rare in Fink's native part of Pennsylvania.[83]

Osborne Perry Anderson, seen in this Library of Congress photograph, escaped Federal forces sent to put down John Brown's raid on Harpers Ferry, Virginia, in 1859. Anderson, one of Brown's lieutenants, made it to York, where a "good Samaritan," believed to be former slave William C. Goodridge, aided his escape. He eventually reached Canada.

This advertisement from the *York Democratic Press* in 1843 shows one of ex-slave William C. Goodridge's business ventures. His rail line is believed to have been instrumental in conveying fugitives along the Underground Railroad.

This is the bird's-eye view from the top of Webb's Hill looking to the north, toward York. In this vicinity, the Confederate army's big guns commanded the town in late June 1863. The terrain would have been similar to that seen in this image from *Art Work of York*, published by the W.H. Parish Publishing Co. in 1893.

Mary C. Fisher, a teacher-turned-nurse, wrote with great insight about how the Civil War affected York and Adams counties. When the Confederates occupied York, she wrote, "We knew not how soon might come a signal to unleash the dogs of war in our midst and give your homes a prey to the invader." She's shown later in life in this York County Heritage Trust photograph.

This portrait of Jeremiah Sullivan Black, a leading U.S. lawyer in the Civil War era, hangs in the York County Administrative Center. York County Controller Robb Green supplied this photograph of the former chief justice of the Pennsylvania Supreme Court and attorney general and secretary of state under President James Buchanan. Black had one of the most respected legal minds of his day, arguing many cases before the U.S. Supreme Court. His mansion, "Brockie," in the hills south of York, serves as a reminder of this prominent 19th-century leader. Brockie burned in the early 1900s, and the rebuilt mansion stands today.

Captain Edgar M. Ruhl of Shrewsbury was killed at Cedar Creek in 1864 while trying to rally his company in the Union army's Third Corps. He was buried in his hometown. A local Union veterans group, Edgar M. Ruhl Camp 33, was named after this brave officer. This photo comes from the book *Heroes and Builders*, published as part of York County's 250th anniversary.

Chapter 2

'Can it be true that our quiet town has been in the possession of the Rebels, and that for the last two days we have all been prisoners of war!'
– Cassandra M. Small, York, Pa.

Robert E. Lee's Confederate Army of Northern Virginia slipped away from its camps near Fredericksburg the first week of June and headed for the Shenandoah Valley.

After defeating a Federal division — and its 87th Pennsylvania from York and Adams counties — at Second Winchester, the Confederates entered Pennsylvania on June 15.

Rumors spread quickly bearing all sorts of wild tales about the Rebels' intentions. In Hanover, the editor of the Democratic Party's *Citizen* mentioned the prevailing uncertainty:

"One thing we would say to the people, that they shall be composed. It is not necessary that we raise an excitement that may, when the time comes to act, make us the degenerate sons of illustrious sires. It is not necessary that we prove ourselves cowards, by packing up our goods and running for our lives."

The newsman concluded with the admonition: "Stand firm, ready to meet the worst, and if the whole thing proves to be a hoax, we can say that we were willing to do the best we could."

Indeed, it was not a hoax.[84]

**

A veteran soldier from Hanover, Wesley Wagoner of the 76th Pennsylvania, wrote to his father from Port Royal, South Carolina, on June 24. With rumors flying, a company of soldiers had been hastily raised in Hanover for the fledgling state militia.

"I have been looking for a letter from you for several weeks," complained Wesley, "but I suppose the excitement was great in Hanover that you hardly thought of writing… I was glad to see that the Hanover boys are turning out so well for defense of the state."

He added, "I guess some of the people in town thought of packing up some of their things and leaving again."

He expressed his opinion that West Manheim Township might be a Rebel passageway into the heart of the county, adding "I would like to be at home first about this time to see the excitement about town."

He relayed news from a fellow Hanoverian in the 114th Pennsylvania, "Letter from Theodore Bair day before yesterday and he was telling me he know how many were killed out of the company that I knew and how he run down a hill at the battle of Chancellorsville."

Meanwhile, the Army of Northern Virginia, fresh off its triumph at Chancellorsville, had arrived in Pennsylvania. Robert E. Lee's soldiers after crossing the Potomac River had marched northward through Maryland into Franklin

County.[85]

**

On a rainy and raw Friday, June 26, a Confederate division of more than 6,000 combat veterans chased away outnumbered and untrained Pennsylvania emergency militia from Gettysburg and occupied the region.

Rebels captured several of the Hanover volunteer militia company, as well as several soldiers who were students at Gettysburg's Pennsylvania College.

Among those who escaped becoming prisoners was 23-year-old Corporal Jesse C. Koller, the son of a Springfield Township farmer. The York countian was one of the college's best students and had earned a split of the Freshman Prize. He would graduate as valedictorian of his class and a member of the Phi Kappa Psi fraternity. But now on Friday evening he trudged from Gettysburg toward safety in Harrisburg as his regiment retreated from the victorious Confederates.

The Southerners' leader, Major General Jubal A. Early, was one of Lee's best fighters. He had a reputation as a foul-mouthed, vitriolic leader, but he was aggressive and, at that point in the war, usually successful against the Yankees.

While anxious Pennsylvanians scrambled to evacuate the threatened region or took steps to guard their property and animals, soldiers from York and Adams counties with their units in Virginia became concerned when word spread that the enemy was invading their homeland.

"The rebels while I am writing are reported to be in Gettysburg," York resident Abram Rudisill wrote to his father Abraham, an artilleryman in the Army of the Potomac. "The stores are all packing up their goods and sending them away."

He added that soldiers from the military hospital were at that moment marching to the depot in York for transport to Philadelphia.

The hospital stores were moved that morning.[86]

**

Phebe Angeline Smith, the Quaker woman living in Washington Township, wrote her "most cherished sister" a note that same Friday that reveals the uncertainty residents faced as the Rebels advanced through Franklin, Adams, and Cumberland counties toward York County.

"(W)ell sister dear is thare such exciting times out thare," she penned, "it appears that thoes suthern people are braking over and still drawing thare force onward to our country every day but we hope they will soon be checked."

Her neighbors were waiting a day or so before moving horses and other livestock toward the Susquehanna River and apparent safety on its east bank.

"Lewis Larue brought his paps horses down yesterday going on down to cross the river over into Lancaster is whare they are nearly all aiming for," she mentioned, "as thare has bin a proclimation sent on I think by they govener that they men are to take thare stock across they river till he can send men on to clear they rebels out."[87]

**

Philip and Julia Raubenstine lived near southwestern York County's Glenville with their large family, including their young daughter Catherine.

Catherine grew up, married, and lived in the area for most of her life. By the early 1900s, she was a widow living in Spring Grove at her daughter's home.

She often recited incidents that occurred in the Civil War, especially about how her family was compelled by force to feed the soldiers in both blue and gray uniforms. On several occasions, large numbers of soldiers came to the rural home and helped themselves to food, leaving practically nothing for the family.

Multiple blue and gray military units visited southwestern York County beginning Saturday, June 27, with the 35th Battalion, Virginia Cavalry. Lieutenant Colonel Elijah V. White led this unit, later known as "White's Comanches" for its fierce war whoops and lightning-quick mounted raids.

Confederate cavalry under J.E.B. Stuart passed through the area on June 30, as did Union horsemen under Brigadier General H. Judson Kilpatrick. In the next couple of days, Federal infantry columns and David M. Gregg's cavalry division also traversed the area en route to Gettysburg.

For many local residents, this criss-crossing of the armies brought emotional highs and lows.

Fear of the Rebels sometimes turned to surprise when they proved to be well behaved and gracious, and joy when the Federal soldiers arrived would turn to shock and disgust when they openly robbed York countians.

In many cases, the U.S. Army caused as much or more damage to property and livestock than the invading Confederates.

Favorite targets for these raiders included horses and mules, clothing and shoes, chickens and pigs. In particular, soldiers would open larders, pantries, and kitchen cabinets, emptying them of their supplies of food.

As the Raubenstines and hundreds of other York County residents found, hunger knew no distinction, blue or gray.

Nor did thievery, gluttony, and greed.[88]

**

As word spread that the Confederates were marching from Gettysburg toward York County, residents throughout that region began to hide their valuables.

Some placed them in grain bags and lowered them into wells or hid them in springs or creeks. Others tucked items under floorboards or in walls and chimneys.

In York, jeweler Francis Polack and his son packed jewelry and silver from their South George Street store in coffins, planning to bury them temporarily in the nearby Christ Lutheran Church graveyard.

Shoemaker Jacob Emmitt made several trips next door to cabinetmaker George Hay's shop, hiding his stock of leather goods in empty caskets.

One enterprising businessman scribbled the words "Smallpox within" on a sheet of paper and placed it in his window, hoping to deter any thieves.

Several people took elaborate efforts to hide their horses, at times even within houses.

The Holtz family of Hampton in eastern Adams County secreted horses in their cellar. To keep the Rebels from hearing the sounds of pawing and neighing, they had one of their youngest children repeatedly run a toy wagon back and forth across the wooden floorboards of the front porch.

The steady racket drowned sounds from the hidden horses.[89]

**

In western York County's Big Mount, young men and boys hastily collected their families' horses and valuables. They headed for the Conewago hills.

Sixteen-year-old Charles Harlacher and his brother Joseph, two years younger, joined in such efforts. Charlie worked as a clerk in C.A. Raffensperger's general store.

The boys had charge of a two-horse team hitched to a covered wagon loaded with silks and other dry goods such as boots and shoes, the store's account books, and some of Mrs. Raffensperger's jewelry and silk dresses.

Along with a large party of neighbors, they headed eastward through the county, taking with them enough food and horse feed for a two-day absence.

The refugees arrived in Strinestown about 3:30 in the afternoon, Saturday, June 27. There, they learned that Jubal Early's Confederate division occupied their village. Big Mount was in Rebel possession, and they could not readily return home.

They camped for two days in a field just north of Strinestown.

On Monday, June 29, they received word from Big Mount that the Rebels had departed that area for York. They decided to start homeward, because they had all but exhausted their provisions.

Just before leaving Strinestown, they heard a rumor that General Hooker's Union army was nearby and impressing civilians into service. That news "put a scare into the camp."

The Big Mount folks decided to move farther back "into the jungles to a place called 'Buzzard's Glory,'" where they stayed on Monday night.

By now, many of the boys were homesick and could not sleep. Joe Harlacher later recalled, "Hoot-owls and the whippoorwills were hollering all night."

In the morning, the weary party started for Big Mount. They portioned out what was left of their meager food supplies — each man and boy received four crackers for breakfast. They planned a round-about route that would avoid reported locations of Rebels and believed they would be home about one o'clock that afternoon.

Trouble loomed.

They passed through Mount Royal, near Dover, and stopped to water their horses in Conewago Creek at Emig's Mill (now the hamlet of Detters Mill).

About 10:00 a.m., while carrying buckets of water from the creek, someone heard a noise over the brow of a nearby hill. He jokingly announced, "The Rebels are coming!"

To the Big Mounters' horror, the jest suddenly came true. Several cavalrymen spotted them, drew their sabers, and thundered down the hill into the midst of the group.

The older members of the party acted as spokesmen, when a Confederate officer inquired, "Where are you going?"

"Home," they replied.

"Where do you live?" queried the Rebels.

"Near Big Mount," answered the boys.

Asked where they had been and why they were returning, the boys said they had been hiding in the Conewago hills and had received word that General Lee had sent a message to Early to retrace his movements toward Gettysburg.

"That is true," snapped a Rebel, "and we need all of those things that you have to help us win the war!"

The Big Mount outfit was a dejected lot.

They were all hungry by now, having only downed the quartet of crackers several hours ago at breakfast. The Rebels formed a procession around the boys and ordered them to "follow the leader."

The Harlacher boys talked the Confederates into letting them leave Raffensperger's account books at a nearby farm. Everything else was lost. A few cavalrymen rode ahead, and others brought up the rear to prevent the civilians from escaping from the caravan.

They crossed the old covered bridge at Emig's Mill, turned left, and followed Bermudian Creek to Trimmer's Mill. There, they crossed another covered bridge.

By the time the column passed the Bermudian Meeting House, hope for release had faded. They crossed Red Run and headed through Franklin Township on the old Shippensburg Road.

As the unusual procession passed by the Sowers house, some girls of that family began to weep when they recognized the Big Mount boys among the prisoners. At one point, Charlie Harlacher managed to slip away long enough to hide his watch and buggy whip under a rail fence.

At Bermudian, the boys began complaining to the officer in charge that they were very hungry. He allowed them to go into a nearby hotel and order food.

Before it was ready the Rebels moved on, taking the famished civilians with him. The Harlachers later reported that some of the Confederate officers by then were drunk, "swinging in their saddles."

That night, the cavalrymen and their captives camped in the Jacob P. Lerew farm, two miles north of York Springs in Adams County. The officers released the smaller boys and began interrogating the older ones. When finished, they made the youths raise their right hands and swear not to fight against the South.

"Now, boys," one officer teased, "you can go down to those girls that cried when they saw you pass."

The weary party, minus their horses and wagons, finally arrived in Big Mount about midnight.

Storeowner C.A. Raffensperger later filed a damage claim with the state.

He asked for compensation for the stolen horses and wagon, shoes, 50 yards of calico, muslin, cassimere woolens, 10 yards of black cloth, and other items.[90]

**

Scores of residents from Hanover Junction and Seven Valleys, in the path of the invaders, fled to Cross Roads in Hopewell Township in southeastern York County.

About 30 wagons, filled with refugees, their belongings and accompanied by farm animals made the 14-mile trip.

There, they initially camped on a hill above John Logan's and Sampson Smith's properties, near the home of Andrew Maffett. They later moved near Rambo's Mill, staying hidden in a hollow.

Cross Roads served as a hub for information in those difficult days. A thousand people gathered there to hear bits and pieces of information.

With the Union army approaching Gettysburg, the Confederate invaders countermarched from York County, never reaching as far southeast as the Hopewell Township area.[91]

**

A Hanover lad had taken some of the family's horses and cows to safety before the first Rebels, White's Virginia cavalry, entered town on Saturday, June 27.

He joined a large contingent of Hanoverians and farmers from the region in tramping eastward to Cross Roads. There, they met scores of other refugees who stopped there for the night.

After a harrowing evening in which they saw Rebels in every shadow, they were relieved at daylight when no enemy soldiers appeared. The throng moved toward the southeast, to the Delta-Fawn Grove region.

Days later, they returned to Hanover, where several of their neighbors who had not fled now rued that decision. Stables, barns and pastures in the Hanover area were empty. Rebels had raided pigpens and chicken coops.

One Confederate trooper later summed up his comrades' adventures.

"We gave the old dutch in Penn. fits," Marylander Joseph H. Trundle bragged. "Our army left a mark everywhere it went. Horses, cattle, sheep, hogs, chickens, spring houses suffered alike. They cried peace, peace most beautifully everywhere we went."

A Lynchburg, Virginia, newspaper in late July inventoried the take from the campaign: 9,000 head of cattle plus enough beeves to feed the gray army for two months. As for horses and mules, the estimate was 5,000 to 6,000.

Estimates from York County placed stolen horses and mules, no longer available for harvest, at more than 1,100.[92]

**

Daniel Q. Albright and Samuel Trone owned a prosperous retail store in downtown Hanover in southwestern York County.

After White's Comanches raided the town on Saturday, the two merchants moved their inventory to a private home on Mount Olivet, southeast of town. They assumed the nondescript house of George Ginn would be out of the way in case of any other Rebel incursions.

The following Tuesday, General Jeb Stuart's nearly 5,000 Confederate cavalrymen attacked Union troopers at Hanover, and the fighting escalated. That afternoon, Stuart positioned artillery in the cemetery in back of the Ginn home, and Southern saddle soldiers milled about the hilltop to support the big guns.

Several Confederates entered the house and discovered the hidden merchandise. The Rebs hauled off 20 pairs of women's Swiss boots, a dozen pairs of men's kid boots, and 50 pairs of other boots and shoes.

Their take included three pairs of children's shoes, probably intended for a Rebel soldier's loved ones back home.[93]

**

Some Hanover businessmen procrastinated in moving their wares before White's jubilant men rode into Center Square.

Jeweler William Boadenhamer, for one, was frantically leaving on the York Road. Gun-toting cavalrymen overtook his carriage about a mile from town and stole a large box of retail goods.

Resting under a shade tree near a gristmill, they

opened the chest and discovered it contained nearly 100 watches and jewelry pieces. They gave part of the loot to their comrades.

Later that day, a soldier gave a stolen brooch to a little girl he encountered in Jefferson. It is one of the few jewelry pieces known to have been recovered from the entire haul.

In a 1906 letter, White informed former Rebel cavalry officer John S. Mosby that, on the way from Hanover to sacking the railroad depot at Hanover Junction, nothing much happened with one exception. He captured a wagonload of jewelry.

"After supplying ourselves," he wrote, "we buried the balance."[94]

**

Nine-year-old Sarah J. Adams helped around the house of a Hanover doctor and lived with his family.

On Saturday, June 27, she was looking forward to her 10th birthday, only three days away.

She was attending religious education class that morning. News arrived that the Rebels were approaching town, and the teacher dismissed the class and escorted all the children to their homes.

The Confederate cavalry took all the horses in the vicinity but left one for the doctor to use to make house calls. They also took chickens and food.

Sarah's birthday on June 30 was perhaps the most memorable of her young life. The physician's family and Sarah stayed in their house as the Battle of Hanover raged outside.

After the troops left town, the doctor was gone for several days. No one knew where he was.

It turned out that he was busy treating casualties from the battle.[95]

**

George Small of Walnut Street in York worked as an engineer for the Northern Central Railway, operating the locomotive "The Susquehanna." On Saturday, he was dispatched down the railroad to fetch a train of boxcars on a siding near the Mason-Dixon Line.

He was near Hanover Junction on his return to York when he spotted a small party of Rebel cavalrymen galloping along the roadbed of the intersecting Hanover Branch Railroad. The soldiers were trying to head off the locomotive and seize the train.

Small opened the throttle to the limit. Calling to the fireman to follow, he left the unprotected cab for the sheltering side of the tender.

Hurriedly dismounting, the cavalrymen fired shot after shot at the fleeing train. None struck the engine or tender, and Small coolly drove his train into York.[96]

**

In 1853 George Brodbeck purchased a 20-acre property located along the present Route 516 south of Shaffer's Church Road in Codorus Township. A tavern sat at this site, along what was then one of the main roads from York to Baltimore.

The sturdy two-story building boasted several guest rooms and a bar. A trapdoor dropped down into the ground cellar. Business was brisk, and the hotel became a popular stopping place for weary and thirsty patrons.

According to family lore, in late June 1863, blue-uniformed officers — likely from the 20th Pennsylvania Volunteer Militia, which camped at nearby Larue — warned Brodbeck that the Rebels were approaching. He should lock his tavern and under no circumstances give them whiskey.

It was later learned that a squad of White's cavalrymen had been sent to Glen Rock to burn a railroad bridge just north of town.

When he heard the Confederates coming, he locked his door and dropped through the trapdoor into the cellar. He scrambled to the outside basement door and slipped outside into a field. Unseen by the oncoming Confederates, he hid in a nearby wheat field.

Enemy soldiers bayoneted the door until they broke it down. They found his supply of York County rye whiskey and drank their fill.

After sating their thirst, they left the tavern and crossed the road to a barn. They emerged leading several horses but did not disturb the neighboring red brick farmhouse.

Brodbeck later claimed that the drunken Southerners began to quarrel. The angry words degenerated into a scuffle in which one soldier was killed.

He reportedly was buried in the tavern's dirt-floored cellar.[97]

**

In the summer of 1863, the cherry crop was spectacular in southern Pennsylvania.

Union and Confederate soldiers often wrote about the bumper crop of cherries. Many soldiers broke off huge limbs and carried them along as they marched, picking luscious cherries and passing them around.

Near Hanover Junction, little Eliza Weaver was in a tree picking cherries when she heard the plod of horses and the tinkling of swords. She stayed quietly in the branches until the Rebels, likely a patrol from White's battalion, were completely gone.

With the road clear, she came down and went home.[98]

**

On Saturday evening, several Southern cavalrymen paused at the sprawling Jackson Township farm of Andrew J. Menges, located near Roth's Church Road.

They were hot, dusty, and tired from the long day, which had seen them rise at daylight near Gettysburg and wend through the countryside to York County.

They had been on the road since June 3, and were grimy and disheveled. Most of their supply wagons had been left west of South Mountain at Greenwood and Fayetteville, so that Early's division could march and ride faster without the encumbrance of the massive train of slow-moving supply wagons.

Each regiment could only take its ambulances, cook wagons, and a handful of wagons for short-term sustenance. They did take empty wagons to be filled with the abundance of Pennsylvania's produce and forage.

Luckily for Andrew Menges and his wife Caroline, the Confederate soldiers who visited their farm were not "bummers," or soldier-thieves who operated on the fringe.

When they appeared, Menges and his sons were out in the field with their horses, presumably harvesting summer crops.

The Rebels rode into the farmyard, dismounted,

and asked Caroline for food. She and her teenage daughters Agnes and Magdalena served them a home-cooked meal, with fresh-baked pie as dessert.

The commander of the squadron promised they would not take their horses because Menges and his two sons needed them in the fields.

Family lore states that this leader was none other than Brigadier General John B. Gordon. The Menges farm was on the road leading to Gordon's camp and less than a quarter-mile from the Wiest farm where Gordon's cavalry, the 35th Virginia Battalion, camped.

No Confederate records confirm that the veteran general left his main camp at the Jacob S. Altland farm near Farmers Post Office for dinner.

"General Gordon," who might have been a staff officer, shared his impressions of York County versus the South. When the officer and his staff were ready to leave, the 59-year-old Andrew Menges, a devout Christian, led them in prayer. Standing in a circle, the soldiers doffed their hats and bowed their heads.

One young officer left his New Testament with the family.[99]

**

The Coleman family had long been associated with the iron forge that gave the southwestern York County village its original name of Spring Forge, later Spring Grove. Some members of the clan lived near the road to Hanover.

On Saturday, as White's Battalion camped on the Wiest farm near town, the Rebels raided the region for horses and livestock. The Colemans sought to protect a pair of cows by herding them into their house's stone cellar.

The ploy worked.

When Confederate raiders came near the property, they did not discover the hidden cows.[100]

**

A mounted patrol of Confederates stopped at John Ilyes's stone house on Water Street, near New Paradise, later Jacobus.

They dismounted and watered their horses at a trough near the barn across the road.

One of Ilyes's boys started to climb to the attic to shoot the troopers. Luckily, the father stopped him before any harm was done. After their horses drank their fill, the cavalrymen moved on without incident.

The cavalrymen were likely a roving patrol of White's mounted men. Foragers ranged for miles on either side of the main column, searching farms for fresh horses and any supplies of military value. Springfield Township's New Paradise was a prime farming area.

Springfield Township farmers Jeremiah Krebs and Jacob Bowman each reported losing horses that day.

Krebs's encounters with the army were not over. This time, it was riders in blue.

On July 1, a division of more than 5,000 Union cavalrymen rested most of the day on his farm along what is now Route 616, feeding and watering their horses.

They took a ton of hay from his barn without payment.[101]

**

Jacob Wiest lived on a farm near Spring Forge on land his ancestors acquired from William Penn's son in 1747.

He had raised a company of emergency militia during the Maryland Campaign in September 1862, but that threat had subsided thanks to the Battle of Antietam.

Now, a group of White's cavalrymen rode up to the old colonial-era farmhouse and demanded that they be fed and allowed to sleep in the barn for the night. If their demands were not met, they would burn the place.

Wiest reluctantly complied with the threat but stewed inwardly throughout the Confederate occupation.[102]

**

White's cavalrymen roamed through the countryside near Spring Forge in search of fresh horses. They often found success, such as at the farms of Samuel Roth and the Rev. John Roth.

One squadron stopped in Menges Mills to raid the large gristmill along the old road to Hanover. Nearby, the Rebels paused at the Sprenkle farm.

One of the Sprenkle girls had recently received as a gift her own horse and buggy. The 16-year-old was in the farmhouse when she spotted Confederates passing through and taking horses. She begged them not to take hers.

The soldiers told her if she could play *Dixie* on her piano for them, they would be on their way.

To their surprise, she knew the tune, and she played it for them.

The Rebels, true to their end of the bargain, departed without taking her horse.[103]

**

Sometime on Saturday evening Private Charles Brown slipped away from the 8th Louisiana, a veteran regiment in the renowned "Louisiana Tigers" brigade.

The next day, June 28, he entered a farmstead near Big Mount in western York County, perhaps seeking food and/or a horse. Details are sketchy, but Brown wound up dead, likely bushwhacked by an irate farmer.

The unfortunate Confederate's service record only states that he "straggled on the march from Gettysburg to York and supposed to have been killed by the citizens of Penn." No one was ever formally accused of the crime.

Paradise Township lore suggests the lone Rebel was buried near the intersection of East Berlin and Canal roads, but no trace, or record, of his grave remains.

Colonel Clement Evans of the 31st Georgia was philosophical about such occasional civilian attacks.

The future Methodist minister from Atlanta wrote in his diary that the hidden bushwhackers had one benefit: they served to keep the men in line and reduced straggling.[104]

**

Gordon's Georgia brigade marched along the Gettysburg Pike toward York on Sunday morning, raising a massive cloud of white dust visible for miles.

A young Paradise Township girl witnessed the march.

Decades later, she told her grandchildren that she had climbed a hill behind her house to watch the distant Rebels as they trudged past her parents' farm. She remembered seeing them enter the barn looking for horses, but her father had taken them to safety in Columbia on the Lancaster County side of the Susquehanna River.

To her, the procession of marching soldiers seemed "endless."

Charles W. Kline, 15-year-old hired hand, worked on the farm of William Smyser at the Five-Mile House, west of York on the turnpike to Gettysburg. It was a good job for the youth, paying $36 a year.

On Sunday morning, June 28, word came that Confederate soldiers were moving toward York, confiscating horses along the way. Smyser asked young Kline to take his five horses to safety across the Susquehanna River. He strapped $650 in cash around the lad's waist.

Charlie hitched two of the horses to a farm wagon and tied the other three behind it. He loaded about 15 bags of corn and oats and headed toward Columbia. They arrived in late afternoon, not realizing that a significant Confederate force was just behind them.

They waited in line to cross the river on the old toll bridge and finally arrived at Chickies Rock in the early evening. Following the Battle of Gettysburg, Kline's team pulled him back to West Manchester Township, and the youth returned the horses and money to his employer.[105]

**

Thousands of Confederates marched through the tiny village of Weigelstown, on the Carlisle Road outside Dover.

On Sunday, June 28, most of Jubal Early's division passed through that region on their way from Big Mount and Davidsburg, and it was at Weigelstown that Early dispatched Colonel William H. French and his 17th Virginia Cavalry

to ride to York Haven to burn the railroad bridges over Conewago Creek.

One group of invading Confederates rested on Peter Leib's prosperous farm along the Carlisle Road.

They entered the springhouse and drank all the milk they could find. Then they pumped the well empty to refill their canteens and forced the women of the family to bake hotcakes for their meal.

An officer arrived to break up the party and get them moving again. His horse reared, and its front hooves thundered down onto the wooden porch, leaving distinct imprints of the horseshoes.

The Rebels departed, but they took with them five of Leib's horses, as well as his harnesses and all the corn they could carry off. They also went into Mrs. Leib's garden and took her currants to make tea.[106]

**

General Early wanted the two railroad bridges burned at York Haven to sever traffic between York and Harrisburg.

For more than a week, the 20th Pennsylvania Volunteer Militia, a recently organized regiment from Philadelphia, had guarded the Northern Central and its vital bridges and the Howard Tunnel, near Seven Valleys. The emergency militiamen departed before the Rebels arrived.

However, they left their mark.

Several farmers along a 15-mile stretch of the railroad later complained of property damage caused by the defenders and the impressments of horses for use by couriers and officers. One farmer lost "a good chopping axe," undoubtedly used to turn wooden fences into firewood.

Colonel John Hoff, a soldier before the war, was one such victim. His farm along Wago Road near York Haven quartered 400 Union soldiers. Several fields used for their tents and campsites were ruined, and Hoff would be unable to salvage much of his rye, oats, and hay. All of his fence rails were missing, and soldiers burned 2,152 board feet of lumber.

All of Hoff's labor to take down trees and saw them into planks and boards was for naught. And he had to fill in dozens of holes dug by soldiers for use as rifle pits.[107]

**

David F. Spangler's great-grandmother Smith put her young children in a wheelbarrow and pushed them to see the Rebel soldiers marching into York on Sunday, June 28.

Family lore suggests that the elderly woman shook her fist at the invaders and cursed them.

Later, some Confederates came by her home and helped themselves to some of her prized laying hens. After killing them, they brought the chickens to the house and ordered her to prepare them for dinner.

That abuse was heightened by the fact that other Spangler ancestors were away at war and not there to buffer the Confederate demands.

Sergeant Noah Waltersdorf, 76th Pennsylvania Infantry, was wounded in both legs at the Battle of Pocotaligo in South Carolina. He convalesced in an army hospital in Hilton Head, as did another ancestor, Corporal Daniel Smith of the 87th Pennsylvania, who recovered from illness at the same facility.[108]

**

Sixteen-year-old Martin L. Van Baman was there when the Rebels marched into downtown York.

"Sunday morning, June 28, the sun rose high in the clear sky over our peaceful borough," he recalled. "Groups of persons could be seen in eager and anxious discussion in and around Centre Square, while many others were on their way to the various churches and the church bells were ringing in the accustomed manner."

Van Baman observed a cloud of dust rising from the Gettysburg Pike and heard bugle blasts signaling the Rebel approach.

The people of York knew that their town and homes would be at the mercy of the invaders.

General Gordon led the Confederate column into the square. In every direction, "not very presentable" troops could be seen sitting or resting.

The 18-by-35-foot Stars and Stripes floated atop the tall pine flag pole in the center of the town square. According to Van Baman, Gordon "immediately ordered the lowering of the flag" and then proceeded on his way to Wrightsville, expecting to cross into Lancaster County.

About noon, General Early arrived and proceeded to the East Market Street courthouse, where the borough's Committee of Safety was in session, with Chief Burgess David Small, presiding.

"No one but those who were eyewitnesses to the occupation of York," Van Baman wrote, "can have any conception of the extent of anxiety and suspense of our people during the two days' occupation."[109]

**

A gray-clad sentry stood in front of Mary C. Fisher's house.

61

Not all houses had guards in Rebel-occupied York. She asked why the house was posted.

"I must obey orders," came the reply.

She offered him food and water.

"I thank you, madam, we are not allowed to accept anything," the guard said.

She later discovered that the sentinel stood guard against Dr. W.S. Roland's escape. The physician, guest of the Fishers, served as an army surgeon and, thus, was a prisoner of war.

The men in gray were well-behaved, but people in town feared an outbreak at any time.

"We knew not how soon might come a signal to unleash the dogs of war in our midst," Fisher wrote, "and give your homes a prey to the invader."

The guard's vigil continued until the town filled requisitions for meat and flour.

Then the sentry departed for a warm meal.[110]

**

After Mary Fisher's death in 1913, the family of this Civil War nurse kept stories alive about the difficult days that Mary and her husband/county Judge Robert Fisher witnessed the Rebel occupation.

Daughter Mary, a youngster at the time, recalled how a Rebel officer picked her up as he rode through York and said, "I have a little daughter at home with eyes just as blue as yours."[111]

**

Reports circulated that another large body of Rebels was coming toward Weigelstown on the Davidsburg Road. It turned out that this was

Jubal Early's main force, having marched through the morning from its camps near Big Mount.

The owners of Naylor's general store, located on Carlisle Road next door to the family's hotel and tavern, did not remove their inventory to a safe place. They scrambled to carry armloads of smaller merchandise upstairs into the living quarters.

Not long afterward, the Southerners arrived and burst into the store. They rummaged through the remaining items and effectively cleaned out whatever Naylor had left on the shelves.

One Confederate was sitting on a counter when he decided to stuff the contents of a box of lead shot into his pockets. When he jumped down, his pockets ripped open from the heavy weight, and the round-shot rattled around the floor.

Next door, Confederates cleaned out the hotel of its stock of whiskey. Several Rebels even filled their water-buckets with liquor.[112]

**

Shortly after Gordon's brigade paraded through downtown York toward Wrightsville, Jubal Early led the remainder of his division into the vicinity. Louisiana troops camped near Loucks Mill (in the area of today's Harley Davidson factory), with Virginians camping along George Street on various farms between Emigsville and York. Artillery crowned several hills.

Early accompanied a North Carolina brigade into downtown York, where the Tar Heels took quarters in the Army Hospital on Penn Common, the market sheds, and at the old fairgrounds. Confederates soon roamed the streets.

Many of the enemy soldiers were wearing worn-out and threadbare clothing, the *York*

But they obtained enough hats and clothing in York to make them look "genteel."

The newsman believed the soldiers were "the flower of the rebel army, stout and healthy men, in good condition to fight."[113]

**

George Munchel, a successful shoemaker, immigrated with his two brothers from Oberwessen, Bavaria, Germany, to the United States in 1846.

One brother wound up in Indiana, and George and Michael settled in York and established businesses and families.

As the Confederates patrolled the streets of York, General Early threatened to burn the town if his ransom demands were not met. The crusty Virginia general established his headquarters in the sheriff's office in the columned county courthouse.

He ordered an aide, William Thornton, to transcribe a requisition for supplies: 165 barrels of flour or 28,000 pounds of baked bread; 3,500 pounds of sugar; 1,650 pounds of coffee; 300 gallons of molasses; 1,200 pounds of salt; 32,000 pounds of fresh beef or 21,000 pounds of bacon or pork.

Early's chief quartermaster, Major Charles E. Snodgrass, wrote a second requisition for 2,000 pairs of shoes or boots, 1,000 pairs of socks and 1,000 felt hats and $100,000.

George Munchel and other York cobblers spent long hours in their shops crafting shoes and boots for the Confederates.

He always believed their efforts helped spare York from the torch.[114]

Door-to-door collections by York's civic leaders netted $28,610, much of which wound up in the treasury of the Army of Northern Virginia.

Chief Burgess David Small justified the decision to pay the ransom, "The people, conscious of their defenceless position, submitted to imperious necessity, and, in saving their lives and property, did what humanity and common sense dictated... All good citizens, while they deplore the humiliation of the occupation of the town by the enemy, are grateful for our fortunate escape from the horrors of war."

For his part, Confederate commander Jubal Early did not think the Yorkers had given enough money. In fact, they were far short, an opinion he held for years.

"Gen. Jubal Early, who loves to be a bit facetious at times, recently told a Pennsylvania civilian at White Sulphur Springs, West Virginia," the *York Gazette* reported in 1877, "that the city of York, Pa., still owes him $71,400, with interest, on the assessment of $100,000 he made during his war expedition, and that he proposes to put the account into the hands of a collector."[115]

**

Outside York in the country, the Rebels were having their way with the citizenry's property.

The proprietor of a well-stocked country tavern, for example, watched with dismay as ravenous Southerners devoured his entire stock of bacon, beef, and poultry.

They forced his wife to use all of his remaining flour to bake them bread and pies. Soldiers took his forage for their horses, and many catnapped on his beds.

Perhaps most annoying to the innkeeper, his inventory of 10-12 barrels of liquor had been reduced to a few pints as the unwelcome guests finally took their leave, hauling away what alcohol they had not guzzled.

A Georgia colonel, perhaps with a tinge of guilt for all the food and drink the men had consumed, loudly stated that it was a pity that no one else had offered to the distraught hotel owner any compensation for his loss.

He stepped to the bar and laid down a $20 Confederate banknote, looking around at his comrades, as he intoned, "There, my good fellow, take that as my share of our indebtedness."

The quizzical proprietor, in a thick German accent, inquired, "Vot kind of monish is dat?" to which the officer calmly replied, "That, Sir, is a greyback; in other words, a note of the Confederate States of America."

"O stranger," retorted the vexed saloonkeeper, "if you hash not got no petter monish dan dat, you'll better keeps it. I don't vont none of it; it is good for nix; no petter dan plank paper!"

"Sir," rejoined the somewhat indignant officer, "I advise you to take it and be glad for the opportunity. You will soon find that it is the best money in the world. Keep it, sir, keep it, by all means."

"Nein, nein," shot back the persistent innkeeper, "dat monish will never be wort anything here nor anywhere. I would not give von silver thaler for a breadbasket full. I von't be seen mit it in my hand; and if you don't take it along, I rolls it up, holds it at the candle, un lites my pipe mit it."

The colonel snatched up the banknote and returned it to his pocket before leaving.[116]

**

When some Rebel raiders found that the citizens had sent their horses away to safety, they forced them to pay the equivalent value in greenbacks.

In central York County, one unfortunate farmer had to fork over $60 to greedy members of Jubal Early's division.

Just north of York, another countryman who lived near the turnpike gate met the oncoming enemy soldiers, telling them that he, too, was a Rebel. The Southerners looked with disdain at the farmer and ordered him to hand over his pocketbook.

They wanted him to guide them around the countryside to point out his neighbors' farms and the most likely places they would hide horses or other valuables. He objected, knowing that he would forfeit his place in the community if he turned on his neighbors and friends.

Hearing this refusal, they threatened to hang him from a nearby tree. Some Rebels started throwing a stout rope over it when the farmer's terrified wife came to his rescue. She paid $20 for his release.

The Rebels let the man go but sternly threatened to come back and hang him if they lost their way.

Well to the north, farmer Samuel Miller, who lived off Board Road near Manchester and Mount Wolf, had a similar encounter. His did not end in the same manner.

Rebels from the 17th Virginia Cavalry forced him at gunpoint to get on his horse and show them the way to the place where the Northern Central Railway crossed the Conewago Creek. After the Confederates burned the bridges in the vicinity, they released Miller.

They kept his horse, and Samuel had to walk home. A historian later labeled Miller "an intelligent farmer," perhaps for his mental acuity compared to fellow countrymen, or perhaps because he knew better than to argue with enemy soldiers pointing a gun at his chest.[117]

**

Young couple John and Louisa Ann Brillinger worked a large farm just outside Emigsville, not far from the Northern Central Railway.

The Brillingers and other local farmers heard reports the Rebels were coming, and most took their horses and mules to safety.

Brillinger and his brother Will took theirs to New Holland in Lancaster County, and John returned to the farm alone to check on his family.

On June 28, Jubal Early's Confederates arrived. Virginia troops pitched tents and camped on Emigsville Hill along the turnpike to Harrisburg. Frightened residents, including John Brillinger, took steps to protect their property.

He loaded his revolver and placed it on the bureau in his bedroom, on top of a long fabric scarf, which hung down on both sides of the bureau.

When Louisa spotted the gun, she told him to put it away somewhere because she feared that their young daughter, Sallie, might pull the scarf down, and the gun might discharge as it struck the floor.

John agreed but took it outside to fire it where it could not harm anyone (it was likely a percussion cap-and-ball pistol that could not be unloaded without being fired). He walked out in a field and shot it in the air, while little Sallie watched beside her father.

His shot was answered by another from the nearby village. Perplexed, he walked back into the farmhouse and remarked to Louisa, "I think it is funny that someone shot in Emigsville from near the blacksmith shop right after I shot into the air."

To the Brillingers' horror, a group of Confederate cavalrymen emerged on the road from under the railroad overpass and galloped toward their house. Horses leaped over fences as their riders urged them on.

Halting at the house, dismounting, and throwing their reins over a fence rail, the soldiers entered the yard.

"Where's that man who shot after us?" one thundered.

Brillinger replied, "I do not know what you mean."

"Why did you shoot?" demanded a soldier.

"I had my revolver around the house," the farmer replied, "and I shot it into the air so my child wouldn't get it."

The Rebels believed his explanation and were sympathetic. They were thankful the child had not been hit by their return fire.

The soldiers confiscated the remaining firearms in the house and searched again for any others that the farmer may have hidden.

They asked for food, and the Brillingers complied. Soon more men in gray arrived as word spread.

"We fed them all day," Sallie later recalled. "Baked pies, baked bread, killed chickens for 2-3 days, worked day and night to get them fed."

Soldiers lined their 12-foot dining table and

enjoyed the forced hospitality.

"Nearly all of our smoked meat was gone Monday and Tuesday for meals," Sallie wrote.

Reports circulated that Rebels planned to burn the house and barn, but a captain reassured the family: "Go to bed and we will put a guard around the place."

John Brillinger later filed a damage claim that the Rebels had drunk or taken two full 40-gallon barrels of whiskey.

The Brillingers' extended family also suffered during the Confederate occupation of Emigsville.

Louisa's father, John Emig, owned the town's general store, which his son Albert managed. Southerners walked away with large quantities of boots, shoes, hats, cigars, and other merchandise, as well as oats and flour.

Rebel forages also hit little Sallie's future father-in-law and his brother. Both filed claims for lost horses and mules.

George Rutter replaced missing mules with inexperienced draft animals. One of them bolted while Rutter was reaping a field.

The heavy reaper crushed Rutter's legs, crippling him.[118]

**

York native James Brown Harry was noted throughout south-central Pennsylvania as a music instructor. Born in 1828, he began his education career at the age of 18.

For decades he held an annual reunion of former and current students and their families near New Oxford. Nearly 5,000 people attended the October 1858 gala, which featured a balloon ascent on a balmy autumn afternoon.

Professor Harry regularly traveled in his buggy to visit students and friends.

On Sunday afternoon, June 28, he was driving west on the turnpike to York from Wrightsville when he spotted a long column of Rebels in the distance, coming directly toward him.

He hastily reversed course and sped back to Wrightsville. There, he notified the residents and soldiers of the approaching enemy, a message soon confirmed by scouts.

Harry crossed over the bridge to Columbia, where he met Union leaders Colonel Jacob G. Frick of the 27th Pennsylvania Volunteer Militia and Major Granville O. Haller of the 7th U.S. Infantry, overall commander of the defenses of Adams and York counties. The two officers interviewed the professor.

Then they telegraphed the pertinent information to Haller's superior, Major General Darius Couch, in Harrisburg.

Considering that information, Couch ordered the bridge to be destroyed to prevent Confederate passage into Lancaster County.[119]

**

Several carpenters worked with the crews preparing the Columbia Bridge for destruction.

They bored holes into the timbers near the Wrightsville side and placed charges of gunpowder, set for detonation if the Rebels threatened the bridge.

John David Gilbert of Lower Windsor Township toiled for several hours inside the tunnel-like covered bridge. He assisted in boring holes in the superstructure, a draining job in the afternoon humidity.

Four men, one of them a cigar-smoking "old negro" named Jacob Miller, would light the fuses on the evening of Sunday, June 28. The resulting detonations scattered roofing, oak beams, siding, and debris high into the overcast sky.

But the bridge decking remained intact, and authorities resorted to burning the bridge to prevent Confederate passage into Lancaster County.

The superintendent of the bridge demolition, railroad executive Robert Crane, later praised his 16-man team for their hard work and asked them to "accept my own as well as the most heartfelt thanks of this community for effecting the object which prevented the rebels from crossing the Susquehanna at this point."

Among those he commended was John Gilbert.

What makes the story remarkable is Gilbert's age.

He was 14.[120]

**

Prominent York businessman David Etter Small had lost an arm in an 1853 industrial accident when it was caught in a piece of machinery.

This cost him a much-desired opportunity to fight for the Union army in the war.

"If I can bring down a partridge with my gun," he argued, "I certainly can shoot well enough to go to the defence of my country."

"Grandfather Small feared for his family with the eminent approach of Confederate troops to York," great-great-granddaughter Liz Winand said years later. "He eventually felt his family would be safer with the Philadelphia relatives, so he loaded them in their carriage, made for the Wrightsville Bridge, and was one of the last passenger carriages to cross the bridge before it was burned."[121]

**

John Gordon's Georgia brigade of more than 2,000 infantrymen arrived outside Wrightsville about 5:30 on Sunday evening, accompanied by several hundred cavalrymen and artillery crews.

They deployed for battle on Strickler Ridge a couple of miles from the town. General Gordon is believed to have directed his forces from a position near one of the Strickler family's farmhouses.

Lieutenant Harrison Monroe Strickler, a devout Methodist who later became a noted evangelist, rode in the Rebel cavalry. Strickler commanded a company in White's Comanches.

In a strange twist, he was waging war on his ancestor's homesteads.

Monroe was a descendant of Abraham Strickler, one of the three original Strickler immigrants from southern Germany.

Abraham had moved to Virginia shortly after arriving in York County, while his two brothers remained in the area.[122]

**

Just before the escalating fire closed off entry to the Columbia Bridge, Company F of the 27th Pennsylvania Volunteer Militia had marched across the bridge carrying the regiment's battle flag.

A 21-year-old farmer-turned-soldier from Huntingdon County, Wm. Albert Myton, crossed the bridge last.

"Rather than be taken prisoner, he ventured

through the flames in order to join his comrades on the opposite side," according to a newspaper account.

The sight of the burning bridge threw Columbia into a panic, a Union soldier who witnessed the mayhem recalled years later.

"Shot and shell were falling into the Susquehanna. Confederate soldiers could be seen on the York County shore swarming the banks and hills," W.S. Hallman wrote. "Persons living in Columbia today who witnessed this thrilling scene declare that the excitement was so great that men and women became bewildered."

That same night, down in Maryland, a courier arrived in the Army of the Potomac's headquarters to bring orders replacing its commander Joseph Hooker with George G. Meade.

The Spanish-born, Pennsylvania-raised Meade had limited time to bring Robert E. Lee to bay.[123]

**

Jacob and Catherine (Keller) Dietz were married in 1861 and took up housekeeping on a farm a half-mile east of the village of Hallam.

They constructed a new brick house that same year. On June 1, 1863, their first child, Harvey, was born.

Just four weeks later, the Confederates entered York County.

Instead of heading for the congestion at the bridgehead caused by those fleeing the Rebel advance, Jacob and several of his neighbors quickly moved their livestock to "Hidden Valley," on the south side of the Kreutz Creek Valley, about a quarter-mile east of the

Ducktown Road.

There, the animals could graze quietly on the lush meadows and drink spring water while hidden by dense woods from Confederate view. Gordon's Georgia infantry raised a large cloud of dust along the old turnpike just north of the Dietz farm, while to the south some of White's Virginia cavalry traced the railroad tracks which closely followed Kreutz Creek.

Catherine Dietz, at home with baby Harvey, was alone on the farm, skirted by the Confederate force. Luckily, none of the Rebels appeared, nor did they discover the horses and livestock in Hidden Valley.

That changed in late morning on Monday.

Frustrated by the Union militia's burning of the bridge, the Confederates returned westward toward York, foraging for food, horses, and clothing as they went.

This time, Catherine was not so fortunate. Rebel cavalry rode into the farmyard and dismounted. They demanded food.

While they rested on the lawn on the east side of the house, Catherine fed them. In response to her kindness, they in turn mowed the lawn for her and did no harm to the farm.

They never discovered her husband and the livestock in Hidden Valley.[124]

**

The main column of Gordon's infantry retraced their march through Hellam Township along the turnpike to York.

Many had bleeding feet, because the hard gravel turnpike had worn through the leather soles of their shoes.

Foragers visited many farms along the way, including the Samuel Ruby place, later known as the Horn Farm.

Elizabeth Ruby, then in her late teens, was outside the house when a Confederate rode up and asked her for a knife to make a harness repair.

After doing his mending, the soldier inquired, "Where are the family horses?" Lizzie fibbed and told him they were up in the hills. In reality, they had been given to the Union militia guarding Wrightsville.

The Southerner, perhaps a bit homesick, remarked that he had a daughter about Lizzie's age back home.

Despite Lizzie's assertion that there were no horses remaining on the farm, the Rebels nabbed one that day.[125]

**

Mount Herman, later known as the Pleasureville area, served as the elevated locale where Spring Garden Township farmers herded and hid their horses to escape Rebel soldiers.

That well-watered sector of York County was home to numerous horses.

"There used to be horse sheds and water troughs in the Ridgewood Road and Memory Lane area near Pleasureville and for good reasons," Elmer Snyder recalled years later. "Several fine clear water springs can be found in this vicinity."

Southern troops marched through this vicinity looking for such herds of hidden horses. They traveled on what later became known as North Hills Road and then through the old farm lane, Ridgewood Road.

Had the Confederates uncovered the horses, they would have promptly liberated them for their war effort.

But luckily for the North, "Penn's Woods" were still thick and deep in that part of Spring Garden Township, later Springettsbury Township.[126]

**

Nearly a dozen farmers in the Spring Garden region, indeed, lost their horses, according to damage claims filed after the war.

Confederate cavalrymen scoured the region for fresh horseflesh, as did the teamsters of the feared Louisiana Tigers and an artillery battery on Diehl's Hill, the Louisiana Guard Artillery.

Among the many victims in the Spring Garden/Springettsbury region was wealthy farmer Daniel Kohr, who lost nine acres of grass that Rebel soldiers cut down and fed to their horses. He also lost eight barrels of flour that were being stored in Josiah Myers' flour mill along Codorus Creek.

Samuel Dietz, who lived off Ore Bank Road, reported that the Rebels took 85 pairs of horseshoes. His kinsman Michael Dietz, who lived off what is today's Memory Lane Extension, lost an eight-year-old horse. Neighbor John Miller spotted Rebels leading Dietz's horse from a lane where his stable was located.

Nearby, Jonas Fidler lost a three-year-old roan. Wagons arrived at his farm and hauled away 50 bushels of corn from his crib and three tons of dried hay.

Bank director Jacob Brillinger and his family lived in a large mansion, the Elmwood House, east of York.

His farm was the campsite of the 17th Virginia Cavalry. The Southerners grazed more than 500 horses in Brillinger's pastures and fields.

He later claimed 247 bushels of corn, 68 bushels of oats, 22 acres of hay, and "nearly all" his fences, taken down and burned for firewood.

Rebel officers compelled Mrs. Brillinger to cook and serve more than 300 meals to the hungry troopers, washed down with six barrels of homemade whiskey from Brillinger's nearby distillery.[127]

**

A Spring Garden family secreted a fine draft horse in their elegant parlor.

When Major John T. Campbell and a patrol of the feared Louisiana Tigers stopped at the front door, the residents denied even having a horse. Its loud neighing signaled its hiding place.

The Confederates barged inside, seized the frightened animal from beside an expensive rosewood piano, and led it away.

The farmer was left with a fistful of worthless Confederate currency and a parlor that could be confused with a barnyard.[128]

**

The Rebels interrupted the quiet lives of a family named Dietz, living on a homestead, later known as Avalong Farm on Mount Zion Road.

Mrs. Dietz was pregnant and expecting at any time. Her husband had taken the livestock into hiding but had left their best riding horse in the event she should go into labor and needed to reach a doctor.

Confederates visited the farm, and some of them were going to take the horse.

Seeing the Dietz lady's condition, the officer commanded his troops to leave the horse.[129]

**

William H. Bond, a "popular and highly esteemed school teacher" in his younger days, owned a general store in Bottstown, on the turnpike just west of the Codorus Creek. His young son, William S. Bond, had been born on May 9.

Now, just a few weeks later, a party of Confederates stopped at the store, throwing a scare into the Bonds. However, the soldiers proved to be "a good natured lot."

They wanted to pick up the wee lad and hold him.

Little William's parents worried that the soldiers might drop him, but they came to believe the Southerners were good family men.

When the Rebels departed with their arms loaded with merchandise, all they left was worthless Confederate money.[130]

**

Alfred Jessop was a little boy growing up on the family's Springwood farm in York Township when 20 Confederate horsemen paid a visit.

His father and mother were talking with the commanding officer when his brother Charlie stepped outside, dressed in his Union uniform, Alfred later recalled. Charlie Jessop produced his parole papers and the captain carefully read them and returned them.

"All was O.K.," Alfred wrote.

A Napoleon cherry tree near the house bore a fine crop, and the Jessops urged the visitors to help themselves, saying they could get all they could eat without dismounting.

"I never saw men enjoy themselves more," Alfred recounted.[131]

**

When a Louisiana officer knocked on the door of a York clothing store, the storekeeper said he had nothing left to sell.

The Confederate offered gold for some fresh shirts, and the old man opened his store, allowing him to select whatever he wanted. The Southerner returned to his quarters and told his men where they could obtain shirts.

They headed downtown, stopped at the store, and requested shirts. The merchant refused to sell any, so the Rebels pushed him aside and entered the store.

They found the hidden shirts, as well as a supply of aged whiskey and other choice liquors. When the owner refused to give them any alcohol, the Southerners locked him out of his store and proceeded to "indulge in a great spree."

A crowd of onlookers huddled outside his windows, peering in at the commotion. The soldiers emerged with armloads of merchandise and asked the merchant to tally up the bill.

They handed him Confederate currency, assuring the unhappy merchant that the day would come when he would be glad to have some Confederate money in his possession.[132]

**

North Carolina native S. Morgan Smith arrived at York's Moravian Church as a temporary pastor in 1861. The young preacher proved to be an excellent leader of the congregation.

In late June 1863, his congregation reflected the general anxiety that spread through York County with "the Rebels expected every day," as

the 24-year-old Smith wrote in a journal.

"Very few at prayer meeting," he added on the 25th, "The town [is] in great excitement. Hundreds of horses and property being carried through from Franklin County and others. The 'Rebels' daily looked for here. They will certainly come."

And come they did.

On Sunday June 28, the Reverend Smith recorded, "No church in the morning. No evening Sunday School. The cause of this was the appearance of the 'Rebels.' They approached the town at about 10 o'clock about 15,000 strong."

The pastor's estimate was high, but the 6,000 Rebel visitors to a town of 8,600 intimidated townspeople.

More than 1,000 North Carolinian soldiers camped within a few blocks of the Moravian Church. Smith knew several of the soldiers from the Forsyth County Moravian community.

He visited the camp often during the two-day occupation, writing, "As to their behaviour, I hardly know what to say. Upon the whole it was much better than we expected. Our farmers lost hundreds of horses. The demand of money of the town was $100,000 in money and half as much in provisions, etc."

On June 30, the Reverend Smith wrote, "This morning our Rebel friends bade us farewell. They were very calm… The Union army is close and probably captured a large number of prisoners."

He reported to *The Moravian* newspaper in Bethlehem, Pennsylvania, a few days later that he "saw a number of his North Carolina acquaintances during the recent rebel occupation of that city and confirms that the prevailing impression that the North Carolinians are tired of the war."

Evening services were dispensed with, and for the two weeks following the battle at Gettysburg, there were no services. The pastor was doing hospital duty at Gettysburg, and many of the congregation had also gone to view the battlefield.[133]

**

Colonel William H. French's 17th Virginia Cavalry was very active in central York County on Sunday and Monday. Several foraging patrols roamed the region between Dover and York.

One oral tradition speaks to a detachment of Confederates who bivouacked on the old Meisenhelter farm at the end of Angus Lane off Fox Run. Apparently the family had a bell in a tree outside their home and the Johnny Rebs amused themselves by taking pot shots at the bell.[134]

**

Dr. Jacob Eisenhart and his wife, Eliza, lived in a comfortable 1843 stone farmhouse along Taxville Road in West Manchester Township.

Their 97-acre farm offered good meadows, shady woodlots, a small stream, and access to the main roads leading to the west. It was the perfect place for Confederates to camp, particularly because the physician maintained his office in a front room on the first floor.

Gordon's brigade of Georgia infantrymen countermarched to York from Wrightsville in the late afternoon of Monday, June 29, accompanied by a battery of Virginia artillery.

The head of the column arrived in York on East Market Street about 4:00 p.m., and within two hours had marched through York and up the

Carlisle Road. Scouts had selected a series of camping sites for the nearly 2,000 men. The Eisenhart farm was among these sites.

The doctor and his family were home when the first Confederates arrived. They had been busy. Jacob took all the livestock and horses to a safe place, and Eliza and their two spinster daughters, Mary and Henrietta, had buried all the valuables and silver in the yard for safekeeping.

Now, in the early evening, Confederates camped in their fields, perhaps noting that the large stone barn, pigpen, and rolling pastures were empty. A small log cabin might have provided some shelter, although the night was warm and calm.

In the rear of the house was an old-fashioned beehive brick oven. Confederates requested food, and Doc Eisenhart fired up the oven. Mary and Henrietta began baking pies for the soldiers. This act of kindness came not from any Southern sympathies, because the family was devoutly pro-Union.

Jacob had other concerns, as he cared for sick soldiers taken to his office for treatment. Many of Gordon's men had bloody feet — the rough, gravelly turnpike from Wrightsville had worn through their leather soles.

Ambulances full of such men passed through York and camped to the west; it is likely many of these men ended up in Doc Eisenhart's cramped office.

According to descendant Robert Hamme, the family always spoke highly of the graciousness of the soldiers and their general, noting that they were not looted.

On Tuesday morning, June 30, officers told the Georgians to pack up and prepare to march.

General Early had received orders to move his

division to Heidlersburg, as Robert E. Lee began concentrating his widely scattered men to meet the threat of the Union army marching from Maryland.

Before departing the farm, Rebel soldiers gave the Eisenharts Confederate currency in payment for the use of the house and grounds.

The money remained in the family for generations.[135]

**

Michael Miller, owner of a prosperous farm near Davidsburg, went into motion upon learning that the Rebels again were approaching.

He gathered his horses and headed for the Conewago hills for safety.

As Early's Division countermarched westward toward Heidlersburg on Tuesday, June 30, several soldiers paused at Miller's western York County farm. They entered the springhouse and gulped down the milk there.

According to tradition, one of the Confederates left behind his blanket.

On their return, the Millers found the blanket, cut it in two and used it on their beds for a generation.[136]

**

As one Rebel put it, Pennsylvania was a land that overflowed with "such oceans of bread as I had ever seen before."

Food was plentiful, the farms fertile, orchards overflowing with fruit, and the climate fair.

Hundreds of men straggled or deserted in the Gettysburg Campaign, and a few evaded capture and stayed in the area. Some came back to

Pennsylvania after the war and settled down.

Several cemeteries contain the remains of former Confederates who became Keystoners. Descendants of Rebels still live north of the Mason-Dixon Line, including some in York County.

Typical of the deserters who never returned to their families were two Virginians in the Staunton Artillery.

The veteran battery had been posted by Jubal Early south of York on Webb's Hill, with the muzzles of their unlimbered guns facing the town. A couple of crewmen slipped into York and were not present for their next roll call. In fact, they were not seen again by their comrades.

During Robert E. Lee's retreat to Virginia, an angry Captain Asher W. Garber wrote a letter back home to his sister. "[James] W. Fallon — I sent out an inquiry about him," he mentioned. "Him & Michael Duneghee [Donaghee] deserted the company in York City and have not been heard of since."[137]

**

On Tuesday, June 30, about 5,000 Confederate cavalrymen of Jeb Stuart's command rode toward Hanover.

They were headed for York, where they expected to rendezvous with Jubal Early's infantry division.

A woman of Moulstown's namesake family walked with a number of her 10 children from that southwestern York County settlement toward Hanover. As the Mouls moved along their six-mile journey, they saw large numbers of farm animals in barns, barn yards and pastures.

Reaching Hanover, they shopped at several

stores for small items. In one store, they heard a fuss in the street.

Peering outside, Mrs. Moul saw a small man running up the street yelling that the Confederates were coming into town. They were Stuart's horsemen.

She rounded up her children and started the walk back home, up the Moulstown Road.

The farms passed earlier were now empty, with no animals in sight. Horse, wagon, and buggy traffic was heavy. Some Union horsemen would pass them, and then they could see distant Confederates. They also heard gun and cannon blasts coming from the area of Hanover.

Back in Moulstown, everything was in an uproar. Soldiers in gray uniforms rode by with confiscated horses and cattle. They told Moulstown-area residents that if they or their neighbors gave them any trouble, they would burn their farms.

"Now also remember, back then, the Moul family didn't speak any English, it was all German," descendant Gregory E. Moul, Sr. related years later, "I often wondered how they knew what the Confederates were saying to them."[138]

**

The Battle of Hanover on June 30 was the largest military encounter in York County's history.

Thousands of cavalrymen clashed in the vicinity, leaving behind more than 300 casualties. Many suffered saber cuts and pistol wounds from close order combat in which soldiers at times battled hand-to-hand along Frederick Street.

Samuel Althoff witnessed the whole thing.

"I was at my home where I now reside on Baltimore Street when Kilpatrick's men entered Hanover," Althoff recalled. "Like the rest of our citizens interested in seeing them move through town, I went up to Centre Square and watched them passing by and helped to feed them as they moved along on horseback."

Before 10:00 a.m., as he was handing out cigars to the Union horsemen, he heard shooting south along the Westminster road,

He returned to his Baltimore Street home.

His family had gone to the cellar, but he climbed through the attic to the roof. There, he saw mounted soldiers dashing back and forward along the roads and in the fields west of town.

In a grain field, he saw Confederate sharpshooters rising from the tall grain to fire at the Union troops in and around the town.

Rebel cannon on Cemetery Hill and near the Westminster road began to fire shot and shell over the town at Federal soldiers on Bunker Hill.

"About this time, an officer of the New York Regiment rode down Baltimore Street and commanded me to get off the roof of the house," Althoff wrote, "for I was in danger of being shot, so I went down stairs."[139]

**

The Mummert family living in Pleasant Hill, south of Hanover, took action when they learned of the Confederate approach along the Baltimore Pike.

According to family tradition, they hid their horses in nearby caves because of suspicions that the Rebels were taking all the horses they could find.

Their suspicions were right. The Rebels were

living off the land and gathering livestock and other plunder to send to the South.[140]

**

As the unexpected battle began, teenage brothers Sam and John Forney were in the fields on the family farm just south of Hanover.

They had been plowing corn for two hours when about 8:00 a.m. they spotted a long line of Union cavalry on the road from Littlestown.

As the advance guard passed through Buttstown (later known as Pennville), the boys tied their horses and sat on a fence rail along the road to watch the procession.

Near the head of the column rode Brigadier General H. Judson Kilpatrick, a youthful officer surrounded by members of his staff.

Half an hour later, the Forney boys spotted another commander, this one with flowing curls. Sam recalled that George Armstrong Custer was "riding a beautiful bay horse and with two mounted aides on either side of him."

As the soldiers passed, one or two would occasionally halt and engage the farm boys in conversation. It was interesting banter, but Sam Forney spotted trouble.

"But you have a soldier in gray coming yonder," he warned a Federal lieutenant.

"Yes," calmly replied the officer. "He is a scout. We captured him up the road and he is our prisoner now."

A minute later the Confederate stopped his horse and engaged in conversation with the boys.

"So you are plowing corn," he said "I often plowed corn myself down in North Carolina, before I entered the army. I am a soldier now but I wish I were back in my native state, working quietly in the fields like yourselves, for this is a cruel war and I hope it will soon be over."

After the main column entered town, Sam and John returned to the plowing. The horses were moving slowly between the rows of corn, while the 18th Pennsylvania cavalry regiment slowly trotted toward town.

Suddenly, a few minutes after 10 o'clock, loud yells and shrieks were heard on the Westminster road. The Forneys watched spellbound as the 13th Virginia Cavalry dashed down the road and fired a volley at the rear of the Federal troopers.

"In a few minutes," Sam later related to historian George Prowell, "the fields immediately north of the Littlestown road and west of Hanover were filled with mounted soldiers. The Union troops had quickly fallen back through town to the assistance of the rear regiment which had been attacked."

While the air was filled with yells and shrieks, the Forney boys unhitched their horses. While bullets whistled overhead, they hastened with them across fields toward McSherrystown. They escaped to the Geiselman farm, where they remained until late in the afternoon.

When they came back home after the battle, the boys discovered 22 dead horses near their father's farm.[141]

**

Young Ambrose M. Schmidt, his siblings, and mother were on the porch of their Hanover home.

A Union cavalry officer came up to the family. But right about then, a shell exploded on Frederick Street.

The officer ran to his horse, and headed out the

Abbottstown Road, but not before yelling a warning, "My God, woman, the Confederates are on us. Get your children into the house."

Gray and blue horsemen clashed on Broadway, right before the family.

"We ran into the house crying," Ambrose Schmidt later recounted.[142]

**

Rebecca Scheurer, a young Hanover girl, found herself in harm's way when the shooting started.

She reminisced that she was "pulled from between artillery horses by my mother, and hastening home, I secreted myself in a rear room, and realized something of the shock of war, as I heard the whizzing of bullets over the house."[143]

**

Some of Hanover's citizens voiced displeasure with the Rebels riding through their town.

They also took action.

"At Hanover the citizens fired at us from the windows. Why the town was not burnt I don't know," a doctor from the 10th Virginia complained.

Another Confederate agreed that the citizens opened "a hot skirmish fire."

Union General Kilpatrick viewed the townspeople in a different light.

"The main streets were barricaded and held by our troops and the citizens, who gallantly volunteered to defend their homes," he wrote.

The women of Hanover shared equally in the post-battle praise with the men.

"God bless the ladies of our town," the Hanover *Citizen* later commented, "and forbid that their nerves ever again be shocked by the roar of cannon, the clashing of steel, or the ghastly image of murdered men."[144]

**

Lewis Miller, the carpenter/artist from York, captured many scenes of the Confederate occupation of York County.

He drew a scene of an old farmer Rudyseal trying to curry protection from General Kilpatrick near Hanover.

"I am an old Jackson, union man," Miller wrote in quoting Rudyseal. "Come to my house and take some wine, you do me a favor."

Farmers in that sector of the county generally did not support a strong state or federal government. But the Confederate presence produced converts.

"Let us Stand up for the Government, and all bear against the rebel," Miller wrote, again quoting the farmer.[145]

**

Heidelberg Township merchant George Zinn was among the dozens of merchants and shopkeepers attracting Confederate troops. A party of mounted Confederate cavalrymen from one of Stuart's regiments rode up to Zinn's modest dry goods store.

Entering the shop, they proceeded to pick merchandise and food from the shelves and bins. Some paid for their purchases with worthless Confederate money; others simply walked out with their arms loaded.

Years later, Zinn filed a claim with the U.S. government but never received compensation to match his losses. He reported the loss of two watches worth $25, a large box of gold jewelry and earrings, and several silk and woolen shawls, among other items.

The Confederates did not stop there. They also hauled off all the meat they could carry, as well as crocks of hand-churned butter, jars of York County apple butter, and other food. The Southerners also carried off a dozen table knives and forks, as well as 18 spoons.

George Zinn was dismayed, but he was powerless to stop the invaders from taking his merchandise.

Many other merchants in York County would tell the same story.[146]

**

Conrad Myers was just one of a dozen shopkeepers from Jefferson to Dillsburg victimized by the thievery of Stuart's men in a 24-hour period after the Battle of Hanover.

Late in the afternoon of June 30, a group of Confederate cavalrymen dismounted and forcibly entered Myers' locked store in North Codorus Township. They helped themselves to his inventory, taking muslins, calicoes, silverware, hatchets, and other dry goods and sundries.

They also snatched up food, walking off with jars of molasses, bottles of wine, and kegs of whiskey. A stunned Myers watched helplessly as the Rebs carried off goods, later valued at $3,150.

One Confederate took about $20 from a cash drawer, and then, to Myers' additional dismay, other soldiers entered his stable and stole a sorrel.

Another party visited a nearby grist mill,

confiscating 50 bushels of corn belonging to Myers.[147]

**

In search of Jubal Early's column, Stuart's cavalry created quite a stir riding northward from Jefferson toward Dover.

Southern patrols seized all sorts of property of military value — horses, mules, livestock, forage, and supplies.

A young couple, Jacob and Mary (Bubb) Werner, and their small child lived on the Brodbeck farm near Jefferson.

When news arrived that the Rebels were coming, Mr. Brodbeck objected to the idea of having to hide with his horses in the woods.

Instead, he placed a lock about the size of a man's hand on the barn's door.

Undeterred upon reaching the farm, the Confederate soldiers shot off the lock and took everything they wanted.

Jacob Werner hid his horses in the middle of a tall green briar patch, which he had trimmed out to form a sort of cove.

As soon as he felt sure the Rebels were out of sight, Jacob, with his wife and baby and his sister, Mary, piled all they could in their covered wagon and took their horses from their hiding place.

They eventually fled to the West, presumably to Kansas, where Jacob Werner's mother and her second husband, Jacob Koehler, had relocated a year or two before.[148]

**

With night approaching and his men strung out

for miles after leaving Hanover, General Stuart called a staff meeting on the property of John E. Ziegler, near the intersection of the Jefferson and Patapsco roads.

A vacant stone tavern sat at that intersection, northeast of Jefferson. In the late 1930s or early 1940s, the owners tore it down.

As they dismantled the creaking structure, William Kessler of Seven Valleys found an old Confederate revolver hidden in the rafters.

Kessler's young son Wayne played with the pistol as a young boy. He put firecrackers in the barrel on the Fourth of July.[149]

**

Shortly after leaving Ziegler's place, Stuart's men headed northward toward York New Salem. Most locals did not realize they were in the area, and had assumed the threat from Confederates had passed.

After the departure of Early's division and White's cavalry from York County, word reached farmers who had taken their horses to Lancaster County that they could return.

"But this proved unfounded," Harry Gladfelter wrote, "as they discovered when a number of them thus returning rode into the midst of the enemy in the public road near the Daniel Henry mill at Seven Valleys, and had to part with their horses."

Gladfelter saw a man in civilian clothes leaping over a fence to the rear of his family's garden. He ran through the orchard toward the nearby woods.

Three Confederate soldiers on horseback galloped to the Gladfelter gate, not far from Ziegler's Church near New Salem.

"I was out in the yard and they called out to me, 'Say Sonnie did you see a Yankee running this way?' I was about twelve years old and certain their intention was to capture and possibly kill him. I answered them, no, and they rode away," he wrote.

He couldn't tell the size of the Rebel force but heard the clattering or horse hoofs and wagons for most of the night.

"The anxiety, uncertainty, and fear that hung over us all can well be imagined," he recalled. "No one could know what the next hour, the coming night, the next day would bring. I possibly was too young to realize at the time the full force of what our fate might be, but looking back at this time of life I understand why fathers, mothers, and neighbors everywhere bore blanched faces moistened by tears of sorrow and dismay."[150]

**

In the late afternoon and evening, a long line of Confederate troops passed by Henry and Mary Kessler's place on Church Road in the Panther Hill area.

Several troopers pulled from the main column and trotted over to the farm, searching for food and horses.

Mary Kessler had just baked bread that day. Her uninvited Southern guests took all of the bread, as well as several crocks of homemade apple butter.

As for the horses, the Rebels went away disappointed. Word of their approach had reached the Kessler family in time for Henry to gather his work animals and hide them in some nearby woods.

A little earlier that afternoon, Henry's kinsman Solomon Kessler was less fortunate. He lost a seven-year-old gray horse to a foraging patrol.[151]

**

A squad of Confederate cavalrymen, escorting a train of empty supply wagons, rode up to William Ross's farm just outside York on July 1.

When the "Johnnies" departed, the wagons carried away 75 bushels of corn and other items from his farm.

William A. French's 17th Virginia Cavalry had visited Dover resident Mary Roth a day earlier, confiscating 40 pairs of horseshoes and 50 pounds of blacksmith's nails, as well as nine bushels of coal.

The Sprenkle family in West Manchester Township was particularly hard hit by the invaders. George Sprenkle lost a five-year-old sorrel worth $150, a three-year-old black horse also valued at $150, and an old-timer, a 20-year-old dark bay, that he estimated was still worth $50.

David Sprenkle reported that Rebels entered his stable on June 30 and emerged with a dark bay worth $175. Jacob Sprenkle lost a pair of mares, as well as two other horses, totaling an estimated $475. Finally, Levi Sprenkle reported that Rebs procured a bay from his father's barn and never returned it.

With harvest season fast approaching, the loss of all those vital farm horses, many of which were pressed into service to pull Confederate wagons or artillery pieces, meant that York County farmers would struggle to bring in their crops.[152]

**

Jeb Stuart's three weary brigades of Confederate cavalry camped for the evening of June 30 on various farms surrounding Dover.

The next morning Stuart ransomed Dover for money and supplies and sent foraging patrols throughout Dover and Conewago townships to search for horses and livestock. He unlimbered artillery south of town along the Carlisle Road and north at Harmony Grove Road to ensure that the locals complied.

Civic officials pled poverty and Stuart relented, although it is said that he threatened to shell the town. His men cleaned out many of the merchants and businesses, often leaving worthless vouchers on the Confederate government.

A small detachment of Rebels was traveling from Wolf's Church in West Manchester Township to Strayer's Church, later Salem Church, near Dover. They camped on the Deisinger farm overnight.

The next morning they broke camp and prepared to leave. One of their wagons was beyond immediate repair, and the soldiers abandoned it.

To render the wagon unusable to any Yankees in the vicinity, they built a fire under it and left. Deisinger hurried outside and extinguished the blaze.

Later, he had the wagon repaired. Deisinger noted that it "proved more than an ordinary wagon in durability."[153]

**

Elizabeth Hoffman was hanging laundry in the back yard of her Dover home when a group of Confederate soldiers appeared from around the front of the house.

Afraid for her safety, Elizabeth, wife of John Hoffman, offered to make them food, figuring it would save her from harm.

While she cooked, they ransacked her home and

stole all of her chickens and any other food they could carry. Her six-year-old daughter, Mary Jane, hung onto her mother's skirts the whole time.

The men did them no harm, but left them shaken, with little in the larder.[154]

**

Stuart's column camped overnight on various farms surrounding Dover.

On the morning of July 1, the Confederates paroled scores of Union prisoners accompanying them.

Before riding north toward Dillsburg, they released some Hanover area men who had been forced to serve as guides. The Johnnies kept the men's horses.

Ephraim Nace, a civilian detainee, had managed to escape and hide in a haymow. He thought danger had passed when Stuart's main force left town.

But some stragglers accosted him. They gave him "two old worn out nags that had been in the Confederate service for a long time. I rode one of these horses home and led the other."

"One of the horses died within a week and the other I was glad to sell for $10," he wrote. "What became of my faithful horses, I know not. Possibly they were killed in the battle of Gettysburg."[155]

**

Henry and Sarah Kalbaugh Miller had roots in the Quaker and Lutheran churches.

Their prosperous farm south of Dillsburg attracted attention from Wade Hampton's cavalrymen as they rode from Dover.

Like so many other residents of Warrington, Washington, Franklin, and Carroll townships, the Millers took their horses into the woods to hide them from the Confederates.

For the Millers, the ploy worked. For so many others, the results were quite different.

"I had taken my horses seven miles from my home in Dillsburg when I was overtaken by Rebel cavalry," William P. Griffith wrote. The soldiers forced Griffith to accompany them as a guide to Dover and then on to Gettysburg, where they finally released him on July 4 when they retreated.

Griffith, now minus his horse, walked home to Dillsburg in a driving rainstorm.

He took ill from the experience and needed medical treatment in Philadelphia.[156]

**

On July 1 in downtown York, 35-year-old Israel Laucks hitched his seven-year-old bay to his spring wagon.

He probably did not expect any trouble. He had managed to protect his horse during Early's three-day Confederate stay in York, and he must have been relieved when the Rebel division left town the morning of June 30.

Like so many other York countians, Laucks had not expected the arrival of Stuart's cavalrymen.

He entrusted his wagon and horse to his father, George Laucks, and asked him to take the wagon back to his Manchester Township farm. George had driven more than three miles from York when he encountered a patrol of Confederate cavalrymen.

At gunpoint, they forced the large man to get down. A Rebel climbed aboard, and that was the last any of the Lauckses saw of the horse or wagon.[157]

**

John Ritter was a prosperous farmer near Rossville in northwestern York County.

He was a simple man, well versed in the ways of agriculture and harvesting, and was married and had several children.

Like his neighbors, his financial livelihood depended upon raising crops and bringing them to market in a timely fashion. He would not get that chance in the summer of 1863.

Stuart's cavalrymen raided northern York County for horses, as they wearily trekked toward Carlisle and an expected rendezvous with Lieutenant General Richard S. Ewell's Second Corps.

Hundreds of farmers between Dover and Cumberland County had failed to hide their horses from the predators.

A large body of armed Rebels approached John Ritter's roadside farm and confronted him. They forced him at gunpoint to go into his fields and personally round up his work horses and draft mules.

He was compelled to collect the animals in his barn until they were all brought in. Ritter watched the Confederates untether his horses and mules and ride off, leading them by their halters.

Ritter would never see the animals again.

He would be forced to find replacements and rely upon friends and family to help him bring in the summer harvest.[158]

**

Round Top, an impressive tree-covered mountain, dominates the skyline in Warrington Township in northwestern York County.

The mountain was a natural place for local residents to hide their horses. Its dense woods, deep ravines, and out-of-the-way location seemed to invite safety in case of a Confederate incursion into the region.

As Stuart's cavalry passed northward from Rossville on July 1, they, too, could spot the landmark. It did not take long for scouts to determine that the mountainside might be a treasure trove of hidden horses.

A Dillsburg-area farmer was one of those who took his horses to Round Top for safety. He had stayed on the mountain for several days when on July 1 he spotted a mounted patrol nearing his hiding place.

He muffled the horses as best as he could and peered through the timber as the cavalrymen rode past without spotting him or the horses.

Nearby, several of his neighbors were accosted and forced to hand over their animals when a horse began to neigh, which revealed their location to the raiders.

Several farmers later filed damage claims for horses stolen "in a secretive place" on Round Top.

They included Daniel Bailey of Dillsburg, who lost a black horse and two bays, as well as three halters. Other victims included Lewis J. Pressel, James Williams, and James J. Logan, all of the Dillsburg area.

A handful of farmers from Cumberland County had also falsely hoped that Round Top was the right spot to secret their animals.

James Coyle from South Middlesex had taken

his five-year-old bay mare several miles to the mountain region. His luck ran out when Confederates discovered his hiding place and took the horse.

The farmers who lived in the shadow of the mountains fared no better. Michael Duty lost an 11-year-old bay. John Hays had volunteered to hide several of his neighbors' horses in a dense thicket on his property. Rebels found them all. Jacob D. Krall lost two stallions, one of which was only two years old.

He recovered the animal a couple of months later. It had been used by a Rebel in fighting at Gettysburg, and it had suffered an injury to its back.[159]

**

Descendants recall Dover Township farmer Eli Zinn as "a tall, bearded, well-built man," who "was a craftsman in his line and often helped neighbors and farmers nearby to rebuild their barns and houses when destroyed by fire or storm, giving the services of himself and his team without charge."

Thirty-eight years old with a wife and a dozen kids, he was noted for being "always kind to his horses and saw that they were well groomed before stabling for the night."

He needed his horses to be in top condition, because he frequently used them to haul heavy loads of produce to Baltimore and other markets.

In late June 1863, as the Confederates neared his farm near Davidsburg along the Conewago Creek, he feared for the safety of his prized horses.

He had not taken them to safety when the first Rebels appeared in the area. Luckily, he was able to persuade the soldiers to leave his farm unmolested. They went away, and Eli kept his animals.

At least for a moment.

"A little while later," one of his descendants recalled, "when in the vicinity of Emig's Mill, beside the Conewago, they were again short of horses. A man by the name of Sam Krout unwittingly told them that a stable full of horses was to be found upstream a mile or two, at the Zinn place. They immediately came after them and took them all but a colt that was too young." Two dozen or more soldiers approached Zinn's house for food. His wife Sarah went with them to the cellar, and the Rebels ate or took everything that was edible.

The officer in charge ordered that Sarah should not be harmed, for she had treated them kindly.

Eli soon received a glimmer of hope that he might regain his lost horses.

After the Battle of Gettysburg, the Zinns received word about a field of horses near Carlisle. Upon identification, horses could be reclaimed.

Eli, accompanied by his brother-in-law, Peter Lonkert, made the trip but found none of their horses.

"They were offered other horses at a price which was not accepted," the descendant said.[160]

The famed Dempwolf architectural firm of York designed Penn Common's Soldiers and Sailors Monument, among scores of other landmarks in the region. This towering monument, seen here in a photo from *Heroes and Builders*, stands on the site of the former U.S. Army General Hospital. It is the most visible reminder of the Civil War in the York area.

This is an early look at the 19th-century Spring Garden Band, still performing in the 21st century. With the outbreak of the Civil War, this Freystown, east York, band served as the 87th Infantry's band. In its long history, it has played at presidential and gubernatorial inaugurations as well as countless performances in York County. This photograph comes from band leader William Frey's descendant Mike Spyker.

Johnson Kelly Duncan of Chanceford Township became the highest-ranking Confederate officer born in York County. As a brigadier general, he commanded the defenses of New Orleans. He died of malaria in December 1862 while serving in the field in Tennessee. This photograph comes from descendant Jill Jordan.

Samuel C. Ilgenfritz of the 187th Pennsylvania spoke eloquently at reunions of soldiers in the decades after the war. In one speech, he stated, 'This is a nation, not a compact, a rope of sand, that may be snapped asunder by the mere whim of any one; nor set of States, but a nation possessing the power to defend, preserve and perpetuate its life.' He is buried in Prospect Hill Cemetery. This photograph comes from a regimental history.

Wrightsville's James Barton made his mark, lower right, on this enlistment form in Carlisle. He traveled to Camp William Penn in Philadelphia for training, where he contracted a severe case of measles that impaired his health for the rest of his life. Barton recovered sufficiently to serve in the 127th Regiment, United States Colored Troops.

David Etter Small was a member of the most prominent 19th-century York County family. This railroad car manufacturer lost an arm in a factory accident and could not fight in uniform, but he was a determined supporter of the Union army and Republican Party. Another David Small, chief burgess of York and owner of the *York Gazette*, was a staunch Democrat and opponent of President Abraham Lincoln's war policies. This photograph comes from descendant Liz Winand.

Chapter 3

Voices from the Battle of Gettysburg

'I have often made claim that in this way I helped to fight the battle of Gettysburg and for all I know our sharpened sword done more execution than I would be proud of.'

> *- Harry Gladfelter, Seven Valleys, Pa.*

On the morning of July 1, while artillery roared and musketry crackled from the fields and woods north and west of Gettysburg, thousands of soldiers from both armies hustled to the scene.

Brigadier General David M. Gregg's veteran cavalry division was one of those oncoming units, camping near Seven Valleys for part of the afternoon.

Harry Gladfelter recalled, "I then ran down the hill to the George Hamm home where quite a number of soldiers were waiting for bread from Mrs. Hamm and daughters were baking for them."

"One of the soldiers, carrying a sword that appeared very large and dangerous to me, laid his hand on my shoulder, saying, 'Come with me sonny; I want you to do something for me.' My first thought was to run away; a kind smile from him gave me courage to go with him. He led me to a grindstone and asked me to turn it while he ground his sword."

"I have often made claim," Gladfelter wrote, "that in this way I helped to fight the battle of Gettysburg and for all I know our sharpened sword done more execution than I would be proud of."[161]

**

Jacob Bowman was not particularly happy to see Gregg's Union cavalry, because the horsemen camped for part of the day on his Springfield Township farm.

He later filed a Federal damage claim citing his loss.

"A great many horses of Gregg's Div. was pastured on the 3 acres of grass about 6 hours until all was eaten up," Bowman complained.

The cavalrymen had "stopped all afternoon to rest and feed their horses." An officer and several privates rode up to his barn, "dismounted and took the oats and corn." The soldiers transported the haul to the regimental camp and fed it to their horses.

Bowman did get a fleeting glimmer of hope: "They gave no receipt but told me to make out a bill and it would be paid."

It never was.[162]

**

Hametown resident Anna Mary Dise was ten years old that summer. Six years earlier, she had suffered through the tragic loss of her father who was killed in a horse and wagon accident.

Now, on July 1, 1863, she "was in the fields gathering hay. The sky in the west became black," she later recalled, and she could hear the blast of artillery.

A great battle had begun in Gettysburg, one that would alter the course of the Civil War.[163]

**

A group of boys wandered along the banks of the Codorus Creek near Laurel Rocks and Indian Steps. These were popular swimming holes.

But the fighting raging 30 miles away in Gettysburg disturbed the normal solitude.

"At these points," Martin L. Van Baman remembered years later, "the rattle of musketry and booming of cannon during the engagement could be distinctly heard."

Fourteen-year-old Emaline Smeigh also heard the roar from her home in Brownton in southeastern York County.

The sounds they heard meant real death and destruction for tens of thousands of men, many not much older than the York boys and Emaline.

For hundreds of men who had tramped through the York vicinity during Early's raid, the picnic-like atmosphere, the fresh bread and roasted beef, the parade through York, and the York County whiskey had been replaced by the grave or the torture of long hours of lying in agony in once obscure fields and woods or in temporary field hospitals.[164]

**

The thunderous noise of battle could be heard throughout York County. The *Hanover Spectator* reported, "The ground was fairly shaken by the concussion and the whole country for miles around was filled with terrible sounds of warlike strife."

A Welsh slate miner named Enoch P. Swayne, a Delta resident, lived about as far away as you can get from Gettysburg and still be in York County — about 60 miles.

But he heard the strife from the major fight to the west.

The *Delta Star* reported years later that Swayne claimed to have heard gunfire from the battle.

Also near Delta, some members of Anna Macomber's family were pumping water into a slate trough when they could hear rumblings from the west. The ground was shaking, and no one knew at the time the source.

It was not until later that they learned of the Battle at Gettysburg.

Not far away, the trustees of the Rehoboth Welsh Church were leaving a meeting in Bangor, a hamlet just north of Delta. They, too, could feel the strong vibrations in the earth.

Harry Boyer's ancestors were working their farmstead in a Springfield Township valley later covered by Lake Williams.

They could hear the sound of the cannons clearly in that region as it echoed from the hillsides.

Union militia in Columbia, across the river from Wrightsville, clearly heard the rumble of artillery, and at least one soldier claimed that a battle was raging in York.

Others believed it was happening in Dillsburg.[165]

**

Samuel Shaffer and his family lived in a farmhouse he constructed near Red Lion.

When he heard about the Rebel approach days earlier, he took his horses up to Zion's View, where a high wooded ridge offered shelter and concealment from roving Confederate patrols.

His wife, Leah, stayed behind to manage the farm.

Now, the sounds of fighting in Gettysburg reverberated through the Red Lion region.

Henry Grove, whose descendant would later marry one of Shaffer's family members, was busy building a new house for himself. He ignored the noise and focused on his project.

Coincidentally, another man with ties to the Groves, William Arnold, was fighting in the battle that raged in Adams County.

He was shot in the foot but survived his painful injury.

When he died years later, his little granddaughter Mabel Grove recalled that he was dressed in his old Civil War uniform with his sword lying beside him in the casket.[166]

**

One of the Union soldiers battling against Lee's army at Gettysburg was Adam T. Smith of the 107th Pennsylvania.

Born in Wittenberg, Germany, Smith was a shoemaker by trade. He first saw combat at Cedar Run in the Shenandoah Valley in early August 1862.

Less than three weeks later, he was wounded at Second Bull Run and taken prisoner. After being held captive for a month, he was released.

On Oak Ridge in Gettysburg on July 1, the 107th was hotly engaged with Confederates from Robert Rodes' division in a field on the John Forney farm. Smith was wounded in the back of the neck.

Though painful, the injury was not life threatening. When the Federals withdrew into the town, Smith was left lying in the hot sun. Adding to his misery, he suffered from sunstroke.

When the Confederates left on July 4, Smith was one of more than 10,000 wounded men being treated in makeshift hospitals or lying exposed on the quiet battlefield. He was eventually transferred to Camp Letterman hospital, just east of Gettysburg.

Once Smith was well enough, he was taken to the military hospital on Penn Common in his hometown of York.

In 1864, he enlisted again but suffered from poor health and was frequently on the sick list. He was transferred to the Veteran Reserve Corps and guarded railroads and important buildings. After his discharge from the army in late June 1865, he returned to York.

Adam Smith was a broken man.

Although he fathered three children with Mary, his health complications continued to worsen, and Smith died at the age of 31 in 1871.[167]

**

A soldier remembered only as "Uncle John" fought in the area of Culp's Hill in the Battle of Gettysburg.

Years later, Uncle John told young Bessie Gingerich how the Union and Confederate soldiers would sneak to Spangler's Spring at night for fresh water.

Uncle John was shot through the fleshy part of a leg, and he cleaned out the wound by pushing his handkerchief through the hole with a stick.

Though he walked with a limp, he didn't have the leg removed, which often happened in such cases. John became reclusive after the war and moved to the Allegheny Mountains.

He was later mauled by a bear, though he managed to kill it.

He presented one of the teeth to Bessie, who later, as Bessie Gingerich Rudisill, gave it to a grandson.[168]

**

Sergeant Abraham Rudisill of York manned a battery on Culp's Hill on the second and third days of the battle.

He recalled on Friday evening, shortly after Pickett's Charge, "Soon firing gradually ceased more or less for now while I write at the side of cannon No. 1, there is comparatively a great calm. Perhaps the Rebels are charging or falling back. We will see; but the storm may rage again ere long."

He added sentiments that so many soldiers on both sides could have echoed, "Lord Keep Us. Praise the Lord for his goodness. I see men reading the Testament."

The respite was brief.

Soon Rudisill added, "Just in front of me the cannons are booming; now and then as shell passes here; sometimes cutting the limbs of trees."

The following evening, after a night and day of relative calm, Rudisill returned to his dairy. He scrawled, "Praise the good Lord for the great deliverance and victory He has given our troops, although undeserving and unworthy as we are."

He recalled the terror of the massive artillery bombardment the previous afternoon just before Pickett's Charge: "Such a cannonading as took place on both sides was scarce ever witnessed in similar circumstances in the annals of warfare."

That Saturday as he roamed the relatively silent battlefield, he noticed the debris of war. A horse had limped past, guts hanging out on both sides. He informed his son in York, "And I heard the poor horse actually uttering a shriek or clear voice of agony."

The most horrific scenes, of course, were the mangled soldiers, living and dead, that littered the once lush summer fields.

Rudisill stood by the side of a dying soldier, who drank from his canteen just before he breathed his last. The wounded man's entrails protruded from his belly, the handiwork of a shell fragment.

But the Union line had held.[169]

**

When the sound of fighting ceased, Mary Fisher, the nurse at York's military hospital, rushed to the battlefield in Gettysburg.

She encountered a stricken drummer boy from a Rhode Island infantry regiment at the foot of Little Round Top.

She leaned over the boy, who calmly whispered, "Kiss me before I die." Mortally wounded, the lad was dying far away from his New England home and his own beloved mother, and the friendly face of the Pennsylvania woman comforted him in his final minutes on Earth.

She kissed his pale cheek and tenderly held the young soldier in her arms until he breathed his last. His broken drum lay not far from the boy.

In the days following the battle, Jacob Weikert, a nearby farmer, picked up the instrument. The thrifty Weikert found a utilitarian purpose for this discarded martial instrument. For the next 16 years, he used the old wooden drum as a hive for his bees.

In the ensuing months, the drummer boy's grieving mother arrived in Gettysburg to search for her son's burial place. She wanted to recover his body and transport it home to Providence, Rhode Island, for burial.

But she failed in several repeated trips to locate the gravesite.

It was not found until 1867, when the remains were identified and dug up, placed in a coffin, and transported via railcar to Providence.

The young Rhode Island musician had finally come home.[170]

**

In the second and third weeks of July, a seemingly endless caravan of wagons and carriages lined the hard gravel turnpike from York to Gettysburg.

Some carried dusty sightseers or eager battlefield relic hunters.

Other passengers were curiosity seekers, adventurers and Good Samaritans seeking to help the injured soldiers. Refugees finally returning to their homes in Adams County were counted among those passengers.

Many of the Yorkers in the procession brought much needed material goods of value to the volunteer groups ministering to the wounded.

On July 21, 1863, the *Adams Sentinel* published a lengthy list of donations of hospital supplies received from the public: "2 wagon loads of stores from York, one wagon load from Dover… one barrel of ice from York… 1 sack clothing, 9 cushions, 1 bundle shirts and drawers, 2 sacks linen rags, 1 bag beans, 1 bag onions, 1 bundle shirts, 1 box stewed cherries and wines, 1 basket rusks, 1 box eggs, apple butter, pickles and groceries from York… assorted hospital stores from Glen Rock… a wagon load of stores from Freedom, York Co.… 8 packages and hospital stores from citizens of Wellsville… a wagon load of bread and hospital stores from Shrewsbury Township, York county… sheets, shirts, bandages, etc. from Baughmansville, York county… ."

One week later, another list included donations from the tiny village of Seitzland in southern York County, as well as from several individuals in York.

All this came from a border county that had seen its own share of suffering from the 11,000 Confederate visitors less than a week before fighting in Gettysburg.[171]

**

Among the earliest York visitors to the debris-strewn Gettysburg battlefield was the young industrialist A.B. Farquhar, who on June 27 had negotiated a surrender with Confederate General John Gordon to ensure York's protection.

It was an impulsive act that proved controversial, but it came to be appreciated by some Yorkers as the key to keeping the Confederates from harming the town and its factories and homes.

On July 2, while fighting raged at Gettysburg, Farquhar used his recently gained relationships with senior Confederate commanders to enter the vicinity safely, intent on helping to care for the wounded.

He passed from Confederate to Union lines where he was met with suspicion and then talked his way out of trouble by appealing directly to General Kilpatrick.

He eventually located a makeshift hospital, a big shed with a hay loft above. There, the wounded were stretched out on the ground side by side.

"As the surgeons were engaged elsewhere and there seemed to be no one in command," he explained in his autobiography years later. "I took charge myself. We could do but little for the poor fellows except give them water and make their lot perhaps a little easier until they died or came under a doctor's care."

While Farquhar and others cared for the wounded soldiers, cavalrymen rode up and fetched hay from the loft. That scattered dust down upon the wounded.

Ever in charge, Farquhar wrote: "I caused them to stop."[172]

**

In the weeks after fighting ceased, thousands of wounded soldiers passed through Hanover Junction en route to Baltimore, Harrisburg, Philadelphia, Washington and other towns where they could receive medical care.

Scores of civilians also traveled through Hanover Junction. Most were sightseers on an excursion to visit the famous battlefield.

Others were relief agents, medical personnel, nurses and aides, and newspaper correspondents. Cars were overcrowded and unsanitary, with passengers often crowding into freight cars.

"Comfortable cars were not available," Harry Gladfelter related, "and anything on wheels that would run was put into service, ordinary boxcars, stock cars, gondolas, sand and lime cars. Made as comfortable as could be done by layers of hay and straw, all manner of men bearing all manner of wounds could be seen stretched out on the floors of the cars. Some weeping, some praying, some cursing, some holding the stumps of their legs in their hands, some with but one hand to use."

Gladfelter recalled that the movement of the wounded lasted for up to four weeks.

The U.S. Christian Commission worked out of cars on a siding, distributing food and comfort to wounded men.

One time, Harry handed oranges to soldiers from a basket.

"I recall that a veritable host of visitors from all parts of the country passed this way," he recalled, "many of whom doubtless had relatives who fought and were probably killed or wounded, as well as those who went out of curiosity to view the battlefield."[173]

**

A party of young ladies took the train toward Gettysburg one day.

Several young gentlemen who knew the girls and wanted to sit beside them rested on the opposite side of the car. A strange odor emanated from near the ladies' seat, and one of the young men casually mentioned that an amputated limb was in the vicinity.

The coveted seats were soon vacated, and the lads had the girls to themselves. The women were shocked and stunned, and the young men were congratulating each other for their ingenuity in clearing the seats.

It turned out the odor came from one of the

girls' lunch baskets, which contained a box of foul-smelling "Dutch cheese."[174]

**

James Ashworth, born in a rural county in northwest England along the Atlantic coast, immigrated with his parents to the United States.

The family settled near Philadelphia, and after high school, he entered the transoceanic shipping business, working for a firm that operated cargo packets to Liverpool, England.

With the outbreak of the war, Ashworth accompanied General Robert Patterson's force to Maryland as a civilian volunteer. He took up a musket and fought a Confederate raiding party that was attempting to wreck the Chesapeake & Ohio Canal near Williamsport but was arrested by the citizens the next day as a Rebel spy and put on trial.

Ashworth's life was spared when some of his Pennsylvania comrades happened into town, learned of the spy charges, and testified to his loyal patriotism and volunteer service in the skirmish at Dam #5. He was acquitted and returned to Philadelphia.

In August 1862, he raised a group of volunteers that became part of the new 121st Pennsylvania Infantry. Ashworth and his comrades saw their first action at Fredericksburg in December.

He became sick but rejoined his unit as it moved toward Pennsylvania in June 1863. In the fighting west of Gettysburg along McPherson's Ridge, he was wounded 11 times. He struggled for life behind enemy lines and was finally stabilized by Confederate doctors.

When the Rebels departed on July 5, Ashworth was left behind in a temporary field hospital in Gettysburg. After he was stable enough to be moved, Ashworth and several other patients were taken for recuperation at York's military hospital.

Ashworth never fought in a battle again, but his survival tale was not yet over. He returned home to recover and was commissioned as a colonel before being reassigned to the Veteran Reserve Corps as a captain.

Ordered to a post in New Orleans, he embarked on a steam ship, which wrecked off the coast of Florida. A U.S. Navy gunboat rescued Ashworth and other survivors.

At war's end, Ashworth was ordered back to York, where he was in charge of discharging convalescent patients.

Ashworth later worked for the Freedman's Bureau in Louisa, Virginia, before resigning from the army and returning to the shipping company he worked for before the war. His health failing due to lingering effects of his war injuries, Ashworth moved to Florida, hoping the warm weather would help him. But he died in Gainesville less than a month later.

James Ashworth survived a potential death sentence for spying, a severe illness, 11 wounds at Gettysburg, and a shipwreck off the coast of Florida, the same state where he would finally expire years later from those war wounds.[175]

**

The military hospital in York treated nearly 2,000 wounded Union soldiers after the Battle of Gettysburg.

But the surgeon in charge, Dr. Henry Palmer, refused to allow stricken Confederates to be housed in his hospital wards, so they were taken to the Odd Fellows Hall.

Most of the Southerners were transported to

prisoner-of-war camps when they were able to travel.

Not all recovered.

James P. Norton, a private in the 8th Alabama Infantry, fought in the fields between Seminary and Cemetery ridges.

In the second day of fighting, the 8th Alabama attacked the Union Third Corps along the Emmitsburg Road. In that engagement, Jim Norton was wounded in the leg.

After fighting ended, he was picked up and taken to a field hospital and then to York's hospital for long-term recuperation. His condition worsened, and he died in November, joining a number of Union soldiers who also perished at York in the months after Gettysburg.

Before the war, young Norton had attended Mount St. Mary's College in Emmitsburg, Maryland.

His body was prepared for shipment and transported to the college cemetery, where it was interred next to another Confederate casualty of the Gettysburg battle.[176]

**

After the fighting at Gettysburg, a large number of looters and relic collectors swarmed the festering battlefield, grabbing guns, swords, and other military and personal effects.

According to contemporary accounts, "a number of nondescript scavengers of mixed nationalities" from the Spring Forge region of southwestern York County were persistent in traveling some 24 miles to the battlefield, collecting rags and clothing by the wagonload, and driving back caravan-style to the small hamlet.

There, they sold their contraband to the Jacob Hauer paper mill, operated by a Philadelphia firm contracted by Hauer's heirs after his death in August 1855.

Since its founding in 1852, the single-machine mill on the west branch of the Codorus Creek had been supplied by these vagabond peddlers, who had provided a cheap but legal source of cotton fiber for the 1,500 pounds of paper produced each day.

The raw material supply had dwindled during the Civil War as fabric had been diverted to the military. Now, with the debris of battle not far away, the rag dealers were harvesting a windfall of discarded clothing, bandages, and slings.

The scavengers did not endear themselves to the local populace.

"They even resurrected corpses from the shallow entombment in the hope that some valuables might be found on the festering body," one eyewitness stated.

Militia patrolled the Gettysburg area to prevent recurrences of such theft. Two weeks after the battle, a squad of 21st Pennsylvania cavalrymen accosted a trio of these rag dealers as they were departing for Spring Forge with their latest haul.

They were quickly escorted back to Gettysburg, turned over to the provost marshal and summarily punished for their transgression of public orders against looting.

In particular, the thieves were ordered to dispose of the rotting remains of dead horses that still littered the battlefield. Some estimates suggest as many as 5,000 horses died during the battle, making the task of their disposal arduous and lengthy.

Using ropes and chains, the thieves used their draft animals to drag the dead military horses into piles, which were then burned. The foul stench soured the air for miles. In several cases, the erstwhile peddlers also dug pits and buried the horses.

Their supply of contraband rags now cut off and with the supply of clean rags and clothing diverted to the military, the paper mill sank into insolvency.

In December 1863, the 101-acre complex was sold for $14,000 at an Orphans' Court sale to Philip Henry Glatfelter, a York countian who had seven years of experience at a Maryland paper mill owned by his future brother-in-law.

The greatly expanded Spring Forge, later Spring Grove, mill later became widely known as the Glatfelter paper company.

As for the rag thieves?

"The dose the rag gatherers received was an ample sufficiency to give them the shivers from all future life at the barest glimpse of a blue uniform," one resident wrote. "Their plunder was confiscated, their teams and they themselves put to work. The work they did was hard work; it was menial and repulsive work; but there were glittering bayonets to enforce activity and diligence in their tasks. It was a long time before the trio ever saw Spring Forge. When they did they were sadder men; likewise wiser. They had lost all desire for battlefield plunder."[177]

**

Nearly 2,000 wounded men from the Battle of Gettysburg were transported mostly by rail or wagon to York's military hospital.

Twenty-year-old Jacob Wagner, a private in the 44th New York Infantry, was one of the York patients.

On July 2, a Confederate bullet crashed into his upper arm near the shoulder. After being stabilized, he walked partway to York before catching a train into downtown.

Although he did not lose his arm, Wagner suffered for almost a year in the army hospital with various complications. When he felt well enough, he helped as a nurse with less fortunate patients.

Wagner married Henrietta Engle in 1864, the same year he was discharged from the hospital.

Like many other convalescing soldiers, he was transferred to the 16th Regiment of the Veteran Reserve Corps. He performed light duty until discharged in July 1865.

Now a civilian, Wagner returned to York. He divorced his wife in 1868, and two years later, he married a local woman named Mary Riehl.

He worked as a laborer, kept a store, and raised five children. He was active in the Grand Army of the Republic, a national veterans group with a chapter in York.

Jacob Wagner lived well into his 80s. But it was a painful existence.

His pension record states he suffered from "the following disabilities: Shot through arm, have trouble with it. Backache; Swelling of the legs."

Many who were wounded in the Civil War carried their pain to their deathbeds.[178]

**

More than 150,000 soldiers in blue and gray fought at Gettysburg, and more than ten percent of them marched or rode through York County.

A handful liked the area so much they decided to stay.

On July 1, Private William Vaughn deserted the Confederate army in Dover Township. He hid under a wooden bridge on Jacob Swartz's farm along Shippensburg Road.

He stayed in Dover and found employment as a hired hand for Edward Jacobs. Another servant, a girl named Raffensburger, took an interest in young Vaughn.

According to tradition, Jacobs often scolded the pair for not getting any work done when they were together. One day, they disappeared from Dover.

Some accounts suggest they got married and settled in York, where they raised a large family and made and sold pretzels for a living. More than 100 other deserters were rounded up by Union cavalry and taken to Columbia to be processed as prisoners of war.

Tradition suggests that a few, like Vaughn, managed to escape detection or find shelter with local families.[179]

**

In a few cases, soldiers returned to the region after their military service expired. Graveyards in the area are dotted with veterans who adopted the area as their new home.

Felix M. Drais, a Columbus, Ohio, native in the 12th U.S. Infantry of the regular army, was one such veteran. He was badly wounded in both legs at Gettysburg and was taken to Littlestown to recuperate.

He subsequently fell in love with his nurse, Laura Will, and returned in 1864 to marry her. They moved to Ohio and raised seven children but moved back east to Gettysburg, where they had additional children.[180]

**

For a handful of York County civilians, the Gettysburg Campaign brought death after the fighting had ceased.

Samuel Wehring, formerly York's police chief, was picking up discarded firearms from the battlefield when a gun accidentally discharged, killing him. His body was transported back to York for burial in Prospect Hill Cemetery.

A few others succumbed to diseases contracted from the battlefield or hospitals.

John Shenberger lived in East Prospect in eastern York County. He must have been excited when he found a relic of the fighting in Wrightsville, an intact Confederate artillery shell.

He brought it home, apparently assuming the powder had been removed. Samuel Wright's *Columbia Spy* recorded the tragic consequences:

"The children were playing with it, when by accident it rolled into the fire, and soon exploded with tremendous force, injuring the two children, Caroline and William, aged respectively 6 and 8 years, so that they died the same evening.

"The affair cast a deep gloom of sorrow and regret over the whole neighborhood. This is but another sad warning to parents and others not to keep these dangerous missiles exposed."[181]

**

Rumors of the Rebel occupation of York County spread slowly among the far-off Federal soldiers who hailed from the area.

Down in South Carolina in the 76th Pennsylvania, Hanover's Wesley Wagoner wrote on July 8 to his father, "We heard here that the Rebels have possession of Hanover &

York but I do not believe it."

He concluded with, "Write soon from your affectionate son. Wesley."

John Wagoner never heard from his son again.

Confederates captured Wesley, along with other York County soldiers of the 76th Pennsylvania, on July 11 during the Battle of Fort Wagner. He was marched overland to the Belle Isle prison in Richmond, Virginia, where he died of pneumonia and dysentery on Nov. 15, 1863.[182]

**

The effects of the Confederate operation hit the Bair family of the Stoverstown area 100 years after the last Rebel left York County.

One night around 1960, Reuben Bair and his wife heard a noise in their home. Mrs. Bair investigated and almost walked through a gaping hole, according to historian Armand Gladfelter's account.

As it turned out, the house had been weakened when Reuben's ancestor, also named Reuben Bair, and his helpers carried grain from the family's nearby mill into the attic of the house to hide it from the Confederates.

The weight of the grain caused the floor joists to buckle, pulling them from the walls. Bair later installed iron rods to pull the walls together.

That jury-rigging worked for 100 years, and its failure did not immediately trouble Reuben.

He looked at the black night visible where the wall had been, lay back and said to his wife: "Come on back to bed, we can't do anything until morning."

The house was later torn down.[183]

COL. FRANK J. MAGEE.

Wrightsville school principal Frank J. Magee was away serving as an officer in the 76th Pennsylvania when Rebels visited his parents' home during the Gettysburg Campaign. His sister, Mary Jane Rewalt, served Confederate General John B. Gordon breakfast as a thank-you for saving the family's house from flames. In a roomful of Rebel officers, she firmly avowed her allegiance to the Union army.

Daniel Smith served in Company D, 87th Regiment. Smith photographs are courtesy of his descendant David F. Spangler.

The 87th's Daniel Smith was promoted to corporal in April 1862 in Cockeysville, Maryland. He later served in South Carolina, where he contracted an illness and convalesced in an Army Hospital in Hilton Head.

Second Lieutenant Jonathan J. Jessup, member of a prominent York County family, was one example of thousands of fighting men from both sides who suffered from war wounds for years after the war. He lost a leg from a wound sustained in fighting as part of the 187th Pennsylvania at Petersburg, Virginia. This photograph comes from a regimental history.

These are Daniel Smith's credentials for the 50th reunion of the Battle of Gettysburg in 1913.

John Sechrist served in the 195th Pennsylvania in the Sixth Corps of the Army of the Potomac. This post-war photograph of the Felton resident comes from descendant Wayne Sechrist.

Chapter 4

Late War Voices

'Although we have not yet seen the end of the Rebellion, you have nobly performed your duty, and your services will be recorded on the bright pages of history … .'
– Henry L. Fisher, York, Pa.

The Battle of Gettysburg and Ulysses S. Grant's July 4 capture of Vicksburg, Mississippi, garnered most of the war news in the summer of 1863.

But another campaign was taking place down in the humid coastlands of South Carolina.

York County soldiers, both black and white, took part in a series of ill-fated attacks on Fort Wagner near Charleston.

Several black soldiers from the Wrightsville region participated in the 54th Massachusetts' celebrated but unsuccessful attack that left their commander, Colonel Robert Gould Shaw, and scores of men dead.

The 76th Pennsylvania, a white regiment, also took considerable casualties in the attempt to seize the Confederate fort. Captain Cyrus Diller had the sad duty of writing a letter to the *Hanover Spectator* to inform his neighbors and friends of losses from the fighting.

For some loved ones, the news brought despair and grief. For others, Diller's letter created fear and uncertainty: "The following members of Company D were left on the field: Lieut. C.I. Bittinger, reported to be wounded in the side, Sergeant Jacob Duck… " and so on.

In the haste to retreat under fire, Diller had been forced to abandon his dead and wounded, almost 20 men, to the enemy.
Lieutenant William Miller, the 76th's acting

adjutant, was "supposedly killed." Diller had no information on the rest of the men left lying in the sand along the Carolina coast.

Their families could only react with shock and concern when they read Diller's terse note in the newspaper, dated July 11.

Some Hanoverians would never see their sons and husbands again.

The victorious Confederates buried the fallen Yankees in long trenches dug in the sand.[184]

**

Another contingent of York County soldiers was fighting out west in Grant's army as it consolidated its grip on Mississippi.

Part of the 45th Pennsylvania had been raised from Wrightsville and east-central York County.

Before the war William A. Roberts had served as an apprentice in the *Wrightsville Star*. The private described the terrible conditions the men endured during the campaign.

On July 24, he wrote his parents from Snyder's Bluff, Mississippi: "It is impossible to describe our sufferings since my last letter to you. Of course you have heard that Vicksburg fell on the 4th of July. The same day the Ninth Corps and all the other troops in this vicinity made a forced march after Joe Johnston's army.

"It was one of the hottest days we experienced during the Mississippi campaign, and in a short while it was hard to tell whether we wore blue or gray, so thickly had the dust settled upon our clothing, which was saturated with perspiration. We marched all that day (July 4th) and long into the night."

The suffering continued even as the regiment was withdrawn to Cincinnati to rest and recuperate.

William Roberts recalled that Theodore Wilson of Wrightsville died on the way to Cincinnati from disease contracted in Mississippi.

"We were well acquainted as boys many years before the war. He was a fine young man and a splendid soldier," Roberts wrote.[185]

**

In mid-November 1863, a reporter for the *Philadelphia Public Ledger* traveled to Gettysburg to attend the dedication of the new National Cemetery, an event marked by a speech by famed orator Edward Everett and a few remarks by President Abraham Lincoln.

He was not impressed by either the Gettysburg Railroad or the Hanover Branch Railroad or by their preparation for the throngs of out-of-town visitors who flocked aboard the trains to Gettysburg.

"While the hospitality of the citizens of Gettysburg was most generous and noble," he opined, "the railroad accommodations from Hanover Junction to Gettysburg appeared quite unworthy of the occasion. No doubt, the unusual crowds, for days together, may apologize for much of this, but either some committee of arrangements, or the Railroad Company, or the State authorities should have better protected the citizens."

The reporter noted that a crime wave suddenly hit Hanover Junction, "The most systematic robbery of purses by pickpockets we ever heard of was greatly increased by the apparent absence of police at Hanover Junction, and the want of all time and system in running the cars. The thousands of dollars stolen from the pockets of ladies and of gentlemen in the boldest manner, without any apparent attempts to check the evil or guard against it, needs explanation."

The pickpockets were annoying, but other York countians took crime to a new level.

Days earlier, they used a crowbar to pry open the door to the store of McConkey & Bro. in southeastern York County's Peach Bottom. They drilled the lock from an iron safe and took $900. When they left, they carted off goods worth another $700.

It was perhaps the largest haul during the Civil War in York County by anyone not named Jubal Early.[186]

**

Abraham Lincoln changed trains at Hanover Junction on his way to and from Gettysburg to deliver his famous address.

Along the way he passed through York County's countryside, steaming through Jefferson and Smith's Station before pausing in Hanover.

During that stop, the Rev. M.J. Alleman called out to him: "Father Abraham, your children want to hear you."

The president came out, with normal self-deprecation.

"Well, you have seen me," the *Hanover Spectator* reported, "and according to general experience, you have seen less than you expected to see."[187]

**

While Lincoln was at Gettysburg for the dedication ceremonies on November 19, at least two young York County women present in the audience left written comments.

One was newspaper reporter Mary Shaw Leader, whose mother owned and managed the *Hanover Spectator*. Mary deemed Lincoln's brief talk as "a remarkable speech," a sentiment some other correspondents did not share.

Fifteen-year-old Louisa Vandersloot of Hanover performed a solo as part of a church choir. The president later rewarded her with a handshake and a fatherly kiss.

Before she met Abraham Lincoln, Louisa considered him unattractive. Now, after looking into his kind and sympathetic eyes, she revised her opinion. He indeed was "pleasing to look upon," as she later recalled.

Years later, Louisa still recalled the size of Lincoln's hand when he shook hers. She also sensed the authority in his mannerisms.

"When Lincoln talked, he said something," she stated.[188]

**

In the fighting at Mine Run, Virginia, in late November 1863, Major Noah G. Ruhl was in command of skirmishers in front of the 87th Pennsylvania.

Early in the morning of the 30th, he ordered the man in charge of his two horses to bring up "Billy," a fine-looking animal. The hostler wanted him to take the other horse, "for Billy," he believed, "will be killed today, Major, if you take him."

"But bring him up, John," Ruhl calmly replied. "I guess the horse and rider will both be dead before night."

Then the major solemnly handed his watch and other valuables to the chaplain, with the request that they be sent home. He never expected to return from the important duty of that day.

But the assault was not ordered. Both horse and rider returned to the regiment unharmed.

Ruhl went to recover his personal effects from the chaplain.

Ruhl would survive the war. But his son, Captain Edgar M. Ruhl, did not. He perished at Cedar Creek.

His father brought the body home to Shrewsbury for burial.[189]

1864

The 87th camped for the winter of 1863-64 near Brandy Station not far from Culpeper, Virginia.

Some of the officers and men brought their wives and families down from southern Pennsylvania.

"To see ladies here does us all good," one soldier said. "The hard every-day life of the army is hostile to the cultivation of refinement of manners. Their presence softens the nature of the soldier, who has been separated so long from home and all its endearments."

George Prowell related a much more sobering event: the execution of two deserters at division headquarters. Many of the 87th went to witness it.

The deserters were pardoned on the day of the execution.

One member of Company G, who had deserted and been captured, was sentenced to loss of pay and his hair to the razor.

He was drummed out of the military, marching through all the camps of the brigades. A board on his back read, "Utterly worthless."

"He was then marched to the train, and sent away from camp," Prowell wrote, "never to return."[190]

**

As the war entered its fourth year, a number of groups in York County and throughout the North organized fund-raisers to assist Union soldiers.

The citizens set up home-front "sanitary fairs" to raise money and supplies for the boys in blue.

These included speeches, plays, music, and tents with displays, literature, art galleries, and various exhibits. Sometimes they included meals, sales of donated items and auctions.

The money typically assisted the U.S. Sanitary Commission in its efforts to minister to the troops. Fairs in Philadelphia and New York each raised more than a million dollars.

York County's fundraisers were proportionally smaller but successful.

In February 1864, York's Ladies Aid Society "inaugurated a series of entertainments in connection with their fair, consisting of concerts, tableaux and other exhibits, by which large amounts of money were raised for the sanitary fund."

That was Mary Fisher's description, and she further considered the fair at the Odd Fellows Hall "a gratifying success."

It raised $4,675.[191]

**

By the spring of 1864, thousands of new recruits had replenished the ranks of the Union armies, thanks in part to a renewal of the draft and by the enrollment of black volunteers into special regiments of U.S. Colored Troops.

Advertisements aimed at the soldiers and their families filled York County newspapers.

"Is it possible that any soldier can be so foolish as to leave the city without a supply of Halloway's Ointment and Pills?" one such ad in the *York Pennsylvanian* asked.

"Whoever does so will deeply regret it. These medicines are the only certain cure for Bowel complaints, Fevers, Sores, and scurvy. Only 25 cents per box or pot."[192]

**

John Aquilla Wilson, known as "Quil," of Fawn Township in southeastern York County, enlisted in the U.S. Colored Troops.

As a teenager, Wilson joined the local militia in Wrightsville and helped prevent the Confederates from crossing the bridge spanning the Susquehanna River in 1863.

A year later, he joined the 32nd Regiment, USCT.

He trained at Camp William Penn in Philadelphia and skirmished with the Confederates in South Carolina before his military discharge in that state in August 1865.

Years later, a Wilson granddaughter, 87-year-old Isabella Phillips, provided insight into why her grandfather, who helped raise her, served.

He believed blacks should be able to own property and vote.

"He wanted to have the same rights as everybody else," she said.

Quil Wilson lived to age 101, then one of the last surviving York County Civil War soldiers.[193]

**

Elijah Berry served in both army and navy uniforms.

The former slave was recruited in Harford County, just south of the York County border, for the 39th USCT in March 1864.

He volunteered near Harford County's Black Horse and was sworn in at Camp Burney in Baltimore. In April 1864, his name was drawn to serve in the Navy. He served on the *Daylight*, but that ship sprang a leak.

From there, he shipped out on the *Brandywine*, but she took fire. He was transferred to the *Shenandoah*.

"While there I done about the same work as on the 'Daylight,' except when in an engagement, when I helped to run in and out the guns and did whatever commanded — sometimes passed shells to the loaders, etc.," he wrote in a pension application.

He was finally discharged after the war at Fortress Monroe and settled in southern York County. He was married in January 1869 at the home of Lewis Tillman, near Stewartstown, by the Rev. J.G. Cowhick.

Berry's applications did not have official papers to back up his pension claims.

"My discharge papers from the Navy and transfer papers from the Army to the Navy have been destroyed," he explained. "They had become worn and torn by being carried in my pocket and one day my children got them and destroyed them. I did not know this until afterwards, too late to save them."[194]

**

Henry Bear, a Native American from York County, served in the 127th USCT, a unit that participated in the final crushing of Lee's army.

He was wounded by a cannon shell while on a skirmish line.

The name Henry Bear was common in the ranks of volunteer soldiers from Pennsylvania. Military records mention at least eight men bearing this name.

There was another Henry Bear from York County, a Caucasian. His story illustrates a military practice where a man with access to money could buy his way out of the army by paying $300 and finding someone to take his place.

The 32-year-old Bear briefly served in the 166th Pennsylvania as a private, enrolling in November 1862.

His military records reveal his service: "discharged by procuring a sub. — date unknown."[195]

**

The wives and families of the 87th Pennsylvania returned home in late March 1864, and the soldiers began preparing for the Northern army's spring offensive.

They now marched under the command of Ulysses S. Grant, who had been sent east to take charge of all Federal armies.

"Our camp is quiet to-night; but the army is preparing for a campaign," Adjutant Anthony M. Martin of New Oxford wrote one day. "Great battles are expected to be fought soon. We hope this campaign will be the death blow to the Confederate cause. If Congressmen at Washington or the Rebel Congress at Richmond, were required to endure the hardships of a soldier's life during one campaign the war would then end."

Martin, popular with the boys from York and Adams counties for his affable manner, added, "The birds entertain us in the morning and the croaking of the frogs is heard at night; but instead of these, we are soon to hear the rattle of musketry and the roar of cannon."

Anthony Martin had only a few months to live when he penned those prophetic lines.

He was killed at the Battle of Monocacy in July.[196]

**

By the spring of 1864, Josephus Burger was a veteran soldier.

A native of the Newberry/York Haven region, he was on his third enlistment, this time with the 187th Pennsylvania.

About 6:00 a.m. on May 21, the newly raised regiment paraded down Pennsylvania Avenue in Washington, D.C., past the Executive Mansion.

A civilian onlooker, described as a "venerable patriot," inquired, "Where from?"

"Pennsylvania," came the reply.

"How long?" the resident asked.

"Three years," came the response.

"Ah! Ah!" the civilian uttered with satisfaction.

The old man had seen plenty of short-term troops pass through the capital. A few more companies passed by, and he called again, "How long?"

"Three years," rang out a chorus of soldiers.

Tickled that these men were committed to a long stint as soldiers, the onlooker cried, "God bless you! God bless Pennsylvania!"

With the man's exhortation ringing in their ears, the 187th crossed the Potomac into Virginia. Burger and his comrades that morning stacked arms at Fort Albany, in the shadow of Arlington House, Robert E. Lee's pre-war home.

It had become a graveyard and a military camp filled with soldiers bent on destroying Lee's army.[197]

**

Ulysses S. Grant accompanied the Army of the Potomac for much of the rest of the war, personally directing that force's movements to finally bring Robert E. Lee's Confederate Army of Northern Virginia to bay.

In late April, Grant began what later became known as the Overland Campaign, a series of maneuvers that eventually brought the Federals to the gates of Richmond.

Several bloody battles marked the spring and summer campaign, including a confused fight in early May in a scrubby, second-growth wooded area of Virginia known simply as the Wilderness.

Lieutenant Ephraim E. Myers of the 45th Pennsylvania was a resident of York after the war.

He later recorded an incident at sundown after fighting at the Wilderness.

His unit had erected temporary breastworks and settled down after rations.

But no one slept that night.

"During the whole night we heard moaning on our front," he recounted. "The next morning some of the company went out and found behind a log Private George W. Gilbert of Company K. They brought him into the lines. As they carried him mortally wounded past me I said to him, 'George, keep up good courage, you will be all right.' But he replied, 'No, I am going to die.' "

East Prospect native Gilbert died about 9:00 a.m.

"A brave soldier was he," Myers said.[198]

**

Perhaps the fate most dreaded by prisoners of war was to be sent to the infamous Andersonville Prison in southern Georgia.

Officially known as Camp Sumter, the 26.5-acre complex housed 45,000 captives taken from the Union armies. Almost 13,000 men died, mostly from disease and starvation.

Levi A. Bowen, a private in the 7th Pennsylvania Reserves, survived the camp.

Rebels had captured the former Fairview Township blacksmith on May 5, in the confused fighting in the Wilderness and sent him to Orange Court House. From there, he began the long journey to Andersonville.

Facing starvation, Bowen kept writing in a diary, providing a glimpse of daily life in the prison camp. Sometimes, the worst enemies also wore the blue uniform.

Here are some selected entries:

May 26 – Catched a ration thief. Shaved half his head and marched him through camp.

May 27 – Saw the boys catch a raider. They shaved his head and gagged him … had quite a riot.

June 14 – The Rebs are just filling up a tunnel that the Yankees have been digging to make their escape. Close by and rainy all day.

June 30 – Traded my ration of pork on a ration of beef. The first that I have eaten since I have been a prisoner.

July 4 – Very hot in the forenoon. In the afternoon very heavy thunderstorms. Boiled beef and corncakes for supper. Very pour grub for the fourth.

July 11 – Very hot and dry. Great excitement in camp. Six men executed on the gallows at 4 o'clock. Verdict guilty of murder and robbery. One broke the ropes and one run but was caught.

Levi was transferred to Florence, South Carolina, in September, perhaps sparing his name from the ever-growing casualty lists.

He was exchanged and shipped north to recuperate in York's military hospital, arriving in December.

He reported his health was "broken down."[199]

**

Samuel B. Gray of Windsor Township, like so many other youths, lied about his age in order to join the army.

He stated he was 16. In reality, he was only 14 when he enlisted in the 87th Pennsylvania in late August 1861.

By the summer of 1864, he was a seasoned veteran and considered a good forager.

"Gray had a lively experience in capturing a hog on the way from Belle Plains to Fredericksburg," historian George Prowell recalled, "He saw a dozen porkers along a stream, and when he got close enough, he bayoneted one of them. His hogship resisted the attack, made a vigorous defense, and came nearly conquering his antagonist.

The pig's squealing attracted another veteran and a new recruit.

"The animal was captured and soon the camp was filled," Prowell wrote, "with the odor of fresh pork being cooked for supper."

Like Levi Bowen, young Sam Gray would be captured and sent to Andersonville.

His war-time imprisonment left him disabled for life, and he virtually lost the use of his left leg.[200]

**

While Sam Gray found several pigs, the men of another Pennsylvania regiment found something of more lasting value — money.

Hard currency at that.

Private Hiram Bixler of the 76th Pennsylvania informed his good friend Milton Ruby in Hellam Township that "The 45th Pa. had good Luck they found over $900 in Gold and Silver that the rebels had buried."

He also reported on the darker side of warfare.

"The Johnnies have a large force in front of Petersburg. Wilson and Kautz Cavalry just came back from their raid. They destroyed about 100 miles of the Danville R.R. But the Rebels captured about 2000 of them & all of their Artillery. But our boys spiked the guns & blowed up the Ammunition & burned up everything. Took the wounded out of the Ambulances & burned them up to prevent them [from] falling into the hands of the Rebels.

About 100 negros women & Children run off and wanted to go along back. But the rebels charged on them & cut them down like dogs."[201]

**

Private Charles E. Gotwalt was yet another Yorker confined at Andersonville.

Firewood was scarce, so he was "hunting around for small wood chips which were lying around on the ground in an effort to collect material for cooking his supper," according to his later reminiscences.

He crawled around on all fours filling his cap with the scraps of wood. At one point, he unwittingly crossed the "dead line," a point beyond which prisoners were forbidden and could be shot by the guards.

He suddenly heard the click of a musket. Now aware of his circumstances, he looked up and saw a guard leveling a musket at him. The Rebel was grinning, perhaps in his eagerness to shoot the Yank if he progressed further.

Gotwalt beat a hasty retreat, still with his precious wood chips in his hat.[202]

**

Several soldiers from northwestern York County in the 7th Pennsylvania Reserves were also held

105

prisoner at Andersonville.

Confederates had seized them in fighting at the Wilderness back in May.

Lieutenant Templeton B. Hurst of Dillsburg tersely recounted in his diary, "This afternoon our regt. advanced on the enemy through a dense 'Wilderness' and became seperated from our brigade. Two regt. of 'Rebs' got in our rear, attempted to escape to the right and left but fired into from all sides. The Col. then surrendered the command and now we are all prisoners."

Hurst was sent to prison in Macon, Georgia, and the enlisted men went to Andersonville.

Three young privates from Monaghan Township — Solomon Smith, Zephaniah Stevens, and Frederick Crumlich — died during their confinement at Andersonville and are buried in the National Cemetery.

They perished from chronic diarrhea.[203]

**

While several York County soldiers languished in Southern prisons and others lay in hospitals or graves, more men back home entered the service.

Some, such as infantryman Casper Henry Kottcamp and 19-year-old cavalry trooper Milton Henry Shenberger of Manchester Township, were volunteers.

Others were draftees.

In the spring 1864 draft, York County's quota stood at 906 men. Eventually, 970 names were drawn across the county in various wards.

Many never had to serve, instead receiving exemptions based upon physical handicaps or by paying for substitutes to take their places.

Henry Ridebaugh was one who ended up in the army.

The Seitzland native became a private in the 53rd Pennsylvania in September.

He would serve through the end of the war, mostly in the trenches surrounding Petersburg, Virginia.[204]

**

New regiments that would serve for only 100 days presented another option in the summer of 1864.

President Lincoln and the War Department asked the states to raise these "Hundred Days Men" for duty as guards to free veteran troops for front-line combat. It was part of an all-out push across all theaters to end the war.

The Hundred Days units stood as an inviting opportunity for ex-soldiers to resume their service to their country without the hardships of a lengthy commitment.

James Clark Channell of Fawn Township, formerly of the 130th Pennsylvania, was among those who re-enlisted.

The veteran of Antietam, Fredericksburg, and Chancellorsville had difficulty walking long distances because of a bad case of varicose veins. The 194th Pennsylvania, with its relatively easy guard duties, was a better fit.

Lieutenant Channell served on Maryland's Eastern Shore and at Fort Monroe, Virginia, where he was reunited with an old friend, diarist Alfred S. Bond of York.

He came back to York County and became a well-known doctor.

His varicose veins plagued him the rest of his life.[205]

**

Like so many York countians, Alfred S. Bond served in the army in multiple units.

He was drafted into the 166th Pennsylvania late in 1862. After his discharge in July 1863, he re-enlisted. Now he was a provost guard near Fort Monroe.

He kept a diary throughout 1864 of his military service.

The duty was mundane, with much of his time spent escorting Confederate prisoners or arresting drunken Union soldiers in the local bars. Occasionally, he wrote about seeing English frigate *Phaeton*, USS *Minnesota*, and other famous warships.

Mostly, he just killed time.

His journal is filled with notes about sightseeing jaunts along the shore or expeditions to pick blackberries. Many nights he went to the black section, Slabtown, to listen to the music and watch the people.

On July 24, he recalled the day he had left his previous regiment before re-enlisting. His words reflect the uncertainty of army life:

"Nothing more than usual going on today. Weather cloudy with rain in the morning. One year ago today I was in Harrisburg waiting to be discharged. Where will I be next year at this time? God only knows these things."

A week later, from Fort Monroe, Bond recorded, "General Grant was here, and the President and family and part of the Cabinet. I seen them all. U S Grant and Abe Lincoln are very common-looking men. Would that our

people wood think of that."[206]

**

At the Battle of Monocacy in July, a ball passed through the cap box and glanced from the U.S. belt plate of Charles H. Spahr of the 87th Pennsylvania.

Another struck his bayonet, nearly knocking the gun out of his hands.

Lieutenant John F. Spangler of York was far less lucky that day in central Maryland. A bullet penetrated his breast and, taking a downward course, lodged in his stomach.

As he lay in agony, orders came for his regiment to retreat and, because it was believed he could not recover, his comrades left him on the battlefield.

Late at night, a relief party found the stricken soldier and took him to a nearby house. There, a widow named Mrs. Doffler, a volunteer nurse from Frederick, tenderly cared for the boy until he died on July 15.

A grieving Jacob Spangler journeyed to Maryland to retrieve his son's body for burial in Union Cemetery in downtown York.

He must have appreciated the loving care that the widow Doffler gave his dying boy.

The two were later married.[207]

**

William and Mary Jane Harris celebrated their 20th wedding anniversary on April 27, 1863, just two months before a long column of Jubal Early's North Carolina infantry snaked past their North George Street house en route to downtown York.

Harris, a veteran of the 130th Pennsylvania, was among scores of former Union soldiers who witnessed the spectacle of a Southern infantry division invade their hometown.

He would have a much different encounter with Early's boys within a year.

The 43-year-old tanner enlisted in the 87th Pennsylvania, despite his age and a family.

Shortly after the Battle of Monocacy, Mary Jane received a dreaded letter.

Company commander Captain Solomon Myers wrote that William "was instantly killed by a musket ball in the brain, near the close of the engagement."

She did not even get the comfort of burying her beloved William. She read further, "As we had to fall back, the battlefield was left to the enemy and we could not bring off his body."

A Marylander by birth, William Harris was likely buried in his native soil, close to where he fell, by Union cavalry that policed the battlefield the next day.

Myers, acting as Mary Jane Harris's legal agent after the war, helped her fill out the necessary paperwork to apply for a widow's pension.

Because the body was never identified, the letter proved invaluable as an eyewitness account of her husband's death, and she was granted a pension of eight dollars a month, with an additional two dollars a month for each surviving child under the age of 16.

A middle-aged widow with eight children to feed, she needed to make the money stretch.

But more tragedy lurked.

On April 10, 1865, just one day after Lee surrendered his army to Grant at Appomattox, Mary Jane's eight-year-old son George William Harris passed away.

Mary Jane went into mourning while the rest of York County celebrated the end of the war.

Death was not finished with her young family. Six months after her son's death, her three-year-old daughter Bertha Serrene also died.

The story finishes with a strange twist.

Among Jubal Early's soldiers who fought Harris and his comrades at Monocacy that fateful July afternoon was a member of the 5th Louisiana Infantry, the famed Louisiana Tigers. Lieutenant Arthur Bryde was wounded and left behind as a prisoner of war when Early marched to the outskirts of Washington, D.C.

Bryde's great-granddaughter would marry William Harris's great-great-grandson.

The Battle of Monocacy proved to be of personal consequence for both men — one wearing blue, one wearing gray.[208]

**

Sergeant John Henry Denig of York served in the Marines. At the Battle of Mobile Bay on August 5, his heroism aboard U.S.S. *Brooklyn* led to a Medal of Honor.

His citation reads: "Despite severe damage to his ship and the loss of several men on board as enemy fire raked her decks, Sergeant Denig fought his gun with skill and courage throughout the furious two-hour battle that resulted in the surrender of the Rebel ram *Tennessee* and in the damaging and destruction of batteries at Fort Morgan."[209]

**

Nathaniel Leithiser was a young lad in Long Level, south of Wrightsville along the Susquehanna River.

In late July 1864, Nat's father, Hartman, and an older brother, George, enlisted in the 195th Pennsylvania, a "Hundred Days" unit.

The Leithisers and the 195th departed York on July 24 aboard the Northern Central Railway, south to Baltimore. Four days later, as part of the Union Eighth Corps, they were guarding the vital railroad interchange at Monocacy Junction near Frederick, Maryland.

In early October, the regiment arrived in Berkeley County, West Virginia, where they performed guard duty along the Baltimore & Ohio Railroad.

Little "Tan" Leithiser was four years old. His mother, the former Salome Ruby, saddled a horse at her Long Level home, scooped Tan aboard, and headed for West Virginia to visit her husband and son. It was a lengthy trip, but she packed plenty of food and a bundle of cookies.

When they arrived at the Berkeley camp, Salome learned that the trip was for naught. Guards would not permit her to see George and Hartman.

A determined Salome Leithiser lifted Tan into the saddle in front of her, turned around, and headed for Washington, D.C., to confront President Lincoln.

When she arrived, she was ushered into the president's office.

Her little boy hooked his fingers over the edge of Lincoln's desk. He pulled himself up on tiptoe high enough to watch Lincoln write a special permit so that he and his mother could visit the two soldiers. His fingers turned white as the blood drained away from exertion.

Satisfied, Salome Leithiser escorted outside, remounted her horse, and began the trek back to the camp of the 195th Pennsylvania. She handed the presidential pass to the army authorities, who permitted her to visit her husband and son. When their conversation was finished, she and Tan once again rode back toward Long Level.

In November, just a few weeks after Mrs. Leithiser's dogged trek, the 195th boarded the B&O and rode back to Baltimore.

From there, they returned to their homes.[210]

**

In September, Daniel Roads and Emanuel Herman sent a letter seeking payment for their military recruiting work.

The treasurers of the Manchester Bounty Fund directed it to Dr. William Bleany, delineating their expenses "to fill quota of Manchester Township."

Local communities often established bounties to help meet their quotas for army recruits. They also incurred other expenses and frequently called upon the army or state officials for repayment.

They specifically noted $24.50 for boarding the prospective soldiers; $5.55 for railcar tickets to Harrisburg; $1.20 for a round trip to Carlisle via train; $8.75 for round trip hack fare to Camp Curtin; and $5 they paid to clerks for examining the muster rolls to procure certificates of credit.

The writer tacked on a surcharge, "I was engaged at the above something over three weeks for which time I will charge the sum of Fifty dollars."

There is no record if Manchester Township ever received the $95.10 submitted by Roads and

Herman.

Emanuel Herman had a personal interest in the welfare of soldiers. His grandfather and namesake had been a captain in the American Revolution, and his son-in-law Samuel Lightner was a second lieutenant in the 166th Pennsylvania.

Sam had contracted a fatal disease while in the Suffolk Campaign in Virginia.

Married to Barbara Herman for less than a year, died in the service of his country.[211]

**

In downtown York, an anonymous businessman grew frustrated that a particular competitor had underbid him for a lucrative supply contract for the army hospital.

On October 24, he complained to Major John S. Schultze in the Department of the Susquehanna, denigrating his rival in the process:

"Since I have written to you the contract for furnishing Beef for the Hospital at York, there has been given to a man who certainly is not a loyal man, his wife was confined about the time of the Rebel invasion of Pennsylvania, when Rebel General Early was in York here, and they named the child which is a boy, Jubal Early Wagner, in honor to General Early being his full name, this Jacob Wagner is the man who is the lowest bidder at $10.50, Ten Dollars and fifty cents per hundred lbs. for furnishing the Beef for the Hospital, and I can prove that that he sold the Hind quarters of the Beef to Butchers, here in York, and took the front quarters to the Hospital, and that he killed Bulls Beef, and refused cattle for the Hospital, he is the man who has had the contract for the past six months, he is one of the worst Copperheads we have here, and our loyal men here are very much put out about it, from what I can learn he

could not furnish good Beef for that amount of money per Hundred lbs. So I thought Maj. Genl. Couch ought to know something about it."

Major Schulze passed the complaint up the military command chain. No action was apparently taken.[212]

**

In early November, citizens across the North cast ballots for president and other offices.

Incumbent Abraham Lincoln was challenged by his former commanding general of the Union armies, George B. McClellan, a Democrat.

Earlier in the war, his men had affectionately nicknamed him "Little Mac." As the war progressed and his ego flared, wags began deeming him "Little Napoleon."

Regulations allowed soldiers to cast ballots, which were counted on site.

At Camp Hamilton and Fort Monroe in Virginia, the interest was heavy. Boatloads of soldiers of the 3rd Pennsylvania Heavy Artillery left the wharf bound for Baltimore, from where they headed home to vote.

Those men who remained in camp could vote at their company headquarters.

York's Alfred Bond penned in his diary:

Tuesday, November 8 – On duty at the Provost Marshals. Voted at Capt Blakes for the Union electors of Abraham Lincoln and Andrew Johnson. The election is very quiet. Weather cloudy.

Wednesday, November 9 – Com. F gave 144 votes for Lincoln and 44 for McClellan. Lieut Cummings detailed to go aboard the flag of truce boat. Retired by John Hartman from being orderly. Weather warm.

Thursday, November 10 – How are you little Mac on the home vote? How do you think the soldiers will treat you? Just as they ought. Lincoln elected for four years. At night weather fair."[213]

**

For the families, wives, sweethearts, and friends of the soldiers, the long periods of separation and uncertainty brought anxiety and concern.

Letters from their soldier boys were eagerly anticipated, particularly after a severe battle. Seeing a letter in familiar handwriting confirmed they were still okay.

Martha Jane Gemmill of Apple Grove, later Winterstown, in southeastern York County, had a brother, Joseph, who had moved to Ohio before the Civil War.

He was serving in the 25th Ohio Volunteer Infantry at Hilton Head, South Carolina. That regiment had been battered on Barlow's Knoll and East Cemetery Hill in Gettysburg the previous year. Now, the unit had engaged in another battle.

She received a welcome letter from Joe in December 1864 shortly after the Battle of Honey Hill, in which dozens of men from his regiment had been killed or wounded after advancing under murderous fire.

Opening the envelope, Martha read, "I seat myself this morning with the greatest of pleasure to inform you by these few lines that I am well at present and hope when these few lines reaches you they may find you enjoying the same good blessings."

Joe was fine. His regiment had driven the Rebels "back slowly about too miles to a batery on honey hill and thare they made a stand. We fought them diligently till dark then we fell back to the church and intrenched our selves. The next day all was quiet. We then layed thare till sunday then our Regt started to capture a batery. We succeeded in capturing it."

Perhaps so as not to worry his far-away sister, Gemmill never mentioned the massive casualties his regiment suffered at Honey Hill, which included 16 commissioned officers and 111 enlisted men.

He described the movements of the 25th OVI in the days following Honey Hill, including an expedition to harass the Confederate-held Charleston & Savannah Railroad.

"I must now bring my few scripted line to a close by asking you to wright soon again. I have only receive[d] one letter [from] you foalks yet. No more at preasant," he wrote.

"But remain your Brother till Death," he concluded.

Martha likely slept better that evening, knowing Joe had survived yet another fight.

The worrying, both in the North and South, would continue until the soldiers came home for good. More than 620,000 men would die in the war.

Joe Gemmill would not be one of them.[214]

**

In 1864, 35-year-old Fairview Township shoemaker Henry C. Springer traveled to York and enrolled in the 202nd Pennsylvania.

He was an experienced soldier, having served in the 166th Pennsylvania in 1862 and in a short-term militia unit the following year.

Springer survived several skirmishes in Northern Virginia, but according to family lore, part of his lip was shot off by a Confederate bullet.

The story went around that "the surgeon sewed it on backwards."
Nevertheless, he lived to be 81 years old.[215]

**

Samuel R. Smith, a harness maker in the Windsor area in southeastern York County, enlisted in 1864 as a private in the 207th Pennsylvania and served in the siege of Petersburg.

By December, he was ill with ague, a malaria-like sickness that produces chills, fever, and profuse sweating.

At a camp near Hancock's Station on the military railroad, he wrote a Christmas letter to his wife Sarah expressing his hope of coming home again, perhaps even that winter. Excerpts from that letter:

"It is with plesher that I drop a few lines that I ant very well at present I have got the aque agane but I hope when the fue lines come to hand that tha ma[y] find you all in good helth."

"I received the box and everything was good but the pies I received it on the 24th. The eggs were all broke."

"Also we except to be paid next month. everything is very dere here butter is 75¢ a pound we have to pay 25¢ for 4 apples not as big as them that you put in mi box we had a little mess of sour crote it was 20¢ a pound."

Sam Smith's poignant Christmas wish to go home to his wife and children again never came true.

In combat along the siege lines sometime before March 1865, he suffered a severe gunshot wound to his left shoulder. Carried to the rear to Hancock's Station, he bled to death while he lay awaiting a train to take him to a military hospital.[216]

1865 and later

Stationed at Camp Hamilton near Hampton, Virginia, artillery Private Alfred S. Bond penned in his diary:

Sunday, December 25 – "Was orderly in the fore noon. Weather pleasant. Christmas passed of[f] very lonely for me."

Most Civil War soldiers would be home before the next Christmas.

But for thousands, this was their last Yule season, as the killing resumed in the spring.[217]

**

Meanwhile, the winter weather back home in York grew nasty by mid-January.

Heavy wind, snow, and ice played havoc with telegraph lines.

In those days, it was common practice for telegraphers to notify their counterparts farther up the line when trains had departed their depot.

With a single track usually between the stations, only one train at a time was authorized to proceed, with others sitting on sidings until the "all clear" message arrived.

Two significant train wrecks occurred in January, as a result of the breakdown of this communication system in the bad weather.

A collision of passenger trains near Summit in northern York County left several citizens seriously injured. A second accident had much deadlier consequences.

With telegraphic communications out between Hanover Junction and York, dispatchers unwittingly sent a passenger train from Baltimore northward to York at the same time that a southbound express left York.

The Northern Central's baggage master, Thomas Gambrill, and two soldiers returning to the front died in the ensuing collision. Nearly 20 other passengers suffered significant injuries.

A Philadelphia correspondent matter-of-factly reported, "The trains were considerably detained, but are now running again."

Adams Express baggage handler William G. Holbrook survived the crash but would never run again, however.

His foot was badly crushed.[218]

**

Zachariah Shepp, born in Manchester Township and a laborer by occupation, married Mary Brunner before the war.

Their first child, Elizabeth, was born in 1860, and Alfred followed in 1863. At the time of Zach's enlistment in the 200th Pennsylvania, Mary was pregnant with their third child.

The 200th mustered into service at Camp Curtin in Harrisburg and, after drilling and training, took the train back through York County toward Baltimore.

After arriving in Baltimore, the regiment marched from the Northern Central Railway station to the B&O, where the men embarked for Washington, D.C. His unit eventually fought in trench warfare near Petersburg.

While her husband was away in Virginia, Mary Shepp gave birth to a daughter on March 4, 1865. She named the baby Alice.

Exactly three weeks later, Zach Shepp took part in one of the campaign's last major fights, the Battle of Fort Stedman on March 25.

Major General John B. Gordon, whose troops in 1863 had occupied York and marched within a few miles of Shepp's home in Manchester Township, launched a pre-dawn attack on the Union-held Fort Stedman. The attack was the last serious attempt by Confederate troops to break the siege of Petersburg. After some initial success, Gordon's men were driven back by Union troops of the Ninth Corps.

Zach Shepp was one of those Union fighting men.

He did not celebrate the victory, which sealed the fate of Lee's army and prevented it from breaking out of the entrenchments.

A Confederate bullet penetrated Shepp's chest and entered his lung. He died later that day.

Shepp's body was shipped back to York County, where it was buried in the graveyard of Pleasureville United Methodist Church on North Sherman Street.

For Widow Mary Shepp, another tragedy loomed. Not only had she lost her husband, but little Alice joined him in death just three years later.

Interestingly, Zach Shepp's brother, Alexander, was drafted in 1864 for the 166th Pennsylvania, but he hired a substitute and thereby avoided service.[219]

**

Charles Henry Ilgenfritz of York was a sergeant

in the 207th Pennsylvania Infantry. He received a Medal of Honor for his valor at Fort Sedgwick, Virginia, on April 2.

His citation reads: "The color bearer falling, pierced by seven balls, he immediately sprang forward and grasped the colors, planting them upon the enemy's forts amid a murderous fire of grape, canister, and musketry from the enemy."[220]

**

Filey's Church, in Monaghan Township, was founded in the early part of the 19th century and has survived serious fires and other problems.

Its quiet cemetery is filled with early pioneers and settlers of the region.

John Yost of the 200th Pennsylvania's marker is among the graves in the cemetery. The blue-eyed Warrington Township farmer enlisted in the army at the age of 44 in York.

In the defense of Fort Stedman, he was struck down and mortally wounded. He died on March 26 and his body shipped home.

His gravestone has this poignant reminder of his brief and tragic Civil War service, "When war its horrors o'er our country cast / When freedom dear with blood and life was bought / For us through care and pain and wintry blast / And until death with dauntless soul he fought."[221]

**

One of the last York countians to die in combat was Lieutenant Samuel Wesley Geesey, a 26-year-old laborer born in York Township.

"While leading on his men in the charge upon the Confederate works, in front of Petersburg, April 2, 1865, he was instantly killed, seven days before Lee surrendered at Appomattox,"

George Prowell later wrote, "His remains were brought home [in November] and buried in the cemetery adjoining Mount Zion church in Spring Garden Township."[222]

**

Robert E. Lee, having abandoned Richmond and Petersburg in the face of overwhelming numbers of Union soldiers, surrendered his army on April 9, instead of continuing his flight toward the west.

The end came in the parlor of the Wilmer McLean house at Appomattox Court House, Virginia.

"I was lying along the railroad tracks near Appomattox Court House and saw Generals Lee and Grant riding side by side along the railroad not more than thirty feet away," Corporal Henry Schultz of the 87th Pennsylvania recalled. "This was on the day of Lee's surrender. He didn't turn to look at me; he must have been ashamed."[223]

**

When news reached York County about the Rebel surrender at Appomattox, Lewis Miller drew a red, white, and blue scene topped by a soaring eagle.

"To our brave footmen, who handled sword and gun," he wrote under the drawing.

He also praised officers of the navy and applauded the great Union generals Grant, Sherman, Sheridan, and Kilpatrick.

"Our gun is pois'd, our aim is Sure, Our wish is good, our End is pure," he wrote, "To virtue we are Sworn allies, And Shoot at folly as it flies."[224]

**

The reports of Lee's surrender touched off celebrations almost immediately.

Joyous citizens rushed into the streets to share in the moment.

In Wrightsville, 29-year-old lumber merchant John Stoner Beidler penned in his diary, "News came that Lee surrendered his whole army to Grant. Bells ringing all around this morning."

The female-owned *Hanover Spectator* also rejoiced, "Certainly the surrender of Lee is a victory such as we never had before to rejoice over."[225]

** **

The celebration did not last long.

As a youth, famed actor John Wilkes Booth had briefly spent time at a York County school.

On the evening of Good Friday, April 14, 1865, he assassinated Abraham Lincoln at Ford's Theater in Washington, D.C.

The shocking news reverberated throughout the North and South. Many York countians reacted by wearing black, placing photos of the late president in their windows, and other memorial tokens.

"News came early this morning that Lincoln was shot last night, Seward badly stabbed. I have still some hope it is not so. 9½ P.M. It is only too true that Lincoln was shot," John Stoner Beidler wrote.

"As soon as the news was confirmed, all the stores in town were closed and business suspended," Beidler noted about Wrightsville. "All or nearly all business places throughout U.S. are closed and many a downcast countenance can be seen and even tears… Copperheads are as silent as the grave. They dare not open their mouth."

Lincoln's death "cast a gloom over the entire army," the 87th Pennsylvania's historian George Prowell stated. "During the night that followed few soldiers slept. They sat around the camp fires for hours discussing the sad news."[226]

** **

After Appomattox, Sallie Leeper Scott wrote a friend, Robert Barnett, in the military at the chief carpenter's shop in Washington, D.C.

She had received a letter from him in which he complained of a headache.

That worried her, and she wrote her "dear friend" on April 15, encouraging bed rest, lest his illness became more severe.

"If you do than then what will become of you away whare you neither have Friends nor relations nor not even a gal to take care of you," she mentioned. "You had better come home for fear you do."

If he would come home, the canal, running along the west bank of the Susquehanna River, offered plenty of work.

She closed the letter that night only to add some lines the next day, April 16.

She referred to a recent letter she reportedly had received from President Abraham Lincoln, although she suggested that Robert Barnett had written it, perhaps in jest.

The next one the president sent, she wrote, "he had better not get you to write it."

Word had not reached that part of southeastern York County that no more letters would be received from "Abe Lincoln."

115

He had died from an assassin's bullet the previous day.

She closed her letter with a routine update.

"I forgot the old hors[e] he is doing well," she mentioned, "only there is something rong with his neck so he cant put his hed down to drink." After his discharge, Robert Barnett did come home and married Sallie Scott. The couple had 11 children.[227]

**

Thomas B. Walton grew up along the Susquehanna River in New Holland, later Saginaw, in northeastern York County.

Before the war, he had moved to Middletown and opened a shoemaking business. Now he was a soldier in the 195th Pennsylvania stationed near Winchester, Virginia.

He penned in his diary on April 15, "News came to camp that President Lincoln was killed—shot in the head," he wrote in his diary on April 15.

The next day, the rumor mill was running wild.

"News that Lincoln is not dead," he penned, "that he has come to his scences again."

Confirmation finally came that the president was dead.[228]

**

Word of the attack on Lincoln reached Abraham Rudisill's camp on Saturday in Virginia.

The initial reports suggested that the president was alive but that Vice President Andrew Johnson had died.

"Oh, I wept for joy and thankfulness that our President was not assassinated — not dead," Corporal Rudisill wrote in his diary.

Two days later, the veteran artilleryman learned the sad truth, "Our Chief is indeed dead."

He then quoted a comforting passage from his Bible, Psalm 45: "Be still and know that I am God."[229]

**

Lincoln's assassination did not move John Gemmill, son of prominent political official Robert Gemmill of Round Hill.

According to the sister of Union soldier John Harvey Anderson, he said, "It served Lincoln right. He should have been shot long ago."

For that statement, he drew the fire of some boys in Stewartstown armed with rotten eggs.

Their ammunition found its mark.

"He was well spattered with the juices of the eggs," she claimed. "The aim of young America on that occasion was straight and true. One of the foul eggs struck him in the mouth, and he beat a hasty retreat."

Immediately after that incident, he was not seen around Stewartstown.[230]

**

Lizzie was the wife of Seven Valleys' butcher, Elmer Hamme. She lived to be 93, although she never learned to read or write.

She maintained a sharp memory and recalled years later about an experience when she was a little girl.

On Friday April 21, her parents took her to view Abraham Lincoln's funeral train as it passed through Seven Valleys on the Northern Central Railroad.

York County had a connection to that train.

Carrolus A. Miller, a Hanover native, had piloted its locomotive between Washington and Baltimore, but he was not at the helm as it passed through York County.[231]

**

To prepare for the funeral train's stop in York, Chief Burgess David Small issued an order that called for:

"1. All businesses to close after 4 p.m. on April 21 and remain closed … as long as the body was in the state.

2. Military and citizens to assemble in York's Centre Square with the procession to march to the North Duke Street rail station.

3. The formation of a line at the station, extending toward Baltimore. 'During the passing of the train the line will remain uncovered (with hats off),' the order stated.

4. Citizens to take their flags and 'drapery of mourning' to Water Street for suspension along the buildings on the railroad line.

5. The tolling of bells while the body was within the borough limits.

6. For Col. J.A. Stahle (formerly the commander of the 87th Pennsylvania) to act as chief marshal."[232]

**

When Lincoln's funeral train stopped in York, Isabel Cassat Small headed a delegation of women who had prepared a three-foot-around wreath of white roses and camellias.

Freedman Aquilla Howard placed the wreath near Lincoln's flag-draped coffin.

A *Philadelphia Inquirer* reporter remembered the contribution from Isabel Small and the women of York.

"The fragrance of the violets," he gushed, "seemed like incense from heaven."

Six-year-old Henry C. Niles, later a York County judge, provided this recollection from his prime perch on the shoulders of his friend, a young black waiter at the Washington House hotel:

"The silent crowd made a way for York's floral expression of patriotism and grief, borne by Aquilla Howard, the tall negro butler of the Philip A. Small family. From John Joice's shoulder, I saw my mother, following Mrs. Samuel Small, pass into one car door and out the other."

Within earshot of the *Inquirer* reporter, an elderly black man proclaimed, "He was crucified for us."

Behind schedule, the train only stayed in York for about 10 minutes before steaming northward to Harrisburg.

John Stoner Beidler regretted missing the train.

"Lincoln went through York about six o'clock," he wrote. "I did not stay to see him, am sorry I did not."[233]

**

After leaving York, the Lincoln funeral train passed through Mount Wolf, York Haven, and other small York County towns before arriving about 8:30 p.m. in Harrisburg.

The booming of cannons and the peeling of bells greeted the train. But that was just the start of it. Rolling peals of thunder and torrents of rain pelted the large crowd that had gathered at the train station to pay their respects.

The *Patriot and Union* reported that the onlookers moved to doorways and under awnings. But the men in uniform stood against a rain that was "almost unendurable."

To the newspaper, the storm typified the national temperament in the aftermath of the chief executive's assassination.

"In addition to bringing with it the greatest discomfort to thousands," the newspaper reported, "it required but little stretch of fancy to imagine it as typical of the national gloom and of heaven's wrath upon the bloody crime that had been committed."[234]

**

Josephus Burger and his comrades in the 187th Pennsylvania were among the last York County soldiers to see President Lincoln's casket.

Stationed at Philadelphia's Camp Cadwallader, they served as the honor guard when the funeral train arrived and the coffin was transported to Independence Hall.

Nearly 200,000 people silently passed by Lincoln as he lay in state.

"Among the first was a woman, no longer young and making no effort to keep back her tears," one of the boys of the 187th wrote. "Speechlessly she handed one of the guard of honor a rudely made wreath, twined by her own hands, from ivy and fir, and he, rising to the truth of that gift, silently hung it among the most honored tributes near the head of the man that dwelt so close to the hearts of the people."[235]

**

By May, with the war over, most soldiers were eager to return home.

From the Army of the Potomac's camp near Fredericksburg, Evan G. Gemmill of the 209th Pennsylvania wrote his sister Martha.

"I told you in my other letter that I thought I would be home soon," he lamented, "but I guess you needent look for me until you see me, for it will be hard to tell when we will be home."

A party atmosphere was building both at home and in the army camps.

"It is in the papers that the Citizens of York Borough are going to give us a feast when we come home," Gemmill relayed. "If they do I want you and Mary Ann to come up for there will be a great time I expect."

"There was a grand illumination of our Corps in the evening of the 13th inst.," he added. "Every man had a candle light and were formed in ranks and marched around the camp — keeping time to the drums and fifes. It was a pretty sight to look at; lasted for about an hour."[236]

**

By June 1865, the 112th Illinois Infantry was a battle-toughened veteran regiment.

As just one test of its mettle, the regiment had participated in the Carolinas Campaign under General William T. Sherman.

The soldiers boarded a train in Greensboro, North Carolina, for the long trip back to Chicago, where the men would receive their final pay and be mustered out of the army.

Instead of the hero's welcome in the Windy City, one soldier would find himself in a Harrisburg hospital.

In late June, the troop train arrived in City Point, Virginia, where the men embarked on a steamship for the James River / Chesapeake Bay voyage to Baltimore. There, they took another train northward to Harrisburg and then to Pittsburgh as they worked their way back home.

Many rode in the cars; others had to ride on the rooftops. Cheering citizens lined the tracks at many places to welcome the boys in blue as they passed through.

"Near York, Pa., as Sergeant William P. Ballentine, of Co. F, was standing on a car, while the train was passing under a low bridge, his head struck the bridge and he was severely injured," the regimental history states, "the only accident that occurred on the ride home."

The unfortunate Ballantine was left behind in the hospital but subsequently recovered and returned home.[237]

**

Dillsburg postmaster A.N. Eslinger recounted a day of festivity on July 3.

With the war finally over, Pennsylvania's Governor Andrew G. Curtin and Major General George G. Meade traveled through Dillsburg en route to Gettysburg for the ceremonies to lay the cornerstone of the Soldiers National Monument.

They remained in town for three hours on July 3, 1865. The ladies of Dillsburg had prepared bouquets of fresh flowers in anticipation of the important guests.

Curtin and Meade ate a meal at the Howard House and chatted with community leaders. Eslinger formally presented the dignitaries with the flower arrangements, in the name of the ladies of Dillsburg.

General Meade simply thanked the women while Governor Curtin, always the consummate politician, expressed his gratitude "in a very appropriate address."[238]

**

A month before the war ended, Private Edward Reiley of North Chester enrolled in the 100th Pennsylvania Infantry.

On May 23, the regiment triumphantly marched in the Grand Review of the Armies in Washington, D.C. In early July, the happy soldiers boarded a train for Harrisburg, where they were to be mustered out of the service.

Ed Reiley would not reach the capital city alive.

As the train steamed through York County on July 9, Private Reiley fell off the top of a railcar.

He was taken to York's military hospital, where he died from his massive injuries.

He is believed to be the last soldier to die in York County during the war.[239]

**

Young John Harvey Anderson of Hopewell Township ended the war in Union uniform in an escort unit for General Sherman.

He, too, marched in the Grand Review.

Letters from his two years in uniform drew responses that tell about life in southeastern York County from 1863 to 1865.

Those were trying times that prompted his sister to write "if they keep on drafting they will have all the men."

Another letter told about political interplay in that rural area among political rivals:

Copperheads, who sought a negotiated peace, and Unionists, who backed Lincoln's war policies.

"Well, we did whip the Copperheads in Hopewell this time at the polls," Anderson stated, "and whipped them with our fists and sent them home with bloody noses."[240]

**

With the war over, Confederate soldiers headed home, often returning to ruined farms and burned-out homesteads.

For those ex-Confederates with Northern ties, returning home presented an entirely different set of problems. Most would never resume their antebellum lives.

George M. E. Shearer is one such example.

Born in Virginia, raised in York County, and educated at Tuscarora Academy in Juniata County, he enlisted in the 1st Maryland Cavalry. Union soldiers captured the captain in the summer of 1864 during a raid on Hagerstown. Two years earlier, as a lieutenant, he was seized by Yankees near Hancock, Md.

Now with the war over, he registered at Hagerstown's City Hotel, proudly signing his name in large bold letters, "MAJOR GEORGE SHEARER, CONFEDERATE STATES ARMY." He and a colleague took a drink at the bar and then left to call on some old friends.

Two members of Hagerstown's Vigilance Committee stopped the duo and politely informed them that if they valued their personal safety the ex-Rebs should leave town as soon as possible.

"He is not personally popular in this region," a Hagerstown newspaper reporter who knew Captain Shearer explained, "and we are

doubtful where General Grant's parole, or any other parole, would be sufficient to make our people respect 'his rights.' "

Unwelcome in his adopted Maryland, Shearer migrated to Idaho.

Many former soldiers simply disappeared, with a large number heading out West in search of a new life.[241]

**

Tens of thousands of Union soldiers remained in the service for months after the surrender of the South's last armies in order to keep the peace and re-establish Federal control in the seceded states.

Most soldiers just wanted to go home.

Among them was York County native William G. Ruhl, the bandmaster of the 10th Illinois Cavalry.

On October 15, 1865, from camp in San Antonio, Texas, he wrote to his father in Stewartstown, "Your welcome letter dated Sept. 25th was received Yesterday Eve. I am happy to hear that you are in good health and I hope you may continue.

You stated brother Nesly had written to me, I have not received any letter from him in a year. I should be very glad to get a letter from him. I should have wrote long ago this but my present accomodiations are so poor that I am scarcity able to do what little I am compelled. It is not necessary for me to make any apoligies you know well of the soldier.

Yesterday there was considerable stir in the city. Our new commander made his appearance there were quite a large number collected in front the Hotel to get a glance at the General. But all proved a failure he was taken to the rear of the house and escorted to his room beastly drunk and after being there some time he undertook to get up and fell to the floor and mashed and bruised his face wonderfully. So much for General [David S.] Stanley our department commander.

You may ask the question what am I doing to kill time, well I get up in the morning Eat my regular hard tack and coffee.

Sometimes write music all day and some time saddle up and go to the city and pass of the day as pleasant I can. This afternoon we have our engagement to play at the beer garden for a concert and select Ball at knight. Probably will feel like sleeping all day tomorrow. Sunday is the general day of amusement in the southern cities, cock fighting, mexician fandangos, gambling, horse racing, and everything that perplexas to the demoralizing of [men].

Thank god theres more care make an impression on me. I have not gamble to the amount of five dollars since I first enlisted Drinking. I drink when I think it necessary but not to any extent. My comrades around me get drunk, gamble, keep bad company but they are the ones that have to suffer, not I.

The last I wrote to you I expected to be a citizen before this but my expectations look mighty far off at present our regiment of our division has left for Brownsville to report to Gen [name unclear] and I fear that we will follow soon. We will have to remain in the service till spring and probably longer.

I shall now close for the present. I had a letter from Mrs R. She is also right she sends her love to you. The Band Boys send their regards to you. Give my love to all inquiring friends. Tell Brother Nes to write as this leaves me in good health. I hope this may reach you the same. Write soon."

On November 22, W.G. Ruhl and his regiment mustered out of the army.[242]

**

Many returning Civil War soldiers had great difficulty in readjusting to civilian life. Lieutenant Ephraim E. Myers of the 45th Pennsylvania recorded his emotions at being home, and then added a touching story:

"We knew that the war was over, Lincoln dead, Lee surrendered, and that we had impressed four years of vigorous young manhood on the battles for our country. We had hoped and prayed for the end of strife; we were overjoyed that we had won the victory and the end had come; as comrades, we were attached by devoted ties, we loved one another; we were dissolving old associations.

"It seemed to me that to be without a musket and with no more camps or campaigns to look forward to, we would be out of an occupation and without a commission. Settling down to routine daily employment in slow shop and store was not favorable to our habits of life; we felt kind of lost.

"Our world of thought and action was breaking up; our accustomed ways in four years of singular existence seemed forsaking us; we were going home of course to friends and scenes we had kept alive the while in our hearts, but after all home life would not be the happy-go-lucky army.

"Illustrative of the fact that we had acquired some peculiar habits, domestic and otherwise, I cannot make my meaning plainer than by stating an absolutely true anecdote.

"In Lower Chanceford, York County, was a good old mother who had three sons in the war. When it was over they came back to her safe; her heart was very glad and proud.

"Their comfort was her constant thought. Every morning early she would quietly open their room door and peep in at them. It distressed her to find the three boys lying on the floor, her soft sweet feather ticks untouched.

"She could not understand it, nor could she stand it any longer, so one morning as she looked in upon their slumber she aroused them with these words, 'Web! Dave! Jack! What are you doing there on that hard floor?' "

"Opening their drowsy lids, staring at her, they replied ruefully, 'We can't sleep in no darn bed, mother.' "[243]

**

After much political postwar wrangling, the state government decided to allow residents of the border counties of south-central Pennsylvania to file damage claims for what they had lost to the Confederate and Union armies.

George Sprenkle, a farmer living in West Manchester Township, had lost some horses from his Bair Station property to Jeb Stuart's men during the Gettysburg Campaign.

Like most other York countians, he never received a dime, although his claim was approved. State budget cuts and financial panics intervened, and the money was not paid out.

George was just one of nine members of the Sprenkle clan to file claims.

As late as 1890, Congress was still debating whether to pay Federal funds to satisfy the still-outstanding border claims.

The House Committee on War Claims voted 6-5 to present the bill for a vote. The claims totaled $3,177,985, of which only $890,000 had been paid by the State of Pennsylvania.

But President Benjamin Harrison "called a halt on the drain on the Treasury, and that the border claims are among the demands upon the surplus that must be rejected."

Several York County families still retain copies of the original paperwork filed by their ancestors and the corresponding claims certificates issued by the state commissioners. They were never able to redeem the certificates for cash reimbursement.[244]

**

Wrightsville's James Barton of the 127th USCT helped man trenches in Petersburg, near the Civil War's end.

Earlier, he had been sent home from his segregated black regiment with a life-threatening case of the measles.

Back with his unit, he was not back to normal. He was not immediately put back on duty. His head and face did not seem right, a fellow soldier observed.

Still, there he was in Petersburg near the war's end, and he served with his unit until September 1865 before receiving an honorable discharge pay of $100, less $24.24 for his clothing.

But his real battle began at that point.

He fought for years for a full military pension.

Barton, one of seven members of his family to fight for black units, eventually received a monthly check of $6.[245]

**

Benjamin Grim, a member of the 200th Pennsylvania, served at Dutch Gap and other places in the 1864 summer campaign to take Richmond and Petersburg.

The preacher's son from Warrington Township suffered a wound in his left hip at Fort Stedman. His records indicated the bullet "still remains and is unaccounted for."

Despite what must have been severe pain, he returned to active duty and marched in pursuit of Lee's army in the Appomattox Campaign. He mustered out in May 1865 and returned home, where he followed in his father's footsteps and joined the ministry.

The Rev. Benjamin Grim spent the rest of his life carrying the Confederate Minié ball in his hip, a constant reminder of how close he came to sharing the fate of scores of fellow York countians.[246]

**

Throughout the spring and summer, regiments continued to muster out and return home. However, a significant number of troops remained in the field to quell any residual Rebel threats or to keep the peace.

With the immediate danger from the Rebels gone, soldiers had more free time on their hands.

Temptations abounded.

In late June from camp in Washington, D.C. James Nickel of the 99th Pennsylvania Infantry wrote his wife Barbara, "You said I shouldn't play cards and do anything bad. I tell you I haven't had a card in my hand yet. Only picked up one and tore that one up to pieces. But they often askt me to with them, but I told them that I did not want to get to playing them."[247]

**

Andrew Jackson Fulton was one of David and Margaret Patterson Fulton's eight children.

He grew up near Stewartstown and moved only a short distance away to Hopewell Township where he and his wife, Elizabeth, raised six children.

When the call came for early responders to protect the Northern Central Railway in Maryland, Andrew Fulton responded. He then enlisted in the 87th Pennsylvania and also served in the 166th Pennsylvania before health reasons forced him out of the service in September 1863.

He resumed his pre-war occupation as a teacher, serving as administrator of a finishing school for young women in Stewartstown.

But the soldier/schoolmaster who avoided taking a bullet in the Civil War could not avoid it after the fighting stopped.

In November 1871, Fulton was hunting and attempted to cross a fence.

His shotgun accidentally discharged, taking his life.[248]

**

Lieutenant Samuel C. Ilgenfritz of York spoke at one of the postwar gatherings of his old regiment.

His passionate speech evoked memories of why he and his comrades went to war: not to eliminate slavery, but to preserve the Union.

"The 187th Regiment contended for a great and far-reaching principle," he stated.

"What is a principle? A truth received, believed and fixed in the mind from which there flows out a corresponding course of action. When this Regiment marched to the defense of the imperiled interest of its country, it received and wrote upon its colors, a great truth, namely, the principle of national sovereignty, i.e.

"This is a *nation*, not a compact, a rope of sand, that may be snapped asunder by the mere whim of any one; nor set of States, but a nation possessing the power to defend, preserve and perpetuate its life."

The price to preserve that nation had been 620,000 lives and more than a million more who would carry the scars of wounds the rest of their lives.[249]

**

An unknown Union soldier rested in a secluded grave at Emig's Grove Camp Meeting grounds, south of Mount Wolf.

"It has been sympathetically remembered by some patriotic members of the Camp Meeting Association, and marked by a neat and appropriate headstone," historian John Gibson wrote 20 years after the Civil War.

"He was clad in the uniform of a Union soldier, the buttons of which contained the coat of arms of Pennsylvania, and his cap the number 65.

There he lay — outlasting the camp ground, which had burned down — until 1902 when undertaker W.L. Denues moved the soldier's remains to Prospect Hill Cemetery.

Sedgwick Grand Army of the Republic Post member Samuel Ilgenfritz inspired the move to a spot not far from a marker of unknown Confederate dead.

The Prospect Hill marker states: "Remembering 5 unknown dead 3 here, 2 near. The Twenty First Century Confederate Legion."

Within a few months of the Union soldier's interment, another distinguished war vet found his final resting place nearby.

Samuel Ilgenfritz's burial spot was within 20 feet of the unknown Union soldier's newly dug grave.[250]

**

York County's Jacob Horlebein was there at the start of the 87th Pennsylvania.

He fought with that regiment for almost three years, finally falling into Confederate hands near Petersburg, in June 1864.

Horlebein was assigned to Andersonville prison and lived to see his liberation.

In poor health, he was transferred to York's military hospital. He did not recover, dying at age 29 in March 1865.

Over the years, weather and acid rain eroded his marker in York's Prospect Hill Cemetery.

He had no survivors, but his service was not forgotten.

Ruhl Camp 33 installed a new marker and publicly dedicated it in remembrance of the soldier who served his country every year of the Civil War.[251]

**

In April 1895 a Glen Rock newspaper reported, "A tourist representing himself as Captain Robert Campbell, 7th Virginia Cavalry, C.S.A., was soliciting alms in the borough on Saturday, apparently with very fair success. He requested the *Item* to thank the citizens for their kindness to an ex-Confederate soldier, which we hereby perform."

Campbell claimed he was with the Confederate army at Gettysburg and had foraged in the Glen Rock, Hanover Junction, and York region. He also purported to be a former college classmate and "chum" of ex-President Benjamin Harrison.

The editor wisely noted, "It is safe to assume, however, that they are not chumming any more, and that his whole yarn is a fake, but it is a clever one, anyway, and gets him more cash than telling the truth."[252]

**

Franklin Ginter fought with the York Rifles, early responders at the firing on Fort Sumter, before joining the 87th Regiment.

He survived the war and, in fact, all other members of the rifle company.

Ginter was also the oldest member of John Sedgwick GAR Post 37 and the last Civil War veteran buried in York's Prospect Hill Cemetery, interred in 1935.

And he met Abraham Lincoln in 1864, a handshake that he remembered the rest of his life.

"One of his fondest memories," one history states, "was shaking hands with President Lincoln at the latter's inauguration."[253]

**

William Henry Gilbert, a farm boy from Craley in Lower Windsor Township, saw two presidents while serving in uniform.

Early in the war, he and some of his comrades in the 187th Pennsylvania entered a home near Arlington, Virginia.

They took some salted fish found in the cellar. The men wanted milk to wash it down, but Gilbert responded "the woman needed that for her baby."

Gilbert heard President Lincoln's speeches on several occasions, and, as he later recalled, Lincoln was "not very much concerned very much as to his dress. He was a tall man and wore a stovepipe hat, which made seem even taller. He seemed odd, both in size and dress and spoke in a high pitched and humorous voice, which so greatly endured him to all who met him."

A bullet claimed one of Gilbert's fingers in the siege of Petersburg, which ended his front-line duty.

In April 1865, he was selected for the Guard of Honor for the Lincoln funeral procession in Philadelphia, and he stood guard at the catafalque where Lincoln lay in state.

There was still one more president to meet.

In 1935, William Henry Gilbert turned 93 years old. The veteran received a tour of the nation's capital, highlighted by an audience with President Franklin D. Roosevelt.

The meeting took place in the same room where Abraham Lincoln had signed the Emancipation Proclamation in 1862.

Gilbert found FDR to be "entirely different" than he expected.

He informed a *York Dispatch* reporter, "The President was so kind he made me feel right at home. I had expected a stern man. He was very social and had such a kind personality, I could see right away he loved the people who had honored him."

Eleanor Roosevelt was "a very gracious lady," in Gilbert's opinion.

After visiting the Veterans' Hospital and the Lincoln Memorial, Gilbert sat for an interview with NBC in a nationwide radio broadcast.

He concluded his 15-minute remarks with "a hope that God, in all his wise providence, provide us, as a nation, with more men like Lincoln, and I further pray that God bless our Nation and President, whom I wish God's speed."

The long day ended with a train ride back to York County.

As he departed Washington, Henry admitted he was tired, but he added, "I surely have had a wonderful day."[254]

**

Dolly Menges of East Berlin is one of those residents who, as a youngster, met veterans in both blue and gray in the 75th reunion of the Battle of Gettysburg in 1938.

She remembers the bearded men walking around the field where they fought.

And she recalls Franklin Roosevelt presiding over the lighting of the Peace Light memorial, a Union vet on one side and a Confederate on the other.

She collected about 10 signatures from the former fighting men, including that of M.D. Vance, a Confederate general from Little Rock, Arkansas.

"They were so glad that we asked for their autographs," Dolly said.[255]

**

Fifteen-year-old Ann Small was another visitor to Gettysburg for that 75th anniversary commemoration.

She remembered the re-enactment of Pickett's charge by veterans in gray, only they were mounted this time.

The re-enactment ended without a mock battle against infantry veterans in blue, but years later Ann remembered that charge by octogenarian vets.

"It sent chills down my spine," she related, "to just witness the re-enactment of what had taken place on that same field, 75 years ago."[256]

**

Franklin D. Roosevelt's speech at the dedication of the Peace Memorial was a secondary event in the memories of one young visitor that day, East Berlin's Robert Mansberger.

The boy observed a bench full of Union and Confederates remembering that terrible charge known to history as Longstreet's Assault or Pickett's charge.

He stood with his father, John Mansberger, near the low stone wall that marked the Union stronghold.

The boy heard the veterans — Union men — remark that their officer urged them to hold their fire until the Confederates were close.

To make sure.

"Shoot the horses first," they were ordered, "then shoot the men."

The horses went down in a "tangled mess," the veterans said.

"The horses just fell among the men," Robert said, recalling the conversation years later.

And then came the hand-to-hand combat in and around that stone wall.

The Northern and Southern men, sitting side by side, Mansberger recalled, "sat there and cried."[257]

**

Robert Doll grew up in the 1920s and 30s in Saginaw.

He remembers visiting the 75th anniversary as part of Troop 51 of the Boy Scouts.

He and his friends helped the old soldiers and acted as their hosts.

"We helped the older gentlemen and pushed their wheelchairs," he recalled. "One thing that stands out — they had wooden walkways on the ground for the veterans to use. It made it easier to push them."

The scouts assisted with meals and cleanup and made sure the soldiers were comfortable and their needs met.

The reward included getting to listen to the old vets swap war stories, many undoubtedly tinged with some exaggeration and embellishment.

Robert remembers standing 20 to 30 feet from Roosevelt, as the president gave his Peace Memorial dedicatory speech to the assembled crowd of veterans, scouts, dignitaries, and guests.[258]

**

That 75th anniversary in 1938 marked the final formal reunion of veterans at Gettysburg.

Most were in their 90s in 1938.
With the 150th anniversary of the Civil War, those scouts, children, and young helpers at that great event in 1938 are now themselves the ages of the soldiers they once helped.

That 20th-century generation is the last link with the men, women, and children of the era of the War Between the States.

They were the last to have actually heard Civil War voices from York County, Pa.

Francis Fix mustered into the 75th Pennsylvania in 1861. He was a house painter from Philadelphia with ties to York County where his descendants now live. He rose from private to sergeant and then to lieutenant in the 75th. Then the French-born Fix accepted a commission as a captain in the 114th Pennsylvania. On July 2, he was severely wounded near the Peach Orchard at Gettysburg. This photograph comes from descendant Jean Fix.

Adam T. Smith of the 107th Pennsylvania is shown with his wife, Mary Ann, and daughter Nancy Catherine. Born in Wittenberg, Germany, in 1840, Smith was a shoemaker in York before the war. Wounded at Gettysburg, he was taken to the U.S. Army General Hospital in York for treatment. This photograph comes from descendant Billie E. Houseman.

Edward Webster Spangler stood five-foot-two, two inches shorter than regulations. But a lenient recruiting officer made him part of the 130th Pennsylvania. He survived the war and became a successful attorney and newspaperman. This photograph is from Spangler's 1904 autobiography, *My Little War Experience: With Historical Sketches and Memorabilia.*

Private James Nickel served in the 99th Pennsylvania and became a prisoner of war. This photograph is from descendant Kathleen Nickel.

Barbara Nickel, like so many women in both the North and South, maintained steady correspondence with her soldier husband, James. This photograph is from descendant Kathleen Nickel.

William R. Smith of Wellsville received this certificate for $1,304 in damages caused by Confederate invaders in 1863. Descendant Senford Smith said his Wellsville relative never received payment. The loss could have been worse. Senford Smith heard a story from his grandmother that family members led a milk cow and team of horses to a rocky area, out of sight of passing Confederates.

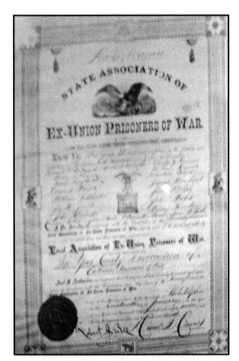

George Stahl of the 130th Pennsylvania served, along with his brothers and father, from Hanover. It was said that he was captured by Mosby's Rangers and escaped twice. He was shot in the leg during the second escape. A plaque in Hanover's Mount Olivet Cemetery lists the names of members of the Stahl family who served in the Civil War. Photograph comes from descendant Ronald A. Reinecker.

This is James Nickel's certificate as part of a distinguished Pennsylvania group of former prisoners of war.

Chapter 5

In their own words

'You can take my life, my land, my home and my possessions, but you can't take my politics.'
– Joseph Kauffman, York County, Pa.

Dozens of York countians left detailed accounts of the Civil War, particularly the Gettysburg Campaign which for many locals was the defining moment of the war. These included legal depositions, personal letters, diary entries, and journals.

Here is a sampling of some of the most descriptive of these written voices.

**

"One old negro to whom was entrusted the duty of igniting the fuse sat very coolly on the edge of the pier, smoking a cigar."

This was a Union cavalryman's account of the scene as civilians sought to mine a span of the Columbia Bridge to stop the Confederate advance eastward. Now, some recently found bank records have revealed the name of the black man who was among the last four civilians working to stop the Confederate advance eastward in the days before the Battle of Gettysburg.

Jacob Miller was the man behind the cigar. One black man had it in his power to stop an entire Confederate brigade — perhaps a whole division — by touching that cigar to a fuse.

He had been recruited to mine a span of the Columbia Bridge over the Susquehanna River. Dropping one span to stop the invading Rebels was preferable to torching the entire mile-and-a-quarter-long bridge.

But the blast did not undermine the span, and Miller and other civilians set fire to the bridge to keep the Confederates from securing the structure and gaining access to the east side of the Susquehanna and the back side of Harrisburg.[259]

Here are two depositions, detailing the defense activities in the face of the Confederate assault on the bridge, recently found in old bank records now in the archives of the Columbia Historic Preservation Society:

"Before me a justice of the peace in and for the Borough of Columbia, County of Lancaster, State of Pennsylvania, personally came Robert Crane of Columbia, who being by me first duly sworn according to law, did depose and say, that in the presence of a written order from Colonel Jacob G. Frick of the 27th Pennsylvania Volunteer Militia, commander at Columbia dated 28th June, 1863, and also in pursuance of a verbal order from Major G. O. Haller of the United States Army, commander at York, York County, re Pennsylvania, I engaged a company of Bridge builders, carpenters, and other persons for the purpose of cutting and throwing the fourth span of the West End of the Columbia Bridge across the Susquehanna between Columbia and Wrightsville.

And that in pursuance of such orders, we went upon the Columbia Bridge, cut the roof downward all the timbers excepting the arches and a small portion of the lower chords on Sunday the 28th day of June, 1863. We bored all the arches and charged them heavily with powder, attached fuses to the powder, and had them all ready for the matches. There were four men placed in charge of the matches and fuses on a given order. An order was given by Major Charles Knox, aid of Major Haller aforesaid, to me to apply the matches to the fuses which was accordingly done. When the blast went off it was effective but not sufficient to throw a span of the Bridge. There was no time to cut the spans down as the Rebel cavalry had entered the bridge from Wrightsville.

Col. Frick then gave orders to the men to set fire to the Bridge which was done as directed, and it was burned down in obedience to his orders. The men in charge of the fuses and blast in the arches were John Q. Denny, John Lockhard, Jacob Miller (colored), and Jacob Rich. Captain Samuel Randall of the City Troop of Philadelphia, aid to Major Haller, had first been selected by Major Haller to deliver the order to me when to apply the match to the fuses.

After our pickets were engaged in front of the rifle pits with the Rebels, Captain Randall came on to the bridge where we were engaged removing the timbers etc. and wished to know of sure if I understood that he Captain Randall was to deliver to me the order to destroy the Bridge. My answer was in the affirmative, when he said he did not so understand it so and said that I had better see Major Haller and have an understanding with him. I then took Captain Randall's horse and rode out to the rifle pits to see Major Haller; when he Major Haller selected Major Charles Knox and detailed him and a few soldiers to aid him in delivering the order and to prevent confusion when [in] the Bridge. Major Knox performed the duties assigned him and gave the orders as above stated.

On the morning of the 29th of June 1863 Major Haller called on me for my report which I made to him in writing, first submitting it to Col. Frick aforesaid for his approval which he gave after perusal with slight corrections, a copy of which report I have given to the Cashier of the Columbia Bank as amended by Col. Frick."

Robert Crane[260]

**

"Before me a Justice of the Peace in and for the Borough of Columbia, County of Lancaster and the State of Pennsylvania, personally came John Q. Denney, who being by me first duly sworn according to the law did declare and say as follows:

I was standing in Black's Hotel on the afternoon of Sunday the 28th of June 1863, when W. Robert Crane came and asked me if I would go along with his party on to the Bridge that he [and] E.K. Smith had been appointed by Col. Jacob G. Frick then commanding at Columbia to cut the timbers of the Bridge, to bore and charge the arches with powder in order to have it in such condition as to blow it up or otherwise destroy it in case our forces stationed at Wrightsville should be attacked by the rebels and repulsed. I told him I certainly would do everything in my power that was considered [acceptable] by Col. Frick.

I with the others went on to the bridge with W. Crane, tore up the planking on one of the spans near the West End, cut off all the timbers that we thought of would have been safe to cut without destroying the possibility of our troops to [hop] over, bored and charged the arches with powder ready for the match if [acceptable]. Jacob Rich, John Lockard, Jacob Miller and myself were appointed to take charge of the lighting of the fuses but a short time, when Col. Frick came and notified us that our forces would retreat and our only safety was to blow up the bridge.

In a few minutes our soldiers retreated and [hopped] over the Bridge and the order was then given by Col. Frick to apply the matches was done. Each of us four, Jacob Rich, John Lockard, Jacob Miller and myself had charge of a fuse and we applied the matches when the order was given; but the explosion failing to blow up or destroy the Bridge as was expected we then under [express] order from Col. Frick set fire to the Bridge by building a fire in the middle of a span near the place where we had charged with powder. We then retreated while the rebels entered the West end of the Bridge and endeavored to extinguish the flames and the Bridge was entirely consumed."

John Q. Denney[261]

**

Arthur Briggs Farquhar was a young businessman when he made initial contact with invading Confederates on June 27, 1863, to surrender the town of York. But he was a veteran captain of industry and friend of U.S. presidents when he penned his memoirs in 1922.

These excerpts from *An Autobiography of A.B. Farquhar* provide insight in to the minds of York countians — and the mind of A.B. Farquhar — at the time of the Civil War:

"The beginnings of the events which developed into the Civil War did not much move us. York was distinctively Northern but not bitterly anti-Southern. The community felt that slavery was wrong in principle. At the same time, being acquainted with many slave owners, we also knew that slavery was better in practice than in theory and that the planter who was cruel to his Negroes was a rare exception. No matter what his personal disposition might be, slaves were so very expensive that it would be as ridiculous to maltreat them as to maltreat a stable of blooded horses.

The situation was not unlike that which obtains in prohibition today. There are fanatics on both sides. The majority of us, I think are distinctly against the sale of intoxicating beverages and especially the saloon, but we would not wreck the country in order to enforce prohibition, That is, from a larger viewpoint, we cannot conceive the regulation of a beverage to be of such overwhelming importance as to make every other issue insignificant. There are others who would prefer a barren waste without liquor to a garden spot where the Rum Demon dwelt.

It often happens that the less you know about a subject, the more fanatical you can become. It is hard to hate a man you know. The fanatical abolitionists and the fanatical slave advocates did not know each other. There they could hate. Some things in *Uncle Tom's Cabin*, for instance, could not have been written if Harriet Beecher Stowe had resided in and been familiar with the South. John Brown's raid, which had as its object the starting of an insurrection among the slaves of Virginia, would not have taken place had he understood the slaves, for he would then have known that the Negroes did not know the meaning of revolt — that they were, in the main, more interested in three meals a day than in political theory; and that, if he had succeeded in stirring them to the point of frenzy, the only result would have been chaos.

We felt that slavery was a political question and we were more concerned with establishing the principle that all new states admitted to the Union — for then the admission of a new state was a personal matter to every citizen as the election of a member to a small club — should be free states. We were concerned with the question that Lincoln put to Douglas at Freeport:

> Can the people of a United States territory, in any legal way, against the will of any citizen of the United States, exclude slavery from its limits prior to the formation of a state constitution?

The debates of Lincoln and Douglas, and Lincoln's great speech at the Cooper Institute in

New York in February, 1860, fired the country. They made known the legal position of slavery and they made known to the East something of the qualities which this wonderful man had in him. His gift of clear thought and Biblical speech convinced the serious citizen, disgusted with the vacillations of Buchanan, that he was the man who might cement together the Union that seemed in a fair way to need the services of a very competent mason. For there was no doubt where Lincoln stood. We needed a strong president with plenty of common sense. And for these reasons Lincoln won the nomination the election.

Only a very few people held him as a potentially great man — not a larger number than hail every president as great. But his speeches and declarations affected me deeply — more deeply than I can well describe. They awoke in me an admiration which, a few years later, after I had met and talked with him, developed into a reverence that has grown with the years. To-day, after having met many of the leading men in most of the countries of the world during the past half century, I believe that he was one of the few supermen. This may sound extravagant but I cannot put down my feeling toward Abraham Lincoln in less emphatic terms. When the most has been said that can be said, only a fraction of the whole man has been revealed."[262]

**

Frances Ellen Watkins Harper was a widely known Civil War-era poet, writer, and lecturer, and a strong voice for abolition and women's suffrage.

But before she reached heights, she was a teacher in York in the 1850s.

While in York, she pondered whether to continue in education and move into the anti-slavery field. "The Slave Mother" is an example of her work:

Heard you that shriek? It rose
So wildly on the air,
It seemed as if a burden'd heart
Was breaking in despair.

Saw you those hands so sadly clasped -
The bowed and feeble head -
The shuddering of that fragile form -
That look of grief and dread?

Saw you the sad, imploring eye?
Its every glance was pain,
As if a storm of agony
Were sweeping through the brain.

She is a mother, pale with fear,
Her boy clings to her side,
And in her kirtle vainly tries
His trembling form to hide.

He is not hers, although she bore
For him a mother's pains;
He is not hers, although her blood
Is coursing through his veins!

He is not hers, for cruel hands
May rudely tear apart
The only wreath of household love
That binds her breaking heart.

His love has been a joyous light
That o'er her pathway smiled,
A foundation gushing ever news,
Amid life's desert wild.

His lightest word has been a tone
Of music round her heart,
Their lives a streamlet in one –
Oh, Father! Must they part?

They tear him from her circling arms,
Her last and fond embrace.
Oh! Never more may her sad eyes
Gaze on his mournful face.

No marvel, then, these bitter shrieks

Disturb the listening air:
She is a mother, and her heart
Is breaking in despair.[263]

**

At the age of 38, Newberry shoemaker George K. Bratton enrolled in August 1862 in the 130th Pennsylvania Volunteer Infantry.

He was 5 feet, four inches, with dark hair and brown eyes, and was married with four children. Bratton was in the battles of Antietam, Fredericksburg, and Chancellorsville along with fellow soldier J.R. Fetrow. He was wounded in the thigh at Chancellorsville on May 3, 1863, and came home to recuperate.

Scarcely more than a year later, on August 23, 1864, George Bratton re-enlisted in the army, this time at Goldsboro in the 200th Pennsylvania. He was promoted to first sergeant the following day.

He was wounded again at the March 25, 1865, Battle of Fort Stedman and spent the rest of the war convalescing.

The recipient of this letter, dated June 16, 1863, from Newberrytown, is believed to be a cousin who was serving in another Union army regiment:

"It is with feelings that I cannot describe and such as I have never experienced before that I seat myself this evening to write you and answer to your welcome letter (which I have neglected to do at the proper time) for which you will please excuse me at this time. Well I supposed you wonder what is the matter or what causes my very agitated state of feelings at this time. Well my dear sir I will tell you as well as I can. We are in a most intense excitement on accounts of reports that the Rebels are in Penna. and some reports say they were at Carlisle today and some say even closer than that and that we may expect

them here tomorrow. The citizens of Cumberland Valley are in a wonderful commotion, hundreds of them are moving horses and cattle out of harm's way if possible. Martin Crull was in Harrisburg today and reports about five thousand men at work throwing up entrenchments and reports that all the horses in the vicinity have been pressed into the service of the Government. These are indeed squirrelly times.

Some of the folks about our town are packing away their valuables in some secret places where they calculate the Rebs wont find them and some more talking of taking their horses away early in the morning perhaps somewhere in the Conewago mountains for security.

The Goldsboro folks are moving their affairs onto Shelly Island calculating that if the Rebels do come along they will hardly take time to visit these places. I can scarcely think that we should be compelled to witness so humiliating a circumstance here. I sincerely hope not but if they do get this far I suppose we will have to abide by the consequences.

What seems to worry me the most is that there is not more exertion made on the part of the citizens to meet them and if possible stop them is they attempt to advance this far. Not one man has volunteered from the neighborhood except John Walters [who] this afternoon took his haversack, I think his knapsack, and started for Harrisburg. Bully for Walters. If I were right well I would go myself but as it is I must remain inactive for at present. But if all reports are true I fear it will not be long before I must again take an active part in the work and do what little I can for my country.

I have not heard how many troops were in the vicinity of Harrisburg but reports say this evening that most of the rest of the 87th [Pennsylvania Infantry] is there but I cannot vouch for the correctness of it. I supposed there will be a battle before they get into the city. I judge Gov Curtain [sic] will burn the bridge before they will be allowed to cross peaceably as the river has raised several feet in the last 48 hours. They may possibly keep them out of the place and if General Hooker is after them as is reported they may find some pretty sharp work to do before they can get back again.

Wednesday, June 17th. This morning things bear a somewhat better aspect than they did last evening. It appears a deal of the commotion was caused by our own cavalry getting through and coming by way of Carlisle and arrived at Bridgeport last evening having traveled one hundred miles without feeding and many of the horses just about out done. Now they think they are pretty well prepared to receive them if they come. A few days ago Geo Yinger, Charly McCreary, Saml Baird, and Joe Updegraff skedaddled off somewhere. It was supposed to escape the draft but they are all back again except Charly. I know nothing about him.

Sam Ensminger did the enrolling in this township and met with no particular difficulties. A proposition is a foot now to enlist men for the defense of the State for six months and give the State credit on the draft and if they rush in as I expect they will I would not be surprised if we were exempt from a draft this time.

Political prejudices and preferences have arisen to an alarming extent and may terminate very unfavorably for all concerned if you can believe one fourth of what we hear. I sincerely hope no such disgraceful things may happen at this time as a political organization to resist the execution of the laws by the present administration and yet some of the outspoken declarations of some of the Rebel sympathizers here seem even to compel us to come to that conclusion.

The weather here is remarkably dry for this part of the season. The grass crops are certainly very short and the grain is in many places although short promises to give as good a yield as last year. Fruit will certainly be scarce in the vicinity this season as most of the trees for some unknown cause did not bloom to any extent. Great expectations have in store for a very large tobacco crop but it looks a little doubtful just now as it is time to plant and no rain. The folks in town are generally well. Grandma Hays is quite perky. Please write soon."[264]

**

Twenty-seven-year-old York lawyer James Latimer wrote his younger brother, Bartow, about events before, during and after the Confederate invasion. James Latimer, a staunch Republican and later a York County judge, took a dim view of the actions by borough authorities to surrender the town:

York, June 15th
10 o'clock P.M.

Dear Bart

"Yours per Miss Lochman I found at the store (Smalls) when I came down this evening.

We had a boro' meeting tonight to devise measures for the defense of the town and responding to the very earnest call for volunteers which Gov. Curtin telegraphed over today. Nothing definite was done, and it is likely nothing will be done.

Our latest intelligence is that the rebels are at Greencastle or were there today and would occupy Chambersburg tonight. This was a dispatch from Col. Scott dated H'burg at 8:35. He says they are undoubtedly advancing on Harrisburg and in large force. It is supposed they will cut the N.C.R. somewhere, very likely here.

We have made no preparations for defence and of course can make none. I will, when the danger becomes imminent try to persuade Ma & Sister to go to Philada. but fear will not succeed. I presume we cant be long without a visit of at least rebel cavalry here and perhaps communication with Ashland may be cut off. If so try to write by Balto & Philada and I will do the same.

This advance of the rebs. is regarded in H'burg not as a raid but as an advance in force of Lee's army. The 87th Regt. is as you probably know at Winchester under Milroy and probably 'gobbled up.'

Write me if anything occurs and I will do the same.

I write tonight because I dont get down street in time for morning mail. I am probably writing very incoherently but am worried. I wish to go to H'burg if a good company goes from here but fear I cant on account of Ma and Sister."

Yrs truly

J.W.L.[265]

**

Thursday Evening
18 June 1863

Dear Bart

"I went to Harrisburg yesterday to try to ascertain the facts in regard to the rebel invasion. Kell went with me. We had a talk with the Governor. He is very much excited and very anxious to secure troops as soon as possible and in as large forces as possible at H'burg. He seemed to think the danger imminent; and as the small forces of rebels at Chambersburg was not sufficient to account for his alarm and anxiety, I concluded he must be acting under secret information from some source—probably Washington. I suppose his idea was that Lee's army is about to cross the Potomac as they did last fall.

They are digging rifle-pits and throwing up intrenchments at Wrightsville to protect the Columbia bridge and say they are acting under orders from Gen. Couch. They have a force of men on the bridge night and day to destroy it if necessary.

A member of the "Committee of Safety" told me this morning that Maj. Haller had been ordered here to obstruct roads and delay the Rebs as much as possible if they should attempt any advance in this direction. He was to consult with Genl. Franklin. The latter was with the Committee last evening and gave it as his opinion that there was about to be an invasion of the State.

With all this there is not the least excitement here. No one is alarmed. Every one seems as indifferent as if there were no rebels within a thousand miles. Either the people Harrisb'g are scared very badly about nothing and are making fools of themselves or there is some considerable danger to be apprehended. Still many people here say it is nothing but a causeless fright among rail-road men.

Mr. Slaymaker had a dispatch from Rob yesterday from McConnellsburg Penna. He is safe. Was with two companies on detached service at Bunker Hill when the rebels advanced. The two companies fought them from the church for several hours and when they fell back for artillery they retreated into Penna.

Col. Schall wrote day before yesterday to say that the 87th had 60 men left. He hoped stragglers would come in enough to make up about two hundred.

Since writing the above I have learned that Col. Slaymaker has come to town. Have not seen him.

Every particle even of interest seems to have died out here. And no one seems to think it worthwhile to inquire where the rebels really are.

This letter is being written by snatches. Rob Slaymaker stopped at our house since supper for a moment. I did not see him. Sister did. He says the two companies at Bunker Hill retreated to Winchester and were with the regiment during the three days fighting on the retreat to Harpers Ferry. His captain was killed on Sunday and the other Lieutenant on Monday. On Tuesday the regiment got scattered in some way among the mountains, and every man looked out for himself. Rob got to Hancock, Md. an(d) found there Stahle (Lt.Col.) and Ruhl and ten men of his company. He told his men they might go home until they could find where their regiment was; and he came home by way of McConnellsburg. Says they were marching six days and fighting three of them. Nothing can be learned of Hen Lanius. Rob says he fought very bravely—on the last charge (of) the Reg't the officers of the Company were killed or wounded & Hen formed his men and led them himself. His conduct attracted attention. There is a report that Emmett was killed. Don't know where it came from. Sister did not ask Rob.

That's all I believe."

Yours truly,

James W. Latimer[266]

**

York
June 24th, 1863

Dear Bart

"The latest intelligence we have here of the rebels is that they are at Shippensburg advancing towards Carlisle. There is little or no excitement here. We have mounted men out in the direction of Carlisle but no preparation for defence here.

I was in the lower end of the County last evening — in Fawn township — on business. Got back this afternoon.

The 87th Regiment is very much reflected on here by some people. I presume the fact is neither that nor any other regiment did much fighting, but probably Milroy is to blame for that more than the men. Rob Slaymaker says that his Company got to Winchester (from Bunker Hill) Sunday morning, went into rifle pit and remained there till Monday morning. He & his Captain went to sleep and discovered accidentally that the evacuation was taking place, went out to their company and found that the 87th which was in the advance had gotten nearly four miles from the town; some one had neglected to inform them and they were nearly left behind. The column was attacked before he over took his reg't. Says they had no artillery and little ammunition but still fought four hours and then the whole division broke and scattered in the woods and every man looked out for himself. He says Schall fought very bravely; but as he says the same with regard to the regiment, and as I gather from what he says that he was considerably scared and took very good care of himself perhaps what he says about their bravery is not very reliable.

Adjutant Emmett is safe of course. He sent here Sunday a list of 190 names of those of the regt who were at Maryland Hights. There are about 200 or 250 of them at Bloody Run in Western Penna., and probably 100 here and in H'burg, so their loss could not have been very heavy. Hen. Lanius is safe.

There is the most extra-ordinary apathy with regard to this invasion. If the information we have here is reliable we may have an attack on Harrisburg in a day or two, and yet nothing is being done here. We have sent one Company. I put my name down to another but it fell thro: If men wont go to the defense of their own State they don't deserve to be called patriots. I am ashamed of myself and my town.

Thats all I believe. Write me.

Whom did Miss Kate Smyser marry"

Yrs truly

James W. Latimer[267]

**

Tuesday morning
June 30th, 1863

Dear Bart

"We have been cut off from the World for two days (it seems like as many weeks), and I hope communication will be resumed soon.

The rebels came into town Sunday Morning about ten oclock. Three brigades were actually in town and another was understood to be at Emigsville & one somewhere south—all constituting Early's division of Ewells corps. The(y) behaved very well did no damage in town to private property, except breaking into one or two houses on the outskirts, paid for what they bought in rebel money & in some instances in Greenbacks; and seemed to be entirely under the most perfect control. Early had his headquarters in the Court-house. He demanded supplies from the Boro' Authorities; Flour, sugar, Coffee, Boots, shoes, hats &c, and $100,000 in money. A Committee went round to collect as much as they could and got $28,000 which was paid to them. The other requisitions were filled.

This morning the last of them left in the direction of Carlisle. I hope we have seen the last of them. They burned a few cars at the depot, but spared the warehouse, Engine house and in fact all the buildings. They destroyed all the R.R. bridges within miles of town.

Ma & Sister stayed. I regretted very much afterwards that I had not sent them off, as of course there was all the time danger of the officers losing control of their men.

The Rebs intended they say to go to Lancaster but the bridge at Columbia was burned Sunday evening by our forces so they could not cross. It is understood that a large part of Wrightsville was burned at the same time.

I hope to be able to send this to W'ville by some private opportunity. Will write further,"

Write me.

Yours truly

James W. Latimer

"Afternoon. No rebs here. The County people are beginning to come in. They were plundered indiscriminately particularly by a Louisiana brigade. Horses and mules taken, houses broken open, and everything the thieves fancied stolen."[268]

**

Columbia
30 June 1863

Dear Bart,

"I came here to mail letters, get news, papers, &c &c. I forgot to say, when you write me, direct to Columbia, till further information. Our Post Office skedadled Saturday night and wont resume for some time probably.

Things look blue. If Lee tries Harrisb'g and is delayed there any time, or if he gets across our place will be on their line, and will be liable to constant visits. I am afraid the rebs will have but little difficulty in going to Philada or any where they please. Our only hope seems to be in Meads Army.

At all events I wish very much Ma & Sister were away from York, tho' I would not let them know I fear anything, for the world. However, no place seems safe.

I may take too gloomy a view of affairs, but things seem at their worst. Write me. Write me and if necessary on two sheets (as heretofore) one to show and one for myself alone.

There is no force here of any account — one Regt and one battery, but I presume there will be no attack or effort to cross here.

Thats about all."

Yours truly
James W. Latimer

"I enclose you the Copperhead account of our Subjugation"[269]

**

York
8th July 1863
Wednesday A.M.

Dear Bart

"Yours of 3rd inst. recd. yesterday.

I suppose the victory of Meade over Lee at Gettysburg, is sufficiently decisive to relieve us of all apprehension of another visit from the Rebs here. The question now seems to be whether they will be able to make their escape over the Potomac.

If there should ever be again the least danger of another rebel invasion I am determined Ma & Sister shall go away. Altho' they behaved very well in town and did no violence to persons or property, their officers might at any moment have lost control over them and then we would have been in a very dangerous position.

You inquire how people behaved here &c. The whole town, men, women, & children were in Main St. when the Rebs came in. People turned out en mass to receive them. There was no expression of sympathy as they marched thro' town except in a very few instances. Handkerchiefs were waved from the Tremont House and Washington House, and from old Pete Ahls and Dr. Nes's. Miss Chapman Mrs. Wickes (Matt Welsh) & one or two others were standing on Henry Welsh's porch & stopped some of the Rebel officers and asked for buttons. But two flags were up when they came in the Boro' flag & one at Pearce's book store. The Rebs took both down and trailed one of them thro' the street. Kirk White helped to take down one of them.

Old Barry had Gen Early to dine with him on Sunday & Dr. Nes it is said had some of them in his house nearly all the time. It was his sister waved her handkerchief as they came in town. Some of the Copperheads were very much alarmed, particularly such men as old Dan Hartman & Tom White and other who had considerable property here. Others gave them all the aid & comfort in their power. Reb. officers said they had many sympathizers here; that they could get any information they wanted. One Copperhead, hearing a Union man asked by an officer for a Map of York Co. which was of course refused, volunteered to take him to his house and give him a map. Early was informed by someone who the prominent Union Men were; and they were marked.

The Rebs were not recd at any private house except Barry and Nes's. Philip Small was excessively frightened — in fact I think he was quite demented for a while. When the Rebs made their demand for money & supplies, a meeting was called of the Committee of Safety & it was determined to endeavor to comply with their demand as far as possible; Ward Committees were appointed to collect money, P. A. & S. Small furnished the groceries and flour, and the hatters & Shoemakers were called on for the shoes & hats; with the understanding that the Boro' would assume the debt & repay the money & pay for the supplies. When the Committee came to our house Mr. P. A. Small was with them & represented that they had given all the money they had, that other people were doing the same, that it would be repaid, & that they wanted all the money we had in the house. We had nearly two hundred dollars in the house, and very foolishly gave them one hundred dollars. I found out afterwards that many other people had not given nearly so much in proportion & that some had refused entirely. I suppose the money will be repaid, by the Boro., but an act of the legislature will be necessary and a vote of the Boro. and that will probably take a year to accomplish. The Banks gave most of the money raised (the whole am't the Rebs got in money was $28,600.); some individuals contributed very large sums.

The merchants had sent off most of their goods & places of business were all closed while the rebs were here; in fact several are still closed. No business scarcely has been done here for two weeks.

Ladies, most of them, had the sense to stay at home. The men went about freely. I did not speak to any of the Rebs except once. Others talked to them & questioned them, but I did not feel like it. I heard nothing of Geo. Latimer or Tom. I am glad to say that at our house no one was visible when they came into town. The parlor shutters were bowed and none of us showed ourselves. I thought the conduct of the people in crowding out to see them was disgraceful. Even Philip Small who should have known better allowed his family to stand on his porch to gaze at them.

I think the Rebel visit to this county will have a wholesome effect on the Copperheads. The Rebs made no distinction. The worst Copperhead Townships such as the Codoruses & Dover suffered most heavily in horses. Men who had

joined the "K.G.C." & paid their dollars to learn the signs which were to save their property, found them of no avail.

The facts with regard to the surrender of the Town are these:

A committee of safety had been appointed when the danger first arose. They made some efforts to raise companies to protect the town against cavalry raids & succeeded in raising one. Dr. Palmer had about 200 convalescents in the Hospital and with these, McGowan's Men, a Squad of the 87th & our company there was some idea of making a defence if threatened by a small force of Cavalry. On Saturday afternoon Farquhar went out to meet them & returning reported them advancing in force with cavalry artillery and infantry. Immediately the Hospital soldiers, 87th Men & McGowans Men, were started on the March to Columbia and all idea of defence was abandoned.

The Committee of safety met and passed a resolution to surrender the town. Dave Small (Chief Burgess), Lat. Small, White & one or two others started about seven oclock, went about nine miles to where the Rebs had encamped, had an interview with Gen. Gordon, received an assurance of protection to persons and private property; but made, it is said, no formal surrender. The next day about ten oclock Gordons brigade marched thro' town, and encamped between here and Wrightsville. Early established his head quarters in the Court House; and in a few hours made the demands for money & supplies. Had the demand been refused, I don't believe they would have done any damage. In Gettysburg they made similar demands which were not complied with & no evil consequence followed. I do not believe such large requisitions would have been made had not the Boro' Authorities behaved so sheepishly in regard to the surrender.

I sent you last week the Copperhead account in

an extra from the Gazette office. Hope you read it and the accompanying letter.

I went to Gettysburg on Saturday, reaching there Sunday at noon, to see the battlefield. Did not see much as the dead had been buried and the wounded removed from the field before I got there. Saw a considerable portion of the army, saw Pleasantons Cavalry going thro' the town to follow up the Rebs. Went over part of the field to see how they arranged a line of battle and saw the marks of severe fighting. Returned on Tuesday morning. Had an upset in an omnibus on the way home. No (one) hurt but Hill Hay who got his nose cut. Was introduced to Gen. Howard 11th Corps. He said the Rebs had lost 18000 in all.

Meade also says they lost about the number, and puts our loss at 15000.

It is understood they will run trains thro' from Balto today or tomorrow to York.

Hope they will. Write me."

Yours truly
James W. Latimer[270]

**

Within 20 years of the Civil War's end, those writing about the war were including York businessman and ex-slave William C. Goodridge among the ranks of Underground Railroad agents.

Robert C. Smedley wrote about Goodridge in his 1883 history, History of the Underground Railroad in Chester and the Neighboring Counties of Pennsylvania:

"Whenever he received information that 'baggage' was on the road that it was necessary to hurry through, he sent word to Columbia the day before it was expected to arrive. Cato Jourdon, colored, who drove a team which hauled cars over the bridge, brought all 'baggage' safely across, where the agents had another trusty colored man to receive it. The fugitives were then taken through Black's hotel yard to another portion of town, and concealed overnight; when Wm. Wright, of that place, generally took them in charge and sent some to Daniel Gibbons, and some direct to Philadelphia, in the false end of a box car; owned by Stephen Smith and William Whipper, colored men and lumber merchants of Columbia. They got off at the head of the 'plane,' near Philadelphia, where an agent was in waiting to receive them."[271]

**

General John B. Gordon's autobiography, Reminiscences of the Civil War, includes three notable encounters with women or girls in York County.

The location of the first meeting is not given in his 1903 work. But its description matches that of Jacob Altland's house in western York County's village of Farmers, down to the spring in the basement under the kitchen:

"With an eye to utility, as well as to the health and convenience of his household, he had built his dining-room immediately over this fountain gushing from a cleft in an underlying rock. My camp for the night was near by, and I accepted his invitation to breakfast with him. As I entered the quaint room, one half floored with smooth limestone, and the other half covered with limpid water bubbling clear and pure from the bosom of Mother Earth, my amazement at the singular design was perhaps less pronounced than the sensation of rest which it produced. For many days we had been marching on dusty turnpikes, under a broiling sun, and it is easier to imagine than to describe the feeling of relief and repose which came over me as we sat in that cool room, with a hot breakfast served from one side, while from the other the frugal housewife dipped cold milk and cream from immense jars standing neck-deep in water."

After that meal, Gordon marched unopposed into York where he took down the American flag flying in Centre Square and then headed toward Wrightsville and its coveted bridge.

On East Market Street, he was approached by a girl, believed to be Mary Ann Small. Gordon writes about that encounter in *Reminiscences*:

"As we moved along the street after this episode, a little girl, probably twelve years of age, ran up to my horse and handed me a large bouquet of flowers, in the centre of which was a note, in delicate handwriting, purporting to give the numbers and describe the position of the Union forces of Wrightsville, toward which I was advancing. I carefully read and reread this strange note. It bore no signature, and contained no assurance of sympathy for the Southern cause, but it was so terse and explicit in its terms as to compel my confidence. The second day we were in front of Wrightsville, and from the high ridge on which this note suggested that I halt and examine the position of the Union troops, I eagerly scanned the prospect with my field-glasses, in order to verify the truth of the mysterious communication or detect its misrepresentations. There, in full view before us, was the town, just as described, nestling on the banks of the Susquehanna."

Defending Union forces burned the Susquehanna River bridge stopping his brigade's eastward march, and that fire spread to buildings in Wrightsville.

Gordon's men helped extinguish the blaze and save many homes including that of Mary Jane Magee Rewalt.

For that act, she invited Gordon and several officers to breakfast. Gordon wrote in *Reminiscences* that he tested Mrs. Rewalt about her sympathy with the North or South:

"She was too brave to evade it, too self-poised to be confused by it, and too firmly fixed in her convictions to hesitate as to the answer. With no one present except Confederate soldiers who were her guests, she replied, without a quiver in her voice, but with womanly gentleness: 'General Gordon, I fully comprehend you, and it is due to myself that I candidly tell you that I am a Union woman. I cannot afford to be misunderstood, nor to have you misinterpret this simple courtesy. You and your soldiers last night saved my home from burning, and I was unwilling that you should go away without receiving some token of my appreciation. I must tell you, however, that, with my assent and approval, my husband is a soldier in the Union army, and my constant prayer to Heaven is that our cause may triumph and the Union be saved. No Confederate left that room without a feeling of profound respect, of unqualified admiration, for that brave and worthy woman."[272]

**

A delegation of ladies from Lancaster volunteered to travel to the distant Gettysburg battlefield to aid wounded soldiers being treated at a myriad of temporary field hospitals in and around the badly battered borough.

The women began their day in Columbia, where they arranged for a boat to ferry them across the broad Susquehanna River because the Union militia had burned the Columbia Bridge.

One of the writers left her impressions of their brief pause in Wrightsville and then a longer-than-planned sojourn in York:

"The morning sun rose in a clear cloudless sky, and the beauty of this noble river never seemed so resplendent. Five o'clock found us at the appointed place, together with many others who had been there the day before, besides large accessions of new arrivals. Fortunately our horses were put on the flat and ourselves in the carriages on the boat. There we ate our breakfast, waited four long hours, and arrived at Wrightsville at ten o'clock.

As soon as we entered the place, we saw traces of our unwelcome guests; a large house near the bridge was destroyed, and in passing through the main street, we saw many houses perforated by shot and shell. All around were rifle-pits thrown up, and there were many signs of war. But after leaving Wrightsville, (though the entire distance was traversed by the foe) there were no depredations committed, not even a rail from any of the fences disturbed, showing the strict discipline under which they were kept, while in this part of the State.

Not however, on account of any regard for us, as one of their Generals asserted while at York; but they knew that if they relaxed their discipline, their army would become so demoralized, that they would lose all control of it. It was twelve o'clock when we arrived at York, where we met some friends returning from the battlefield, who gave us much valuable information as to what we would require. The most pressing want seemed to be tin-ware, wash basins, tin cups, etc., which of course we immediately procured.

Here we dined, and though York had anything but an enviable reputation during the raid, yet we must bear testimony to the loyalty and kind hospitality of Mr. Alfred Gartman, who, though an entire stranger to most of us, gave us a warm welcome, and a dinner, which in after days, when we were our own cooks and when our store rooms were not always luxuriously supplied, we looked back upon with longing eye?

The day had become excessively hot; and we found that if we went through to Gettysburg, we would arrive there at night, which would be very undesirable; so we accepted Mr. Slagel's kind invitation, and found a cordial welcome to one of the loveliest spots and one of the kindest Christian homes that can be met with anywhere. Mrs. Myers and Mrs. Slagel were unremitting in their attentions, not only during our stay with them, but while at the Hospital, supplying our table every week with the best their farm afforded.

We arose invigorated by a good night's rest, and with a solemn feeling pervading our hearts, of the responsibilities of our undertaking and the nearness of our duties. We felt that God had so far smiled upon us, and would not now desert us, and that in His strength we would go forth.

All around was in the height of summer beauty; the birds sang in the clear morning sky, and the stately hills looked down on orchards laden with their crimson fruit. Though late in the season, the harvest was just yielding to the sickle. All here was beauty, quietness and peace, whilst all beyond was desolation, destruction and war. Here we listened to the sweet songs of birds, whilst within a few miles, the air was laden with shrieks of the wounded and groans of the dying."[273]

**

Mary Cadwell Fisher came to York as a teacher but became a seasoned nurse as thousands of wounded Union soldiers flooded the U.S. Army General Hospital at Penn Common in York.

As this account from the Philadelphia Times on Jan. 9, 1883, indicates, those experiences in hospital wards ill prepared her and other York volunteers for the carnage greeting them after fighting stopped at the battlefield in Gettysburg:

"It was impossible for one who lived in the sections of the country remote from the seat of war to realize the meaning of life in the Border States in that time that tried the souls of all men and wrung with anguish the hearts of the devoted women both North and South. Unprotected by military force, with no natural barrier between the seceding and the loyal States, the exaggerated rumors and the constant suspense were appalling in the early days of the deadly struggle.

But soon familiarized to the life we became indifferent to danger, and with the advent of the summer campaign sent away our plate and valuables and calmly awaited whatever might come to us in the fortunes of war. We devoted ourselves to preparing supplies for the Sanitary Corps and to hospital work, which alike filled our hearts with compassion and our hands with labor.

Situated but a few miles from the border, the sick and wounded were often sent to us directly from the field, giving most forcible impressions of the revolting results of every battle; but vivid as those scenes were they paled into insignificance in the presence of the actual battle ground, as I saw it at Gettysburg, immediately after the great combat.

On the morning of Saturday, July 4, 1863, came the glorious news of our victorious arms and of the retreat of the enemy toward the border. We learned that by afternoon supplies could be forwarded to our army. About 3 p.m., I started with two ladies and my oldest son in a two-horse wagon loaded with necessaries of every kind.

About 7 a.m., we reached the first hospital ground. I thought before this that I had learned all the horrors of warfare inside the walls of our crowded hospitals and from the continually passing trains of wounded, bleeding men to whom we carried food and stimulants, as they were on their to distant points. It was a frequent occurrence to receive a telegram announcing hours at which a train would arrive with hundreds of sufferers who would stop to be fed; often coming directly from the fighting ground, the cars dripping with blood from undressed

wounds. Our citizens never failed to respond, laden with coffee, soup and bread.

But here a new revelation of the brutality of war was presented to my eyes. No imagination could paint the picture in that wood. I instinctively recoiled from the sight. Grouped beneath the trees we saw about five hundred men, the wounded from the first day's battle, who had hastily been removed beyond fighting limits. There were lying upon the bare ground, some of them literally half buried in mud. With no shelter, wounded, chilled, starving and racked with pain, how they welcomed us as we carried food and reviving cordial."[274]

**

Several York County physicians were among the relief workers who spent weeks in the makeshift field hospitals, often treating patients in such rudimentary settings as barns and carriage houses.

Medical students contributed as assistants. Robert Beniak Gemmill Jr. was one of those doctors-in-training who went through this trial by fire.

He was one of seven children of a former York County commissioner and grew up on a prosperous farm at Round Hill in Hopewell Township.

In 1864, he graduated from the University of Pennsylvania and then practiced medicine in Pennsgrove, New Jersey, for a year until failing health compelled him to return to York. He died in October 1868. He was only 27 years old.

He is buried in the Stewartstown Presbyterian Cemetery.

Gemmill left a handwritten account of his first impressions of the aftermath of the savage fighting at Gettysburg:

"My esteemed friends who have never witnessed the scene, I would humbly beg of you your feelings and sympathies while I narrate to you a few of my observations on Sunday the 5th while strolling over the blood-stained hills of Gettysburg.

Oh! could the uninterested, the unconcerned, the hardhearted, trace the footsteps of our brave and gallant men over the battlefield, without having his energies, his sympathies, aroused to the highest pitch of exasperation, to think that men high minded, weak in the eyes of their maker will still persist in such abominable, such degraded vices, that are calculated to disgrace any nation, but especially the one which other nations envy and seek to destroy, and which we should be proud of and pray that Almighty God would spare his vengeance and not destroy us from off the face of the earth.

Passing on toward the scene of action our attention was first directed to the desolated country of Adams county; and what was that compared to the state of Virginia, the fences, the grain destroyed. But they should be thankful that their dwellings were not consumed and villages fired, as they had been by our army in other states.

If we only had the assurance that this would be the last battle fought in Pennsylvania no doubt the loss would not be felt so heavily but the idea of this state being the battle ground for the summer is disagreeable to imagine. Still I think some reflection is to be cast upon our state officers. We have responded to every call of the President and Governor, and now we stand with more troops in the field than any other state in proportion to her population.

But, now, when an invasion is made into our own state and we are left to the merciless hand of the enemy. This very great act will make our own men feel an unwillingness to respond any longer to the Administration if our own state is not protected from the ravages of the enemy. Other states saw us in our weakness and sent us aid. We should thank them for their hearty response.

The first hospital we visited was filled very full with the wounded. After delivering our 'paroum doum' to the surgeon we passed around the room and there lay some apparently dead, moaning and weeping with all kinds of wounds and amputation. A writer has well said the sweetest words in the English language are Home, Mother, and Heaven. I heard many say, 'If I were only Home,' 'If I were only Home,' but the poor fellows would never be able to reach their earthly home.

But still there were some that still remembered the Sabbath day. Two were lying on their beds of straw with Testaments in hand reading the word of God. But sad were their physical abilities, their limbs amputated, and the fractures adjusted, very likely they would make an early recovery.

We passed on to the Fifth Army Corps in which the 93rd Reg. P.V. Having some acquaintances in it I was able to visit all their tents. The first poor sufferer that met my gaze was a slender young man who lay on the ground with nothing more but the sky for his mantle and knapsack for a pillow since the battle. He was shot in the breast and the ball had not been dislodged. His comrades that were watching him to sink in the repose of death told me that he had been dying since the day before and just before he died he rose up and told them his late words as I was assisting the surgeon in reporting his division, the dispatch was carried to me of his death.

Another poor fellow was shot in the head and he too was at the threshold of the dark valley and shadow of death. He was perfectly wild, maniacal. He had torn the clothes from off his person and it was enough to melt the hardest heart to tears to see how he was struggling with death.

Numbers of instances of this kind were there, and hundreds much worse. The time passed very slowly to them. They were so delirious and in such a state of coma that they were not conscious whether it was morning or evening.

But the saddest sight was on the field where the battle was fought. It was there I thought of the loved ones who had gone from paternal roofs with the expectation of returning to see their friends again. But, oh! alas they have fallen, and are sleeping in their last resting place, and their friends will not be able to find where they have fallen.

They were not home to receive the farewell kisses of their fathers, mothers, brothers and sisters, when about to be conveyed to the church yard. But right among the din of battle their grave was dug and thrown in as if the wild brutes of creation with no kind friend to mark where they were placed.

But finding the Federals all buried, we passed over a little farther and here lay the Confederates in the bleaching sun with the rocks for their pillows and the sky for a covering while their comrades were not permitted to come, and throw a little clay over their decaying bodies. It was considered treasonable language there to utter one word of sympathy for them, but I could not express my deepest feelings for them as well as for our own men. They too, were away from home and their dead bodies not permitted to be conveyed thither. Yes, the 'Johnny Rebs' as they are termed, received no attention until ours were cared for.

Could any enlightened person that has any regard for the preservation of life have a desire that the iniquitous war should be waged any longer? I know that it is considered treason for peace men to speak but can any intelligent man that knows the stretch of Southern Confederacy and how well they are disciplined, have any hope of making peace by the sword. We might as well try to dam up the waters of the Nile as to subdue the South by force of arms.

It will be just as President Lincoln said in his message of '62, that after much fighting and great loss of life on both sides, we will then have to resort to measures of treaty.

May he who holds the destinies of all nations in his grasp not blot us out of existence. But wilt thou in thine own good way bring back the order and love that once existed amongst us, and as we have been a proud and haughty people, forgive our sins and give us grace that we may live uprightly and obey the commandments of God and man."[275]

**

Lieutenant Robert I. Boyington of the 105th Pennsylvania "Wildcats" was shot and badly wounded at Gettysburg.

In late autumn 1863, he became a patient in York's sprawling military hospital.

He later wrote in his journal:

"About the 1st of Nov. 1863 the Letterman Gen'l hospital was entirely evacuated. I was among the last of the wounded to be removed and as the surgeon advised I be taken to the nearest hospital, Little York was decided on.

As a commissioned officer I knew I would have to pay my way in the hospital, or out of it, so 2 days before I was to be moved Capt. Sam'l McHenry who had been shot through the upper right lung who was with us but able to be around, went to Little York with Mary, where they succeeded in securing a fine large front room near the Gen. hospital on George St., and also board with a fine Pa. dutch family, Jno. Swartz by name. The family consisted of father, mother, 2 grown girls and a younger, Anna, about 12 years old and one boy, the youngest of the

147

family.

One thing I want to note is, the Rebel wounded and sick received the same treatment, the same rations and in every way the same care that I and all the other Union soldiers received, that almost every day they received visits from southern ladies or at least by women who were in sympathy with them and their cause and these same women took pains to express their hatred and disdain in look and language of everything northern and were particularly venomous when in contact with our northern ladies, yet they were allowed the same courtesy and priviledges accorded our own.

Surgeon Gen. Palmer, who was in charge of the Little York hospital, called on us the next day and told me not to employ a surgeon that he had several that didn't have enough to do to keep them busy and that he would detail one of them to attend to Capt. McHenry and myself and Surgeon Purcell of Indiana was appointed. He came down from the hospital to attend us once a day and oftener when it was necessary. He was a competent surgeon and an interesting talker. He would often remain with us a half day at a time and said he was very fortunate to get the appointment. The surgeon Gen. had assured us that there would be no charges made for his services.

Purcell thought we ought to have something to do to amuse us and so break the monotony of our confinement, as he was an expert chess player, he proposed that we learn the game under this tutorage. This, wife and I had done and soon became quite proficient players and it did indeed help us greatly to while away the lonely days and he would stop and play the game for hours with us.

Our landlord wove fancy bed spreads and made cigars of which last, the Dr. was very fond and as I had a box always open. He helped himself whenever he had occasion to smoke. We also received a great many visitors, men and women who lived in the city, who had done all they could to brighten the hours and cause us to forget our isolated condition, but in spite of all, a hungering desire was with us all the time for home and home friends."[276]

**

The Rev. Henry E. Niles was new to the pulpit of York's Presbyterian church when he was called upon to deliver the sermon at the community service on April 19, 1865, commemorating slain President Abraham Lincoln.

Excerpts from his long address follow:

"This is an occasion without parallel. For the first time the business of our whole people is suspended on a bright, sunny vernal day, and badges of mourning are everywhere displayed, and the great heart of a mighty nation weeps because of its murdered head! True, Death has often in been in our high places, and wide-spread sorrow has been felt when we learned that his skeleton foot had stalked the President's floor. But, never before was the hand of violence raised against the man whom our American people delighted most to honor. Never before did the assassin's bullet accomplish such a far-reaching, irrevocable, dreadful result.

And now, as the funeral train at Washington is about to move, hark to the sobs of agony, which, bursting from the rocky shores of New England, are borne along over Ontario's and Erie's waters, and well down the Ohio and Mississippi to the crescent city of the Gulf! Hark! To that mighty dirge of the Atlantic, to which so many millions of hearts beat solemn measure, as it peals across the Hudson, over the Alleghanies and the Rocky mountains, until it breaks in a solemn wail of grief on the golden shores of the Pacific: — While fair young Illinois, pale with weeping, stretches out her arms to receive to her bosom, the mangled corpse of her most favored son, whose glory will make her name illustrious, and whose ashes will make her soil a shrine for liberty's pilgrims, through all the ages to come!

This day shall be forever sacred in the calendar of our nation. It is, as though there was 'not a house in the land, where is not one dead.' This day, when a mighty nation is bowed as by one common impulse of sorrow and shame, shall be remembered as the beginning of increased Union and Loyalty and Fidelity to the truth. Around the coffin of our martyred President, shall a loyal people join hands... in holy league of eternal enmity against that Treason whose root is slavery, and whose horrid fruit is war, starvation, savage butchery and cold blooded murder!

Today, shall they pledge themselves anew, amid the music of funeral hymns, to stand by and uphold by their influence, their prayer, their property, and, if need be, their lives, the government of these United States by whomever administered; trusting in the President of the Universe, our fathers' God, to guide us safely through this whirlwind of confusion and over this sea of blood, into the fair haven of an honorable, a lasting and a glorious Peace."[277]

Fawn Township's John Aquilla Wilson, right, and an unidentified Civil War veteran flank a Lincoln impersonator in this photo from York County Heritage Trust files. Wilson enlisted in the 32nd Regiment, United States Colored Troops, in 1864, one of dozens of York County blacks to wear the blue Union uniform in the Civil War.

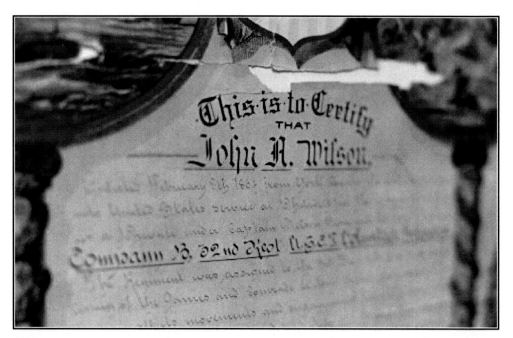

John Aquilla Wilson, 32nd Regiment, USCT, was discharged at Hilton Head, South Carolina, on Aug. 22, 1865. His granddaughter, Isabella Phillips, of Chanceford Township, said Quil Wilson did not talk much about the war. "He was a good Christian man," she said. He is buried in Fawn A.M.E. Cemetery near Gatchellville in southeastern York County. Isabella Phillips made these discharge papers available to the *York Daily Record/Sunday News.*

Henry Schultz of the 87th Pennsylvania was a Spring Garden Township farmer before the war. He was disabled by a gunshot wound in both legs. Photographs of Henry Schultz come from descendant David F. Spangler.

Young Henry Schultz is shown in the 1850s with his mother Mary (Ferree) Schultz. Henry lived to be 96, and was one of the last members of the 87th Pennsylvania to pass away.

Taken at the 75th anniversary of the Battle of Gettysburg, Henry Schultz is on the right, age 95. President Franklin Roosevelt was the featured speaker at the dedication of the Peace Memorial.

Afterword

Green, untested Union troops dressed in blue assembled in York soon after Confederate forces in South Carolina fired the first shots of the Civil War.

York sat in a prime spot in the North.

Steam-powered trains on the Northern Central Railway stopped in York to take on water, and the borough was close to Southern battlefields.

In fact, so many troops arrived in York that quarters at the old York Fairgrounds and other public accommodations overflowed.

York-area residents opened their homes to relieve the strain.

Judge Robert J. Fisher and his wife, Mary, were among those residents.

The Fisher home on East Market Street already bustled. The widower had married Mary Sophia Cadwell in 1853, and children from both marriages were in the household. A unit of Hanover men particularly appreciated their quarters in the Fisher house and others around town.

They met in special session at the courthouse — the judge's domain — just down Market Street from the Fisher residence.

M.F. Mulgrew, one of the Hanover men, resolved:

"That the Hon. R.J. Fisher and his accomplished lady are entitled to the gratitude and lasting remembrance of every soldier from Hanover for their hospitality at their own house, and their extreme kindness in procuring the best quarters in the county, for the soldiers of York and Adams."

**

There was then a bit of excitement in some quarters of York early in the war, a kind of naive energy that often springs forth at the start of wars and dissipates when blood starts flowing.

The welcome offered to those raw recruits came in contrast to a front verging on panic two years later.

Then, 6,000-plus Confederates marched into the county, occupied a surrendered York, and sent a brigade to the banks of the Susquehanna River. The Rebel raid meant physical and mental trauma.

Ditto for the impact of J.E.B. Stuart's Rebel cavalry charge into the tail of the Union column in Hanover and his subsequent 5,000-man ride through the heart of York County in a bid to find commanding General Robert E. Lee.

Fighting in Hanover and Wrightsville caused an estimated 300 casualties. Civilians lost money, food, supplies, and workhorses.

York County lost honor for surrendering the town, an undefended victim without the will or the means to fight back.

But what about the impact of the war after Lee's surrender at Appomattox?

The war distressed and even degraded York County, but did it in some bittersweet way cause York countians to grow as a people?

Did it produce anything of value?

Would the generosity of the Fishers and other townspeople be forgotten?

At the beginning of this 150th anniversary of the Civil War, it's time we explore those county contributions.

**

Indeed, the war left an indelible impression in the hearts and minds and bodies of York countians and their community:

• A link can be made between the U.S. Army General Hospital at Penn Common and York Hospital's opening in 1880.

The venerable Small family in York supported the military hospital — where 14,000 wounded Civil War soldiers were treated — as nurses and in other roles. Samuel Small, one of the family's patriarchs, founded York Hospital in 1880 at a site near where the military hospital once stood.

Some of the physicians who worked in the military hospital served on the staff of the fledgling hospital, their skills honed in their military work. Dr. A.R. Blair, York Hospital's first consulting physician, and Dr. James Kerr, first consulting surgeon, labored at the military hospital.

Dr. W.S. Roland, the first president of the hospital board, performed physicals for men entering the Union army.

• The Civil War placed the spotlight on organized York-area women's community service groups.

Isabel Small spearheaded the York-area women's efforts to provide aid to soldiers.

The women established an organization to recruit others, and the Ladies Soldiers Aid Society was formed.

Female volunteers met in a large room set aside at P.A. & S. Small's Centre Square store.

Isabel Small made that happen. She was the wife of "S." — Samuel Small.

There, women and children sorted donated garments, sewed new clothing, and wound clean bandages.

Farmers opened trunks carried with them across the Atlantic to equip the women with linen to make dressings for wounds.

A similar organization formed in Hanover, particularly aided in the makeshift hospital set up in the Pleasant Hill Hotel after the awful battle in Hanover.

Mark A. Snell has researched pre-Civil War women's service organizations in York.

"Antebellum York must have been very active socially, at least from a white man's point of view," Snell wrote in his 1987 master's thesis, "A Northern Community Goes to War."

For example, York hosted one Masonic and three Odd Fellow lodges, five volunteer fire companies, two benevolence associations, a male temperance society, a mechanics order, and a YMCA, he wrote.

But borough directories of that day did not list any women's charitable, voluntary, or temperance societies. Snell came up with no evidence of any women's associations from county newspapers or church records.

Still, women's service organizations operated before the war, even if outside the official radar.

The Dorcas Society, for example, sponsored a fair in 1830 that included the exhibition of an early American Christmas tree.

York County's Scott Butcher has written that the Dorcas Society of York was an "Association of Ladies" founded around 1820 for the "truly charitable purpose of clothing the poor widow and the friendless orphan."

The terrible war drew attention to how kind York County women worked in concert to nurse thousands of casualties.

• The war claimed untold hundreds of York County fighting men. This and other wartime family disruptions created the need for an orphanage.

The Small family led the movement in 1865 to form the Children's Home of York. Two years later, these youngsters had a new home: a four-story red brick building at East Philadelphia and Pine streets.

After the war, the home broadened its mission to accommodate youngsters from broken homes and otherwise in need.

The Children's Home would house more than 3,000 children to the time of its demolition in 1973, and it continues in newer quarters east of York today.

• The war tore at the community and cultural fabric of York County. But perhaps it was a woven rug that needed a good beating.

In *Faith and Family: Pennsylvania German Heritage in York County Area Fraktur*, June Lloyd observes that many members of the county's dominant German population marched off to war. They saw other places and met other people.

"They were no longer Germans who could get along speaking 'Dutch,'" she wrote, "they were Americans, and their lives could depend on their ability to communicate with fellow soldiers."

The world — and York County — would never be the same.

The material and supplies needed to run a war stoked the growth of Northern factories.

"Young men left their small communities," Lloyd wrote, "to work alongside others in factories."

**

Those seeking to justify the surrender of York to the Rebels in late June 1863 point out that the borough was, in fact, not burned, as General Jubal Early had threatened. An intact city with good rail and road transportation was ready for the postwar Industrial Revolution.

From this point of view, cutting a surrender deal with the Confederates — some would argue the devil dressed in gray — was an investment that paid off handsomely.

The surrender became part of a community battle after the fighting stopped in Gettysburg. Proponents and foes of the deal with the Rebel command formed battle lines.

That battle raged in unsettled silence until relatively recently.

Today, on this 150th anniversary of the Civil War, historians are increasingly writing about the Civil War and probing the surrender decision, an act that relegated the Civil War to third chair behind the American Revolution and World War II, whose heroes York County commemorates with music.

**

This major anniversary provides a moment for York County to recognize the effects, often for the better, coming from this most deadly of all American wars.

In writing about the Civil War in his book *Patterns of Our Past*, Tom Schaefer observed

154

that many residents hung their heads in shame or turned their backs in contempt when the Confederates approached.

Others cheered and aided the Rebels.

"It was not York County's finest moment," he wrote.

No, it wasn't.

But ironically, the raw and brutal Civil War spawned many fine moments.[278]

James McClure
York Township
York County, Pennsylvania

Chronology

1860

Nov. 6 — Abraham Lincoln is elected U.S. president, gaining 180 of 303 electoral votes and 40 percent of the popular vote. York countians cast more votes for his opponents than for Lincoln.

Dec. 20 — South Carolina secedes from the Union. Mississippi, Florida, Alabama, Georgia, Louisiana and Texas soon follow.

1861

Feb. 9 — The Confederate States of America forms with Jefferson Davis as president.

March 4 — Lincoln is sworn in as 16th president of the United States.

April 12 — Confederates open fire upon Fort Sumter in Charleston, South Carolina. The Civil War begins.

April 15 — Lincoln calls for 75,000 volunteers. Fighting men from the York Rifles and Worth Infantry respond to a call for guards against saboteurs along the Northern Central Railway, linking York and Baltimore.

April 17 — Virginia secedes from the Union, followed within weeks by Arkansas, Tennessee, and North Carolina. An 11-state Confederacy forms.

April 20 — Robert E. Lee resigns from the U.S. Army and goes to the Confederate capital of Richmond, Virginia, accepting command of military and naval forces there.

July 4 — Congress authorizes a call for 500,000 men. By this time, thousands of Union soldiers are training at the old York Fairgrounds in preparation for orders to move to the South.

July 21 — The Union army suffers a stunning defeat at Bull Run. Confederate General Thomas J. Jackson earns the nickname "Stonewall" as his brigade resists Union attacks.

July 27 — Lincoln appoints George B. McClellan as commander of the Army of the Potomac.

1862

Feb. 6 — General Ulysses S. Grant achieves victory in Tennessee, capturing Fort Henry and, 10 days later, Fort Donelson.

March 8-9 — The Confederate ironclad *Virginia* (formerly the USS *Merrimac*) sinks two wooden Union ships and battles the ironclad *Monitor* to a draw off Norfolk, Virginia.

March — The Peninsula Campaign begins as McClellan's army advances from Washington, D.C., to the peninsula south of Richmond, then begins an advance toward the Confederate capital.

April 6-7 — Confederate surprise attacks on Grant's troops at Shiloh on the Tennessee River result in a bitter struggle with 13,000 Union soldiers killed and wounded. The rebels suffer 10,000 casualties.

April 24 — Seventeen Union ships under the command of David Farragut take New Orleans, an important Southern port. York County native Johnson Kelly Duncan is a key Confederate commander in the battle.

June 25-July 1 — The Seven Days Battle begins as Lee attacks McClellan near Richmond, resulting in heavy losses for both armies. McClellan withdraws toward Washington.

July 11 — After four months as his own general-in-chief, Lincoln hands over the task to General Henry W. Halleck.

Aug. 29-30 — Confederates under Generals Stonewall Jackson and James Longstreet defeat 75,000 Union troops under General John Pope at the Second Battle of Bull Run.

Sept. 4-9 — Lee invades the North, heading for Harpers Ferry in western Virginia, 50 miles northwest of Washington.

Sept. 17 — York County prepares for possible invasion. McClellan's Union forces stop Lee's army at Antietam Creek in Maryland in the bloodiest day in U.S. military history, resulting in 26,000 casualties. Lee withdraws to Virginia. Physicians at York's military hospital, opened in late June at Penn Park, treat hundreds of those casualties.

Sept. 22 — Lincoln issues a Preliminary Emancipation Proclamation freeing all slaves in territories held by Confederates.

Dec. 13 — General Ambrose E. Burnside's Union Army of the Potomac suffers a costly defeat at Fredericksburg in Virginia with a loss of 12,653 men after 14 assaults on well-entrenched rebels.

1863

Jan. 1 — Lincoln issues the final Emancipation Proclamation and emphasizes enlistment of black soldiers in the Union army.

Jan. 25 — The president appoints General Joseph ("Fighting Joe") Hooker as commander of the Army of the Potomac, replacing Burnside.

Jan. 29 — U.S. Grant receives orders to capture Vicksburg, Mississippi.

March 3 — The U.S. Congress enacts a draft, covering male citizens ages 20 to 45, but also exempts those who pay $300 or provide a substitute.

May 1-4 — Hooker's army is decisively defeated by Lee's much smaller force at the Battle of Chancellorsville in Virginia.

June 3 — Lee launches his second invasion of the North, heading toward Pennsylvania in a campaign that will soon lead to Gettysburg.

June 13-15 – Confederate troops rout Union forces in the Second Battle of Winchester, opening the way through the Shenandoah Valley to Pennsylvania. York County's 87th Pennsylvania is among the defeated defenders.

June 27 — Confederate soldiers, part of General Jubal Early's division, step onto York County soil. Elijah White's Comanches moved through Hanover and Jefferson to the rail and communications center of Hanover Junction. York's fathers surrender the town to General John B. Gordon in Farmers, west of York.

June 28 — Lincoln appoints General George G. Meade as commander of the Army of the Potomac, replacing Hooker. Early's division invades York. Union militia burn the Columbia Bridge to keep Gordon's Georgia Brigade from crossing the Susquehanna River.

June 30 — Lee recalls Early's division from York County, part of a concentration of rebel forces in Adams County. In Hanover, Union forces stop Jeb Stuart's horsemen from rejoining Lee's army in a major cavalry battle on the town's streets.

July 1-3 — The tide of war turns against the South as the Confederates are defeated at Gettysburg.

July 4 — Vicksburg, the last rebel stronghold on the Mississippi River, surrenders to Grant after a six-week siege, splitting the Confederacy in two.

July 18 — Black troops of the 54th Massachusetts Infantry under Colonel Robert G. Shaw assault rebels at Fort Wagner, South Carolina. Shaw and half of the 600 men in his regiment, some from York and Lancaster counties, are casualties.

Oct. 16 — Lincoln appoints Grant to command all operations in the Western Theater.

Nov. 18 — Lincoln stops at Hanover Junction and Hanover en route to Gettysburg. He jokes with the crowds.

Nov. 19 — Lincoln delivers a two-minute Gettysburg Address at a ceremony dedicating the battlefield as a national cemetery.

Nov. 23-25 — The Rebel siege of Chattanooga ends as Grant's Union forces defeat Braxton Bragg's army.

1864

March 9 — Lincoln appoints Grant to command all of the armies of the United States. General William T. Sherman succeeds Grant as commander in the west.

May 4 — A massive, coordinated campaign involving all the Union armies begins. In Virginia, Grant advances toward Richmond to engage Lee's Army of Northern Virginia. In the west, Sherman moves toward Atlanta to engage Joseph E. Johnston's Army of Tennessee.

June 3 — A costly mistake by Grant results in 7,000 Union casualties in 20 minutes during an offensive at Cold Harbor, Virginia.

June 15 — Union forces miss an opportunity to capture Petersburg, south of Richmond, and cut off Confederate rail lines. As a result, Grant's forces begin a nine-month siege.

July 9 — Early's drive to seize Washington,

D.C., is delayed for a day by Union forces near Frederick, Maryland. York County's 87th Pennsylvania plays a key role in the Battle of Monocacy.

July 20 — At Atlanta, Sherman's forces battle the rebels now under the command of General John B. Hood, who replaced Johnston.

July 31 — Early orders a raid on Chambersburg, 60 miles west of York, resulting in the torching of 500 structures in that town. York County prepares for another Confederate invasion, as refugees reach the town, but Early's detachment returns south.

Aug. 29 — Democrats nominate McClellan for president to run against Lincoln.

Sept. 2 — Sherman's army captures Atlanta. The victory helps Lincoln's bid for re-election.

Oct. 19 — Union cavalry General Philip H. Sheridan scores a decisive victory in the Shenandoah Valley over Early's troops.

Nov. 8 — Lincoln is re-elected, carrying all but three states with 55 percent of the popular vote and 212 of 233 electoral votes. The Southern states did not participate. McClellan easily carries York County.

Nov. 15 — After destroying Atlanta's warehouses and railroad facilities, Sherman, with 62,000 men, begins his "March to the Sea."

Dec. 21 — Sherman reaches Savannah, Georgia, leaving behind a path of destruction 300 miles long, all the way from Atlanta.

1865

Jan. 31 — Congress approves the 13th Amendment to the U.S. Constitution, to abolish slavery.

March 4 — Lincoln participates in inauguration

ceremonies in Washington.

March 25 — The last offensive for Lee's Army of Northern Virginia begins with a doomed attack on the center of Grant's forces at Petersburg.

April 2 — Grant's troops break through Lee's lines at Petersburg. Richmond is evacuated.

April 4 — Lincoln tours Richmond, where he enters the Confederate White House.

April 9 — Lee surrenders his Confederate army to Grant at Appomattox Court House in Virginia.

April 14 — The Stars and Stripes is raised with ceremony over Fort Sumter. Lincoln and his wife, Mary, see a play at Ford's Theater. John Wilkes Booth shoots the president in the head.

April 15 — Lincoln dies in the morning. Vice President Andrew Johnson assumes the presidency. York County joins the rest of the nation in mourning, and York churches later hold a memorial service at First Presbyterian Church.

April 18 — Johnston surrenders to Sherman near Durham in North Carolina.

April 21 — As part of a national tour, Lincoln's funeral train passes in York County, stopping at York and then proceeding to Harrisburg.

April 26 — Booth, who attended a York school as a youth, is shot and killed in a tobacco barn in Virginia. York native Ned Spangler is implicated in the assassination, charged with holding the reigns of Booth's horse while the assassin was inside the theater. He is convicted and imprisoned.

May — Remaining Confederate forces surrender. The nation reunites as the Civil War ends. More than 620,000 Americans died in the war.
May 4 — Lincoln is laid to rest in Oak Ridge Cemetery, outside Springfield, Illinois.

Dec. 6 — The 13th Amendment, passed by Congress on Jan. 31, 1865, is ratified. Slavery is abolished.[279]

This undated photo shows Civil War veterans from the Mount Wolf and Manchester areas. Emelyn Blymire, owner of this photograph, identified the following, from left: No. 1, Jacob Smith; No. 7, Jacob Kunkle; No. 10, ? Bare; and No. 11, Zebulon Pike Rodes, Emelyn Blymire's relative.

After the battle ended, York countians began heading west to visit Gettysburg. Initially, the trips were largely to provide medical help. Later, Gettysburg became a draw for excursions. In this undated photograph, members of York County's Yeagley family are seen on such a visit. The date of 1898 is detectable at the base of the monument honoring Union General John F. Reynolds. The monument appears to be under construction. The visitors in this photograph from *Builders and Heroes*, from left, Dr. John H. Yeagley; Finley Torrens, related to the Yeagleys by marriage; Dilbert Yeagley, a Kansas farmer and John's brother; and Dr. Henry Yeagley, John's father.

U.S. Grant gets the center stage of the 50th anniversary program cover for the 87th Pennsylvania, made up most of soldiers from York and Adams counties. Colonel J.W. Schall was listed as president of the reunion. The Colonial Hotel, on the southwest corner of York's Centre Square, offered a menu that started with "bean soup, army style" and ended with coffee and cigars.

160

Ninety-three-year-old Civil War veteran William H. Gilbert visits the Lincoln Memorial during his 1935 trip to Washington, D.C., where he met President Franklin D. Roosevelt. Earlier that day he sat for an interview with NBC in a nationwide radio broadcast. Photo courtesy of granddaughter Martha Fellenbaum.

Civil War veterans, including William H. Gilbert, pose for a photographer in front of the Grand Army of the Republic's meeting place. Gilbert was one of the last of the more than 2,000 men who served in the 87th Pennsylvania Infantry. Photo courtesy of granddaughter Martha Fellenbaum.

ENDNOTES

Chapter 1

[1] Jezierski, John V., *Enterprising Image: The Goodridge Brothers, African American Photographers, 1847-1922.* (Detroit: Wayne State University Press, 2000), 18-19.

[2] McClure, James, *Almost Forgotten: A Glimpse at Black History in York County, Pa.* (York, Pa.: York Daily Record, 2002), 21; York County Heritage Trust files.

[3] Spangler, Edward Webster, *My Little War Experience: With Historical Sketches and Memorabilia.* (York, Pa.: York Daily Publishing Co., 1904), 10-11.

[4] Harry I. Gladfelter manuscript, Casper Glattfelder Association of America. Courtesy of Dr. Charles Glatfelter.

[5] Phebe Angeline Smith to Most Cherished Sister (Ruth Walker Bloom), June 26, 1863. Courtesy of James W. Brown.

[6] *York Gazette*, April 18, 1861. Collection of the York County Heritage Trust (YCHT).

[7] Spangler, *My Little War Experience*, 15; Snell, Mark A., "If They Would Know What I Know It Would Be Pretty Hard to Raise One Company': Recruiting, the Draft, and Society's Response in York County, Pennsylvania, 1861-1865," in *Union Soldiers and the Northern Home Front: Wartime Experiences, Postwar Adjustments*, edited by Paul A. Cimbala and Randall M. Miller. (New York: Fordham University Press, 2002), 74: *Hanover Spectator*, May 10, 1861.

[8] W.P. Karr to Dear Sir (Milton Ruby), May 22, 1861. Courtesy of Joseph Brillhart.

[9] Journal of the York First Moravian Church, April 1861, microfilm at YCHT.; *York Gazette*, April 18, 1861.

[10] Krepps, John T., *A Strong and Sudden Onslaught: The Cavalry Action at Hanover, Pennsylvania.* (Orrtanna, Pa.: Colecraft Books, 2008), 15; Anthony, William, *Anthony's History of the Battle of Hanover.* (Hanover, Pa.: Self-published, 1945), 144.

[11] David Givens biography, http://www.reocities.com/43rdpa/bios/givensd.html. Courtesy of descendant Benjamin M. Givens, Jr.

[12] Joseph W. Ilgenfritz to Dear Brother (Samuel Ilgenfritz), July 17, 1861. Courtesy of James W. Brown.

[13] *Columbia Spy*, May 19, 1866. Collection of the Lancaster County Historical Society (LCHS).

[14] Neubaum, Victor A., *Our Boys: Northern York County in the Civil War.* (Dillsburg, Pa.: s. n., 1989). 7-9.

[15] Farquhar, Arthur Briggs, "The Heart of America," in *McClure's*, Vol. 54, No. 2, April 1922, 111.

[16] McClure, James, *East of Gettysburg: A Gray Shadow Crosses York County, Pa.* (York, Pa.: York Daily Record/York County Heritage Trust.), 16.

[17] *Philadelphia Times*, Vol. VI, No. 44, 1883; McClure, *East of Gettysburg*, 111.

[18] McClure, James, *Nine Months in York Town, American Revolutionaries Labor on Pennsylvania's Frontier.* (York, Pa.: York Daily Record/York County Heritage Trust, 2001); McClure, *East of Gettysburg*, 13; Spangler, *My Little War Experience*, 162-63.

[19] Brandt, Dennis, "Database of Civil War Soldiers: York/Adams Counties," YCHT, http://www.yorkheritage.org/la_sc.asp

[20] Stewart, Rev. Alexander M., *Camp, March, and Battlefield: Or, Three Years and a Half with the Army of the Potomac.* (Philadelphia: James B. Rodgers, 1865), 272.

[21] *Philadelphia Inquirer*, May 4, 1861.

[22] *Beaver Weekly Argus*, June 26, 1861; *Philadelphia Times*, Vol. VI, No. 44, 1883; McClure, *East of Gettysburg*, 111; *Philadelphia Press*, June 16, 1863.

[23] Dowley, M. Francis, *History and honorary roll of the Twelfth regiment infantry, N.G.S.N.Y., containing a full and accurate account of the various changes through which the organization has passed since the date of its formation (1847) to the present.* (New York: T. Farrell & Son, 1869).

[24] Cook, Benjamin F., *History of the Twelfth Massachusetts Volunteers (Webster Regiment).* (Boston: Twelfth (Webster) Regiment Association, 1882), 24.

[25] Moss, James W., Sr., *A History of the Civil War as Presented by the Church Advocate*, Vol. 1. (Harrisburg, Pa.: s.n., 2009), 324-25.

[26] Henry Schultz reminiscences courtesy of great-great-grandnephew, David F. Spangler.

[27] Prowell, George R., *History of the Eighty-seventh Regiment, Pennsylvania Volunteers*. (York, Pa.: The Regimental Association, 1903), 16.

[28] *York Gazette*, October 1861.

[29] Samuel Snyder to Scott Mingus, August 26, 2010; Brandt, Dennis W., *From Home Guards to Heroes: The 87th Pennsylvania and Its Civil War Community*. (Columbia, Mo.: University of Missouri Press, 2007), 126-27.

[30] Prowell, *History of the Eighty-seventh Regiment*, 16-17.

[31] Hall, Hillman A.; W.B. Besley; and Gilbert G. Wood, *History of the Sixth New York Cavalry (Second Ira Harris Guard)*. (Worcester, Mass.: Blanchard Press, 1908), 362.

[32] Hiram E. Bixler to Milton Ruby, January 29, 1862. Courtesy of Ruby's great-grandson Joe Brillhart

[33] Harry I. Gladfelter manuscript, Casper Glattfelder Association of America. Courtesy of Dr. Charles Glatfelter.

[34] Jonathan Stayer, Pennsylvania State Archives, to Scott Mingus, May 18, 2009.

[35] Charles and William Hoffman accounts courtesy of descendants Karen Shellenberger and Carol Reidel Norman.

[36] Conn family information courtesy of Jeanie Delouis. Jesse Conn was paroled at Paducah, Kentucky, in May 1865. He died in October 1906. His obituary in the Dresden, Tenn., *Enterprise* notes that Conn "was one of the first settlers in that part on the country and was one of the most substantial, influential men to be found in that whole country."

[37] Ovid Reno information courtesy of his great-grandson's wife, June Lloyd.

[38] *Hartford (CT) Daily Courant*, April 1, 1862.

[39] Albert, Allen D., ed., *History of the Forty-fifth Regiment, Pennsylvania Veteran Volunteer Infantry 1861-1865*. (Williamsport, Pa.: Grit Publishing Co., 1912), 274.

[40] Hiram E. Bixler to Milton Ruby, April 26, 1862, courtesy of Ruby's great-grandson Joe Brillhart

[41] McClure, *East of Gettysburg*, 22.

[42] Kane, Paul J. *A History of St. Paul's Lutheran Church*, (York, Pa.: 1986), 8.

[43] Henry Schultz reminiscences courtesy of great-great-grandnephew, David F. Spangler.

[44] Gibson, John, *History of York County, Pennsylvania: A Biographical History*. (Chicago: F. A. Battey, 1886).

[45] Lloyd, June. Universal York blog, "York Berger Family Musicians Make It Big," Jan. 4, 2009, http://www.yorkblog.com/universal/2009/01/york-berger-family-musicians-m.html.

[46] Charles E. Gotwalt manuscript, *Adventures of a Private in the American Civil War*, YCHT.

[47] Harry I. Gladfelter manuscript, Casper Glattfelder Association of America. Courtesy of Dr. Charles Glatfelter.

[48] Goodhart, Briscoe, *History of the Independent Loudoun Virginia Rangers, U.S. Vol. Cav. (scouts) 1862-65*. (Washington, D.C.: Press of McGill & Wallace, 1896), 69.

[49] Farquhar, Arthur B., and Samuel Crowther, *The First Million: The Hardest: An Autobiography of A. B. Farquhar*. (Garden City, NY: Doubleday, Page & Co., 1922), 71.

[50] Spangler, *My Little War Experience*, 26-27.

[51] Bates, Samuel P., *History of Pennsylvania Volunteers, 1861-5*, Vol. 1 (Harrisburg: B. Singerly, 1869), 880-84; Brandt, "Database of Civil War Soldiers: York/Adams Counties," YCHT.

[52] *East Berlin News Comet*, December 8, 1916; Brandt, "Database of Civil War Soldiers: York/Adams Counties," YCHT. Edward Fisher survived the war and later moved to Indiana. His life proved tragic. After his wife died, he married her sister. When she, too, died, he married a third time but was forced to divorce her because of her "cruel treatment" of him. He wound up with a fourth wife only to later watch his house burn to the ground in 1920.

[53] Files of the Antietam National Battlefield; Brandt, "Database of Civil War Soldiers: York/Adams Counties," YCHT.

[54] *Baltimore Sun*, August 8, 1863. Waring later helped clean up the Gettysburg battlefield. He died there when a loaded musket he picked up suddenly discharged.

[55] *York Democratic Press*, December 28, 1862.

[56] Lydia Jane Larew to Ruth Anna Walker and Phebe Angeline Smith to Ruth Anna Walker, undated but believed to be in September 1862, both courtesy of Elizabeth Valent; *Friends Intelligencer and Journal*, Vol. 56, May 27, 1899.

[57] McClure, *Almost Forgotten*, iv.

[58] Clark, James H., *The Iron-hearted Regiment: being an account of the battles, marches, and gallant deeds performed by the 115th Regiment N.Y. Vols.* (Albany, N.Y.: J. Munsell, 1865), 35.

[59] Lamanda Sweitzer account courtesy of great-granddaughter Gladys M. Smith.

[60] Henry W. Miller account courtesy of Louise Waldman; York U.S. Army Hospital files, YCHT.

[61] *Hartford (CT) Daily Courant*, October 1862.

[62] RG-2, Records Relating to the Civil War Border Claims, York County Damage Claims #6177-89, Records of the Department of the Adjutant General, Pennsylvania State Archives, Harrisburg, Microfilm reels 19-31 (a searchable database is on the York County Heritage Trust's website), Levin Willey claim.

[63] George W. Stahl account courtesy of Ronald A. Reinecker. Stahl later fought at Chancellorsville and Second Fredericksburg before being mustered out in May 1863. He prospered after his tour of duty, serving as a foreman at Hanover's Winebrenner Cannery for the next 36 years.

[64] Brandt, "Database of Civil War Soldiers: York/Adams Counties," YCHT; *Delta Herald and Times*.

[65] United States Army Military History Institute (USAMHI), Carlisle, Pennsylvania.

[66] William G. Ruhl to Sam Ruhl, December 20, 1863. Courtesy of Ron Dise. On August 7, 1864, Ruhl wrote that his late brother Sam's personal effects consisted of "one pocket book, three postage stamps, one pr socks, one neck tie, one locket, one knife and fork, one spoon, one dollar."

[67] Moss, *A History of the Civil War*, 205-206.

[68] Jonathan Schenberger to Mollie A. Schenberger, January 18, 1863. Courtesy of Scott Mingus.

[69] *Columbia Spy*, February 14, 1863.

[70] Brandt, "Database of Civil War Soldiers: York/Adams Counties," YCHT.

[71] Rev. John A. Gere account courtesy of descendant Jill Jordan.

[72] McClure, *East of Gettysburg*, 29; *York Gazette*, March 24, 1863.

[73] The Abraham Lincoln Papers at the Library of Congress, Series 1. General Correspondence. 1833-1916. George W. McElroy, et al. to Abraham Lincoln, Saturday, April 04, 1863.

[74] Grove, June R. and Richard K. Konkel. *"A History of Chanceford Township, York County, Pennsylvania, 1747-1997."* Brogue, Pa.: Brogue Community Lions Club, 1997, 92-93.

[75] *The National Preacher*, April 1863.

[76] Samuel Boll account courtesy of great-great-granddaughter Jean Delouis; Brandt, "Database of Civil War Soldiers: York/Adams Counties," YCHT.

[77] Hotchkiss, Jedediah, *Make Me a Map of the Valley: The Civil War Journal of Stonewall Jackson's Topographer.* (Dallas, Texas: Southern Methodist University Press, 1973), 116.

[78] William B. Barr to Elizabeth Ruby, May 11, 1863. Courtesy of Elizabeth's great-grandson James C. Strickler.

[79] Courtesy of researcher and author Alice L. Luckhardt, who owns a series of wartime correspondence between John and Wesley Wagoner.

[80] *York Gazette*, May 26, 1863.

[81] James Nickel to Barbara Nickel, May 7, 1863. Courtesy of great-granddaughter Kathleen Nickel. The original James Nickel letters are in the YCHT Library/Archives.

[82] Hanover Junction files, YCHT.

[83] Prowell, *History of the Eighty-seventh Regiment*, 227-28.

[84] *Hanover Citizen*, June 18, 1863, as cited in Krepps, John T., *A Strong and Sudden Onslaught: The Cavalry Action at Hanover, Pennsylvania.* (Orrtanna, Pa.: Colecraft Books, 2008), 16.

[85] Wesley Wagoner to John B. Wagoner, June 24, 1863. Courtesy of Alice L. Luckhardt.

[86] Breidenbaugh, E.S., ed., *The Pennsylvania College, Books 1832-1882.* (Philadelphia: Lutheran Publication Society, 1882), 280; Rudisill, James J., *The Days of Our Abraham.* (York, Pa.: The York Printing Co., 1936). Theology student Jesse Koller later pastored churches in Glen Rock and Hanover before becoming administrator of the Lutheran Theological Seminary in Gettysburg.

[87] Phebe Angeline Smith to Most Cherished Sister, June 26, 1863. Courtesy of James W. Brown.

[88] Scott Mingus, Cannonball blog, "The Empty Larder," October 16, 2007, http://www.yorkblog.com/cannonball/2007/10/an_empty_larder.html

[89] Civil War files, library, YCHT; *East Berlin News Comet*, September 17, 1943.

[90] *East Berlin News Comet*, April 24, May 1, and May 8, 1942; York County Damage Claims, Raffensperger deposition.

[91] Hershner, Ronald L., *Cross Roads: A History and Reminiscences.* (York, Pa.: York Graphic Services, 1999).

[92] Trundle, Joseph H., *Gettysburg Described in Two Letters from a Maryland Confederate* (Montgomery County, Md.: Montgomery County Historical Society, 1959), 211-12; *Lynchburg Press*, July 1863.

[93] York County Damage Claims, Albright and Trone depositions. Albright and Trone reported their loss to the state as $895.50, a princely sum for 1863. They never received compensation.

[94] York County Damage Claims, Boadenhamer deposition; Mosby, John S., *Stuart's Cavalry in the Gettysburg Campaign* (New York: Moffat, Yard & Co., 1908), 156.

[95] Sarah J. Adams account courtesy of granddaughter Jeanne M. Saylor. Sarah J. Adams genealogy, "Descendants of Jacob Egg/Eck," Family Tree Maker, http://familytreemaker.genealogy.com/users/w/a/l/Robert-G-Walsh-i-Easton/GENE5-0145.html; *Hanover Spectator*, June 30, 1938.

[96] Undated transcript by P. H. Small of a newspaper article in a 1905 issue of the *York Dispatch* announcing the retirement of engineer George Small upon his 70th birthday; courtesy of Ray Kinard.

[97] George Brodbeck account (from his granddaughter Lettie May Rebert in the 1920s) courtesy of Evelyn Kern of the Spring Grove (Pa.) Historical Society.

[98] Eliza Weaver account (from her daughter Lettie May Rebert in the 1920s) courtesy of Evelyn Kern of the Spring Grove Historical Society.

[99] Overmiller, Howard A., *York, Pennsylvania, In the Hands of the Confederates* (York, Pa.: s. n., undated), 2-4.

[100] Files of the Spring Grove Historical Society.

[101] John Ilyes account courtesy of great-grandson Paul Ilyes, Jr.; York County Damage Claims, J. Krebs and J. Bowman depositions.

[102] Jacob Wiest account courtesy of great-great-grandson Matt Markel. In September 1864, Captain Wiest and a group of local men enrolled in the 200th Pennsylvania Infantry, a nine-month regiment. He and his comrades fought in the siege of Petersburg and the Appomattox Campaign before mustering out of the service in May 1865.

[103] Sprenkle family account courtesy of courtesy of great-great-granddaughter Diane Myers.

[104] Booth, Andrew B., *Records of Louisiana Confederate Soldiers and Louisiana Confederate Commands.* Vol. 1. (Spartanburg, S.C.: Reprint Co., 1984), 141-42; Stephens, Robert Grier, Jr., ed., *Intrepid Warrior: Clement Anselm Evans.* (Dayton, Ohio: Morningside Press, 1992), 218.

[105] *Gettysburg Times*, December 12, 1940. A year later, when he reached the age of 16, Charlie Kline enlisted in the 200th Pennsylvania Infantry. He participated in the siege of Petersburg and took part in the battles of Fort Stedman, Dutch Gap, and Butler's Point. He would witness the surrender of Robert E. Lee's Army of Northern Virginia at Appomattox Court House.

[106] Botterbusch, Ronald, *Blood Roots: An Oral History of Dover, Pennsylvania.* (Dover, Pa.: Dover Area High School, 1978-1981); York County Damage Claims, P. Leib deposition. After the war, Peter Leib filed a damage

claim with Pennsylvania for losses incurred to the invaders. He asked for $765 for the theft of five horses and mules. He did not mention the loss of the shelled corn or his wife's currents.

[107] York County Damage Claims, J. Hoff deposition.

[108] Smith, Waltersdorf, and Spangler accounts courtesy of descendant David F. Spangler. Another great-great-grandfather, George I. Spangler, served in the 200th Pennsylvania.

[109] *Gettysburg Compiler*, June 28, 1911.

[110] McClure, *East of Gettysburg*, 64.

[111] *Legacies: Remembrances of York County Women* (York, Pa: York Branch AAUW), 30.

[112] Botterbusch, *Blood Roots: An Oral History of Dover, Pennsylvania*; York County Damage Claims, Naylor deposition.

[113] Civil War files and *York Pennsylvanian* microfilm collection, YCHT; York County Damage Claims, Loucks, King, Stevens, Schall, and Baisch depositions.

[114] George Munchel account courtesy of great-grandson Chuck Munchel, September; Early's demands are from the files of the York County Heritage Trust and from Prowell's *History of York County*.

[115] James W. Latimer to Bartow Latimer, July 8, 1863, YCHT; *York Gazette* microfilm collection, YCHT.

[116] Richard Miller, *The Pictorial Book of Anecdotes and Incidents of the War of the Rebellion, Civil, Military, Naval and Domestic*. (Hartford, CT: Hartford Publishing Company, 1867).

[117] Prowell, *A History of York County*.

[118] Brillinger and Rutter accounts based upon an interview conducted by George H. Kain II with Sallie Rutter on Thanksgiving Day, 1953, courtesy of George Hay Kain III.

[119] *Gettysburg Star and Sentinel*, November 2, 1918.

[120] John D. Gilbert story courtesy of great-grandson Stephen H. Smith. Earlier that summer, Gilbert had started an apprenticeship with a Columbia carpenter, and one of his first major tasks was to help destroy the bridge. He later became a carpenter in York. Coincidentally, his son-in-law Luther S. Smith became a bridge builder for the Pennsylvania Railroad, and his grandson was among a crew that regularly painted the replacement covered bridge.

[121] David E. Small account courtesy of great-great-granddaughter Liz Winand.

[122] Strickler account drawn from Harrison M. Strickler's post-war memoirs and from family information provided by descendant Morgan G. Brenner.

[123] *Huntingdon (Pa.) Daily News*, July 3, 1923; *The War of the Rebellion: A Compilation of the Official Records of the Union and Confederate Armies,* 70 volumes in 4 series. (Washington, D.C.: United States Government Printing Office, 1880-1901), Series 1, Vol. 27, Part 1, pg. 114.

[124] Jacob Dietz account courtesy of great-great-grandson Gerald Dietz.

[125] Elizabeth Ruby account courtesy of great-grandson Morgan G. Brenner. Samuel Ruby's heirs later filed a damage claim with the state for $250 for a missing roan.

[126] Elmer Snyder remembrances courtesy of Jeanie Delouis.

[127] York County Damage Claims, D. Kohr, J. Myers, S. Dietz, M. Dietz, J. Miller, J. Fidler, J. Brillinger depositions.

[128] William T. Seymour account courtesy of the library of Gettysburg National Military Park.

[129] Dietz account courtesy of great-great-grandson Gerald Dietz.

[130] Gibson, *History of York County, Pennsylvania*, 520; Wiley, Samuel T., *Biographical and Portrait Cyclopedia Nineteenth Congressional District Pennsylvania containing Biographical Sketches of Prominent and Representative Citizens of the District together with an Introductory Historical Sketch*, 1897.

[131] Alfred Jessop to Jonathan Jessop, 1930, collection of YCHT.

[132] Gibson, *History of York County, Pennsylvania*, 209.

[133] Journal of the York Moravian Church, YCHT; general church history courtesy of church secretary Christine Dobron. In 1864, Reverend Smith became chaplain of the 200th Pennsylvania and served until the end of the war.

[134] Courtesy of James Smoker, who currently lives on another of the Meisenhelter family's old farms.

[135] Hamme, R.E., "The History of Kin Mar," typescript / Dr. Jacob Eisenhart account courtesy of Ron Hamme, a great-great-grandson of the Eisenharts, and Zee Kehr, who currently lives in the old Eisenhart house.

[136] Botterbusch, *Blood Roots: An Oral History of Dover, Pennsylvania.*

[137] Driver, Robert J., *The Staunton Artillery – McClanahan's Battery.* (Lynchburg, Va.: H. E. Howard, 1988), 32.

[138] Moul account courtesy of descendant Gregory E. Moul, Sr.

[139] *Hanover Record Herald*, July 1, 1905.

[140] Reta Markish, interview with James McClure, November 2010. The cave might have been an iron mine shaft or small quarry.

[141] *Hanover Record Herald*, July 1, 1905; courtesy of Samuel Forney's great-grandson David Cleutz.

[142] Anthony, William, *Anthony's History of the Battle of Hanover.* (Hanover, Pa.: Self-published, 1945), 136. "Civil War Comes to York County" exhibit, York County Heritage Trust. A virtual website developed concurrently with this exhibit is available at the York Daily Record/Sunday News history site, http://media.ydr.com/interactive/cw-ycht.

[143] Krepps, *A Sudden and Strong Onslaught*, 44.

[144] *O.R.*, Series 1, Vol. 27, Part 1, 992; Anthony, *Anthony's History*, 40.

[145] Lewis Miller files, YCHT.

[146] York County Damage Claims, G. Zinn deposition.

[147] York County Damage Claims, C. Myers deposition.

[148] Jacob Werner account courtesy of great-granddaughter Lamanda Warner Heil via Gerald Dietz.

[149] Wayne Kessler account courtesy of Ray Kinard.

[150] Harry I. Gladfelter manuscript, Casper Glattfelder Association of America. Courtesy of Dr. Charles Glatfelter.

[151] Henry Kessler account, transcribed by descendant Wayne Kessler, courtesy of Ray Kinard.

[152] York County Damage Claims, M. Roth, G. Sprenkle, D. Sprenkle, J. Sprenkle, L. Sprenkle depositions.

[153] Botterbusch, *Blood Roots: An Oral History of Dover, Pennsylvania.*

[154] Botterbusch, *Blood Roots: An Oral History of Dover, Pennsylvania.*

[155] *Hanover Record Herald*, June 30, 1904; Krepps, *A Sudden and Strong Onslaught*, 93.

[156] Henry Miller account courtesy of great-granddaughter Marilyn Geesey Kern; York County Damage Claims, W. Griffith deposition.

[157] York County Damage Claims, I. Laucks deposition.

[158] York County Damage Claims, J. Ritter deposition.

[159] York County Damage Claims, various depositions.

[160] Eli Zinn account courtesy of great-great-great-granddaughter Donna "Dee" Zinn Waugh; Grass, E. Maurice, *Genealogy of the Zinn Family of York & Lancaster Counties, Penna.*, (s.n., 1962), 74. Zinn later filed a $700 damage claim citing that during the night of June 30, Rebels had taken four expensive horses from his stable.

Chapter 3

[161] Harry I. Gladfelter manuscript, Casper Glattfelder Association of America. Courtesy of Dr. Charles Glatfelter.

[162] York County Damage Claims, J. Bowman deposition.

[163] Anna Mary Dise Moody account courtesy of Ron Dise. Anna's son Harold Dise Moody (1890-1971) became a reporter for the *York Gazette & Daily*. He recorded the information and passed it on to Ron Dise.

[164] *Gettysburg Compiler*, June 28, 1911.

[165] *Delta Star*; Anna Macomber Orr account courtesy of Charles Lowe; Harry Boyer account courtesy of Lee Matthew; Mingus, Scott L., Sr., "The 1863 Diary of 4th Cpl. Daniel D. Dillman, Co. A, 27th Pennsylvania Volunteer Militia," in *The Gettysburg Magazine.* (Dayton, Oh: Gatehouse Press), Issue 32, January 2005.

[166] Samuel Shaffer, William Arnold, and Henry Grove accounts courtesy of great-great-granddaughter Nancy Rutledge.

[167] Adam T. Smith account courtesy of descendant Billie Houseman.

[168] Bessie Gingerich Rudisill account courtesy of grandson Gerald Dietz.

[169] Rudisill, *The Days of our Abraham*; McClure, *East of Gettysburg*, 108-110

[170] Gilbert, J. Warren, *The Blue and the Gray: A History of the Conflicts during Lee's Invasion and Battle of Gettysburg*. (Harrisburg; Evangelical Press, 1922), 140.

[171] *Adams Sentinel*, July 221, 1863.

[172] Farquhar, *The First Million: The Hardest*, 91-92.

[173] Harry I. Gladfelter manuscript, Casper Glattfelder Association of America. Courtesy of Dr. Charles Glatfelter.

[174] Boritt, Gabor, *The Gettysburg Gospel: The Lincoln Speech That Nobody Knows*. (New York: Simon & Schuster, 2006), 66.

[175] *History of the 121st Regiment Pennsylvania Volunteers*. (Philadelphia: Catholic Standard and Times, 1906),139-40.

[176] Blum, Edward J., and W. Scott Poole, eds., *Vale of Tears: New Essays on Religion and Reconstruction*. (Macon, Ga.: Mercer University Press, 2005), 196-97; Mount St. Mary's College Archives, Emmitsburg, Md.

[177] *Harrisburg Telegraph*, September 20, 1907.

[178] Jacob Wagner account courtesy of courtesy of great-great-granddaughter Marcia Forbes.

[179] Botterbusch, *Blood Roots: An Oral History of Dover, Pennsylvania*.

[180] Felix M. Drais account courtesy of great-grandson Randy Drais. Felix and his wife purchased the 178-acre Granite Hill Farm near Fairfield, before retiring to a house they built in Gettysburg. The transplanted Buckeye and several family members are buried in Gettysburg's Evergreen Cemetery.

[181] *Columbia Spy*, March 2, 1866.

[182] Wesley Wagoner to John B. Wagoner. July 8, 1863. Courtesy of Alice L. Luckhardt. A grieving John tried unsuccessfully to claim Wesley's body and bring it back home to Hanover. Wesley Wagoner (spelled Wagner in some records) remained buried with many other soldiers in and around the grounds of hospital in Silkmound (General Hospital #21 in Richmond). He may have been reinterred later in the Richmond National Cemetery. John G. Wagoner himself had less than two years to live. He died March 18, 1865, at his home in Hanover.

[183] Gladfelter, Armand, *The Flowering of the Codorus Palatinate*. (North Codorus Township, Pa.: Sesquicentennial Commission, 1988), 181.

Chapter 4

[184] *Hanover Spectator*, July 11, 1863.

[185] Albert, Allen D., *History of the Forty-fifth Regiment Pennsylvania Veteran Volunteer Infantry, 1861-1865*. (Williamsport, Pa.: Grit Publishing Co., 1912), 395-96.

[186] *Philadelphia Public Ledger*, November 20, 1863.

[187] *Hanover Spectator*, November 27, 1863.

[188] McClure, *East of Gettysburg,* 126.

[189] Prowell, *History of the 87th Pennsylvania*, 105.

[190] Prowell, *History of the 87th Pennsylvania*, 109.

[191] Gibson, *A History of York County*.

[192] *York Pennsylvanian*, various issues, March 1864. Halloway's Pills were perhaps the best known "patent medicine" of the era, having been introduced in1837. Inventor Thomas Halloway claimed his pills and ointment could "cure anything." The formulation contained opium.

[193] McClure, *East of Gettysburg, 152; York Daily Record,* Oct. 12, 2010.

[194] Elijah Berry service records courtesy of Rebecca Anstine.

[195] Brandt, "Database of Civil War Soldiers: York/Adams Counties," YCHT.

[196] Prowell, *History of the 87th Pennsylvania*, 117.

[197] Josephus Burger account courtesy of Mike McAdams.

[198] Albert, *History of the Forty-fifth Regiment*, 286.

[199] Levi Bowen diary entries courtesy of great-grandson Philip Dodson.

[200] Prowell, *History of the 87th Pennsylvania*, 141.

[201] Hiram E. Bixler to Milton Ruby, July 3, 1864, courtesy of Ruby's great-grandson Joe Brillhart

[202] Charles E. Gotwalt manuscript, *Adventures of a Private in the American Civil War*, YCHT.

[203] Templeton B. Hurst diary, Manuscript Group 6, Pennsylvania State Archives, Harrisburg.

[204] Henry Ridebaugh account courtesy of great-great-granddaughter Gloria Miller. In some other accounts his name is spelled Radebaugh. Henry Kottcamp and Milton Shenberger accounts courtesy of great-granddaughter Marilyn Ruth. Shenberger enlisted August, 27, 1864, as a private in company in the 3rd Pennsylvania Calvary. He later fathered 14 children.

[205] Brandt, "Database of Civil War Soldiers: York/Adams Counties," YCHT.

[206] Alfred S. Bond 1864 diary courtesy of great-grandson Rodney Bond, transcribed and annotated Aug.-Nov. 2010 by Scott Mingus

[207] Prowell, *History of the 87th Pennsylvania*, 186, 292; Brandt, Dennis W., *From Home Guards to Heroes: The 87th Pennsylvania and Its Civil War Community*. (Columbia, Mo.: University of Missouri Press, 2007), 204. Lt. John F. Spangler left a widow and two children.

[208] William Harris account courtesy of great-grandson Dean M. Messerly.

[209] USAMHI, Carlisle.

[210] *York Sunday News*, February 7, 1960.

[211] Daniel Roads and Emmanuel Harman to Wm. Pleany, September 15, 1864. Courtesy of James W. Brown.

[212] "Your obedient servant" to Maj. Jno. S. Schultze, October 24, 1864. Courtesy of Scott Mingus.

[213] Alfred S. Bond 1864 diary courtesy of Rodney Bond.

[214] Gemmill, Joseph S. Gemmill to Dear Sister (Martha Gemmill), December 19, 1864. Courtesy of the family of Elsie Brose through Sharon Ebaugh.

[215] Henry C. Springer account courtesy of his great-great-grandson Ralph Roberts.

[216] Samuel R. Smith to Dear Wife, beloved wife, December 25, 1864. Courtesy of descendant Lester M. Laucks, Jr. A copy is in the Center Square Museum of the Red Lion (Pa.) Historical Society. Private Smith is buried in the City Pont National Cemetery near Hopewell, Virginia. According to Jan Barnhart of RLHS, "Upon Samuel's death, his widow was left to raise her family alone. She never remarried and died in Bittersville on March 12, 1909, in the same house in which she and her husband were married. She left 122 descendants at the time of her passing. She was buried in the Salem Church Cemetery in Lower Windsor Township."

[217] Alfred S. Bond 1864 diary courtesy of Rodney Bond.

[218] Hanover Junction files, YCHT.

[219] Zachariah Shepp account courtesy of Jeanie Delouis.

[220] USAMHI, Carlisle.

[221] Brandt, "Database of Civil War Soldiers: York/Adams Counties," YCHT; Gravestone, Filey's Christ Lutheran Church, Monaghan Township, York County, Pa.

[222] Prowell, *History of the 87th Pennsylvania*, 308. Prowell spells the name as Keasey.

[223] Henry Schultz reminiscences courtesy of great-great-grandnephew, David F. Spangler.

[224] Lewis Miller files, YCHT.

[225] John Stoner Beidler 1865 diary, transcribed by descendant Charles Wilcox, YCHT; *Hanover Spectator*, April 11, 1865.

[226] Beidler diary, YCHT; Prowell, *History of the 87th Pennsylvania*, 222.

[227] Richard K. Konkel, "A Civil War Love Letter," *Chanceford Clarion*, June 4, 1999. Courtesy of June R. Grove.

[228] Taylor, Robert A., ed., *A Pennsylvanian in Blue: The Civil War Diary of Thomas Beck Walton*. (Shippensburg, Pa.: Burd Street Press, 1995), 8.

[229] Rudisill, James J., *The Days of Our Abraham*.

[230] Hershner, Ronald L. *Cross Roads, A History and Reminiscenses.* (York, Pa.: York Graphics Services, 1999), 33.

[231] Lizzie Hamme account courtesy of Terry Koller.

[232] McClure, *East of Gettysburg*, 145; Files of York County Heritage Trust.

[233] McClure, *East of Gettysburg*, 146; Beidler diary, YCHT.

[234] *Harrisburg Patriot and Union*, April 22, 1865; *Apprise* magazine, April 1990.

[235] Josephus Burger account courtesy of Mike McAdams.

[236] Evan G. Gemmill to Dear Sister (Martha Gemmill), May 15, 1865. Courtesy of the family of Elsie Brose through Sharon Ebaugh.

[237] Thompson, Bradford F., *History of the 112th Regiment Illinois Volunteer Infantry, in the Great War of the Rebellion 1862-1865.* (Toulon, Illinois: Stark County News Office, 1885), 332, 347.

[238] Eslinger, Augustus N., *Local History of Dillsburg, Pa.* (Dillsburg, Pa.: Dillsburg Bulletin Print, 1902), 25.

[239] Muster rolls of Company A, 100th Pennsylvania Infantry; National Archives. Reiley, a native of Washington County, ironically had joined the army as a paid substitute for a draftee.

[240] Hershner, *Cross Roads, A History and Reminiscenses.*

[241] *Philadelphia Press*, August 9, 1865; Sharf, J. Thomas, *History of Western Maryland.* (Philadelphia, 1882; reprinted by the Regional Publishing Co. of Baltimore, 1968), 1255-56; *Idaho County Free Press*, October 18, 1889, and January 10, 1890.

[242] W.G. Ruhl to John Ruhl, October 15, 1865. Courtesy of Ron Dise.

[243] Albert, *History of the Forty-fifth Regiment*, 302-303.

[244] York County Damage Claims, G. Sprenkle deposition; 1890 *Congressional Record*.

[245] James McClure, *East of Gettysburg*, 133, 152.

[246] Benjamin Grim account courtesy of his great-granddaughter Nancy E. Hoskin Laird.

[247] James Nickel to Barbara Nickel, June 21, 1865. Courtesy of great-granddaughter Kathleen Nickel. Original Nickel letters in YCHT Library/Archives.

[248] Brandt, "Database of Civil War Soldiers: York/Adams Counties," YCHT; *Builders and Heroes.* (York, Pa.: York Daily Record and York Dispatch/York Sunday News), 158.

[249] Gibbs, James M., *History of the First Battalion Pennsylvania Six Months Volunteers and 187th Pennsylvania Regiment Pennsylvania Volunteer Infantry.* (Harrisburg, Pa.: 187th Regiment Survivors Association, 1905), 159.

[250] Gibson, *History of York County*, 620; *York Gazette*, May 13, 1902, and May 11, 1906; Fourhman-Shaull, Lila, *A Walking Tour of Civil War Era: Residents at Prospect Hill Cemetery, York, Pa.,* (York, Pa.: York County Heritage Trust, 2005); James McClure, York Town Square blog, "Tomb of unknown soldier in York, too," March 10, 2007, www.yorkblog.com/yorktownsquare/2007/03/post-29.html.

[251] *Builders and Heroes.* (York, Pa.: York Daily Record and York Dispatch/York Sunday News), 170.

[252] *Glen Rock Item,* April 19, 1895. Courtesy of Charles H. Glatfelter. Research by Wayne Motts of the Adams County Historical Society has not yielded any "Robert Campbell" in the roster of the 7th Virginia, which never entered York County. Similar research by Scott Mingus shows no one by that name in the 35th Battalion, Virginia Cavalry, which did visit Hanover Junction and approach Glen Rock.

[253] Fourhman-Shaull, *A Walking Tour of Civil War Era.*

[254] Gilbert, Melvin Lester, *The Gilberts of Conejohela Valley*, privately printed, 1980), 94-101. Other information courtesy of great-grandnephew William B. Anstine, Jr. and from granddaughter Martha Fellenbaum.

[255] James McClure, York Town Square blog, "Headline: 'Beards on Parade at Gettyburg (Battle) Field,'" Aug. 14, 2008, www.yorkblog.com/yorktownsquare/2008/08/post-187.html.

[256] Niess, Ann Small, *Elmwood House.* (Naples, Fla., 2007).

[257] Robert Mansberger interview with James McClure, November 2010.

[258] Robert Doll interview with Scott Mingus, November 2010.

Chapter 5

[259] Frazer, Persifor, Jr., "Philadelphia City Cavalry, Service of the First Troop Philadelphia City Cavalry during June and July, 1863," *Journal of the Military Service Institution of the United States*, Vol. 43 (1908), 289.

[260] Robert Crane deposition, Columbia Historic Preservation Society, Columbia, Pa.

[261] John Q. Denney deposition, Columbia Historic Preservation Society, Columbia, Pa.

[262] Farquhar, *The First Million*, 62-65.

[263] McClure, *Almost Forgotten*, 21.

[264] George K. Bratton presumably to his cousin, June 16, 1863. Courtesy of Phil Dodson.

[265] James W. Latimer to Bartow Latimer, June 15, 1863, courtesy of YCHT. These letters on the web at the York Daily Record/Sunday News history site: http://media.ydr.com/interactive/cw-ycht/jlatimer.html. An extensive diary providing another account of the occupation by Cassandra Small can be found in James McClure's *East of Gettysburg*.

[266] James W. Latimer to Bartow Latimer, June 18, 1863. Courtesy of YCHT.

[267] James W. Latimer to Bartow Latimer, June 24, 1863. Courtesy of YCHT.

[268] James W. Latimer to Bartow Latimer, morning June 30, 1863. Courtesy of YCHT.

[269] James W. Latimer to Bartow Latimer, evening June 30, 1863. Courtesy of YCHT.

[270] James W. Latimer to Bartow Latimer, July 8, 1863. Courtesy of YCHT.

[271] Smedley, Robert C., *History of the Underground Railroad in Chester and the Neighboring Counties of Pennsylvania*. (Lancaster, Pa.: John A. Heistand, 1883), 45-46.

[272] Gordon, John B., *Reminiscences of the Civil War*. (New York/Atlanta: Charles Scribner's Sons, 1903), 141, 143, 148.

[273] Patriot Daughters of Lancaster County, *Hospital Scenes After the Battle of Gettysburg July, 1863*. (Lancaster, Pa.: Daily Inquirer, 1864), 8.

[274] *Philadelphia Times*, Jan. 9, 1883.

[275] Robert Gemmill account courtesy of descendant Gene Gemmill.

[276] Robert I. Boyington, *Army Life Journal (1861-1865)*, Wilbur E. Ford Collection, used with permission of Robert W. Ford.

[277] "Rev. Mr. Niles' Address, on the Occasion of President Lincoln's Funeral Obsequies, in York, Pa." April 25, 1865. York County Heritage Trust files.

Afterword

[278] Adapted from a *York Sunday News* column, Nov. 11, 2010.

Chronology

[279] Chronology adapted from that found in James McClure's *East of Gettysburg*.

Further Reading

Books, Pamphlets, and Magazine Articles

Albert, Allen D., ed., *History of the Forty-fifth Regiment, Pennsylvania Veteran Volunteer Infantry 1861-1865.* Williamsport, Pa.: Grit Publishing Co., 1912.

Anthony, William, *Anthony's History of the Battle of Hanover.* Hanover, Pa.: Self-published, 1945.

Birnstock, H.O., *Wrightsville's Book of Facts: A Souvenir Inspired by the Sixtieth Anniversary of an Event of the Civil War Which Occurred at Wrightsville, York County, Pennsylvania.* York, Pa.: Historical Commission of Wrightsville, 1923.

Van Baman, M.L., "Confederate Invasion of York Just Fifty Years Ago Today," *York Gazette,* June 28, 1913.

Botterbusch, Ronald, *Blood Roots: An Oral History of Dover, Pennsylvania.* Dover, Pa.: Dover Area High School, 1978-1981.

Brandt, Dennis W., *From Home Guards to Heroes: The 87th Pennsylvania and Its Civil War Community.* Columbia, Mo.: University of Missouri Press, 2007.

Butcher, Scott D., *Civil War Walking Tour of York, PA.* York, Pa.: York County Heritage Trust, 2006.

Clarke, Anna Mumper, "Confederate Spies in Dillsburg." Dillsburg, Pennsylvania: Northern York County Historical Society, 2003. From a typescript interview by James J. Logan with Mrs. Clarke in August 1930.

Eslinger, Augustus N., *Local History of Dillsburg, Pa.* Dillsburg, Pa.: Dillsburg Bulletin Print, 1902.

Farquhar, Arthur Briggs, "The Heart of America," in *McClure's,* Vol. 54, No. 2, April 1922.

Farquhar, Arthur B., and Samuel Crowther, *The First Million: The Hardest: An Autobiography of A. B. Farquhar.* Garden City, NY: Doubleday, Page & Co., 1922.

Fourhman-Shaull, Lila, *A Walking Tour of Civil War-Era Residents at Prospect Hill Cemetery, York, Pa.* York, Pa.: York County Heritage Trust, 2005.

Gibbs, James M., *History of the First Battalion Pennsylvania Six Months Volunteers and 187th Pennsylvania Regiment Pennsylvania Volunteer Infantry.* Harrisburg, Pa.: 187th Regiment Survivors Association, 1905.

Gibson, John, *History of York County, Pennsylvania: A Biographical History.* Chicago: F. A. Battey, 1886.

Gilbert, Melvin Lester, *The Gilberts of Conejohela Valley,* privately printed, 1980.

Glatfelter, Dr. Charles, *The Story of Jefferson Codorus, Pennsylvania,* Codorus, Pa.: Jefferson Community Centennial Inc., 1966.

Grove, June A. and Richard K. Konkel, eds., *A History of Chanceford Township, York County, Pennsylvania, 1747-1997.* Brogue, Pa.: Brogue Community Lions Club, 1997.

Hall, Clifford J. and John P. Lehn, *York County and the World War: being a war history of York and York County and a record of the services rendered to their country by the people of this community.* York, Pa.: s.n., 1920 (contains a chapter on York in the Civil War).

Hall, George D., *Wrightsville Centennial Celebration of the Invasion of Wrightsville by the Forces of General Robert E. Lee and the Burning of the Bridge, June 28-29, 1963.* York, Pa.: Self-published, 1963.

Hershner, Ronald L., *Cross Roads: A History and Reminiscences.* York, Pa.: York Graphic Services, 1999.

Jezierski, John Vincent, *Enterprising Images, The Goodridge Brothers, African-American*

Photographers, 1847-1922. Detroit, Mi.: Wayne State University Press, 2000.

Kauffman, Charles Fahs, *History of Dover Township*, volumes 1 and 2. York County, Pa.: 1961.

Kauffman, George P., *York and York County and the Civil War, from Glimpses of Historic York*. York, Pa.: typescript manuscript, undated, 1970s.

Krepps, John T., *A Strong and Sudden Onslaught: The Cavalry Action at Hanover, Pennsylvania*. Orrtanna, Pa.: Colecraft Books, 2008.

Lehman, Donald I., Sr., *Wrightsville: Gateway to the West*. York, Pa.: Historic Wrightsville Association, 1976.

Lloyd, June, *Faith and Family, Pennsylvania German Heritage in York County Area Fraktur*. York, Pa.: York County Heritage Trust, 2001.

McClure, James, *Almost Forgotten: A Glimpse of Black History in York County, Pa*. York, Pa.: York County Heritage Trust / York Daily Record, 2002.

-----------------------, *East of Gettysburg: A Gray Shadow Crosses York County, Pa*. York, Pa: York County Heritage Trust / York Daily Record, 2003.

McLaughlin, Alycia and Harry J. McLaughlin, *The Gettysburg Campaign in York County*. York, Pa.: Susquehanna Broadcasting Co., 1986.

Mellander, G.A. and Carl E. Hatch, *York County's Presidential Elections*. York, Pa.: The Strine Press, 1972.

Mingus, Scott L., Sr., *Flames Beyond Gettysburg: The Confederate Expedition to the Susquehanna River, June 1863*. El Dorado Hills, Ca.: Savas Beatie, 2011.

---------------------, *The Louisiana Tigers in the Gettysburg Campaign*. Baton Rouge: Louisiana State University Press, 2009.

---------------------, "The 1863 Diary of 4th Cpl. Daniel D. Dillman, Co. A, 27th Pennsylvania Volunteer Militia," in *The Gettysburg Magazine*. Dayton, Oh: Gatehouse Press, Issue 32, January 2005.

---------------------, "J.E.B. Stuart Rides through Dover, Pennsylvania," in *The Gettysburg Magazine*. Dayton, Ohio: Gatehouse Press, Issue 38, January 2008.

---------------------, "Jenkins' Raid through Northwestern York County," in *The Gettysburg Magazine*. Dayton, Ohio: Gatehouse Press, Issue 44, January 2011.

---------------------, "Jubal Early Takes York," in *The Gettysburg Magazine*. Dayton, Oh: Gatehouse Press, Issue 37, July 2007.

---------------------, "White's Comanches on the Warpath at Hanover Junction," in *The Gettysburg Magazine*. Dayton, Ohio: Gatehouse Press, Issue 42, January 2010.

Mingus, Scott L, Jr. and Thomas M. Mingus, *Human Interest Stories of the Civil War*. Gettysburg, Pa.: Ten Roads Publishing, 2010.

Moss, James W., Sr., *A History of the Civil War as Presented by The Church Advocate*, 2 volumes. Harrisburg, Pa.: self published, 2010.

Neubaum, Victor A., *Our Boys: Northern York County in the Civil War*. Dillsburg, Pa.: s. n., 1989.

Nye, Wilbur S., and John G. Redman, *Farthest East*. Wrightsville, Pa.: Wrightsville Centennial Committee, 1963.

Overmiller, Howard A., *York, Pennsylvania, In the Hands of the Confederates* (York, Pa.: s. n., undated. Copy in the collection of the York County Heritage Trust.

Prowell, George Reeser, *History of the Eighty-seventh Regiment, Pennsylvania Volunteers*. York, Pa.: The Regimental Association, 1903.

----------------------------, *History of York County, Pennsylvania*. Chicago: J. H. Beers, 1907.

----------------------------, "The Invasion of Pennsylvania by the Confederates Under Robert E. Lee and Its Effect Upon Lancaster and York Counties," in *Historical Papers and Addresses of the Lancaster County Historical Society*, Vol. 29, No. 4 (1925), 41-51.

----------------------------, *Encounter at Hanover: Prelude to Gettysburg*. Gettysburg, Pa.: Historical Publication Committee of the Hanover Chamber of Commerce, Times and News Publishing, 1962.

Robison, Gerald Austin, Jr., *Confederate Operations in York County*. Millersville, Pa.: graduate thesis, Millersville College, 1965.

Rohrbaugh, Carroll G., Jr., *Operation Underground Railroad in York County*. Gettysburg, Pa.: Gettysburg College, 1953.

Rudisill, James J., *The Days of Our Abraham*. York, Pa.: The York Printing Co., 1936.

Rummel, George A., III, *Cavalry on the Roads to Gettysburg: Kilpatrick at Hanover and Hunterstown*. Shippensburg, Pa.: White Mane, 2000.

Sheets, Georg R., *To the Setting of the Sun: The Story of York*. York, Pa.: Windsor Publications, 1981.

Snell, Mark A., *From First to Last, the Life of Major General William B. Franklin*. New York: Fordham University Press, 2002.

-------------------,"'If They Would Know What I Know It Would Be Pretty Hard to Raise One Company': Recruiting, the Draft, and Society's Response in York County, Pennsylvania, 1861-1865," in *Union Soldiers and the Northern Home Front: Wartime Experiences, Postwar Adjustments*, edited by Paul A. Cimbala and Randall M. Miller. New York: Fordham University Press, 2002.

-------------------, "A Northern County Goes to War: Recruiting, the Draft, and Social Response in York County, Pa., 1861-1865," Master's Thesis, Rutgers University, 1987; York County Heritage Trust archives.

Spangler, Edward Webster, *My Little War Experience: With Historical Sketches and Memorabilia*. York, Pa.: York Daily Publishing Co., 1904.

Vosburg, Brent L., "Cavalry Clash at Hanover," *America's Civil War*, January 1998.

Wittenberg, Eric J. and J. David Petruzzi, *Plenty of Blame to Go Around: Jeb Stuart's Controversial Ride to Gettysburg*. El Dorado Hills, Ca.: Savas Beatie, 2006.

Websites

Dennis R. Brandt's York County Civil War Soldiers database at YCHT
Scott Mingus's York County Civilian Damage Claims database at YCHT
        (Both at http://www.yorkheritage.org/la_sc.asp)
Scott D. Butcher's Windows into York blog (www.yorkblog.com/window)
June Lloyd's Universal York blog (www.yorkblog.com/universal)
Jim McClure's York Town Square blog (http://yorktownsquare.com)
Scott Mingus's Cannonball blog (www.yorkblog.com/cannonball)

Index

Ensminger, Sam 136
Eslinger, A.N. 118
Evans, Clement 59
Everett, Edward 99
Ewell, Richard S. 81, 139

Fairview Township, Pa. 34, 104, 111
Fallon, James W. 73
Falmouth, Va. 39
Farquhar, Arthur Briggs 17, 31, 89-90, 133-134, 141
Farmers, Pa. 58, 142
Fawn A.M.E. Cemetery 150
Fawn Grove, Pa. 55
Fawn Township, Pa. 101, 106, 138, 150
Fayetteville, Pa. 57
Fellenbaum, Martha 160
Felton, Pa. 98
Fetrow, J.R. 135
Fidler, Jonas 69
Fifth Army Corps 146
Filey's Church. See Christ Lutheran (Filey's) Church, Monaghan Township, Pa.
Fink, Harry 45-46
Fisher, Edward 33
Fisher, Henry L. 98
Fisher, Mary 62, 152
Fisher, Mary Cadwell 18, 19-20, 29, 48, 61-62, 88-89, 101, 144-145
Fisher, Robert J. 18, 62, 152
Five-Mile House 60
Fix, Francis 128
Fix, Jean 128
Florence, S.C. 104
Ford's Theater 115
Forney, John 75, 87
Forney, Sam 75
Forrest, Nathan Bedford 26
Fort Albany 103
Fort Delaware 26
Fort Donaldson 26

Fort Monroe 102, 106, 107, 110
Fort Morgan 108
Fort Pickens 26
Fort Pulaski 27
Fort Stedman, Battle of 113, 114, 123, 135
Fort Sumter 11, 13-14, 17, 125
Fort Wagner, Battle of 95, 99
Franklin Township, Pa. 54, 80
Fredericksburg, Battle of 17, 32, 33, 38, 40, 50, 91, 105, 106, 135
Fredericksburg, Va. 118
Frederick, Md. 107, 108
French, William H. 60, 72, 79
Frey, William 83
Freystown, Pa. 83
Frick, Jacob G. 66, 131-132
Fugitive Slave Law 11, 12
Fulton, Andrew Jackson 123
Fulton, David 123
Fulton, Elizabeth 123
Fulton, Margaret Patterson 123

Gambrill, Thomas 113
Garber, Asher W. 73
Gartman, Alfred 144
Gatchellville, Pa. 150
Gates, Horatio 18
Geesey, Samuel Wesley 114
Geiselman farm 75
Gemmill, Evan G. 118
Gemmill, John 116
Gemmill, Joseph 111
Gemmill, Martha J. 111, 118
Gemmill, Mary Ann 118
Gemmill, Robert 116
Gemmill, Robert Beniak Jr. 145-146
Gere, John A. 41
Gettysburg Campaign 18, 25, 26, 28, 51, 53, 54, 60, 73, 80, 82, 85-95, 96, 97, 98, 122, 125, 126, 127, 128, 131, 143, 145-146, 151

About the Authors

Scott L. Mingus Sr. has written *Flames Beyond Gettysburg: The Confederate Expedition to the Susquehanna River, June 1863*; *The Louisiana Tigers in the Gettysburg Campaign*; six other Civil War books, and numerous magazine articles. He is a sanctioned Civil War guide for the York County Heritage Trust and writes the Cannonball Civil War blog for the *York Daily Record*.

He is a scientist and executive in the paper and printing industry and is a graduate of Miami University in Oxford, Ohio.

James McClure is the author of *East of Gettysburg: A Gray Shadow Crosses York County, Pa.*, *Almost Forgotten: A Glimpse at Black History in York County, Pa.*, and three other books on York County history.

He earned a master's degree in American Studies at Penn State Harrisburg and is editor of the *York Daily Record/Sunday News*.

Other Books by Colecraft

Civil War Artillery at Gettysburg by Philip M. Cole

Command and Communication Frictions in the Gettysburg Campaign by Philip M. Cole

Human Interest Stories of the Gettysburg Campaign
by Scott L. Mingus, Sr.

Human Interest Stories of the Gettysburg Campaign - Vol.2
by Scott L. Mingus, Sr.

Human Interest Stories from Antietam
by Scott L. Mingus, Sr.

A Concise Guide to the Artillery at Gettysburg
by Gregory A. Coco

Remarkable Stories of the Lincoln Assassination
by Michael Kanazawich

A Strong and Sudden Onslaught: The Cavalry Action at Hanover, Pennsylvania by John T. Krepps

The Campaign and Battle of Gettysburg by Col. G. J. Fiebeger

YOU'LL BE SCARED. Sure—you'll be scared. Fear, Stress, and Coping in the Civil War by Philip M. Cole

For Ordering Information:

Visit us at colecraftbooks.com

or

e-mail us at: colecraftbooks@embarqmail.com

Wholesale orders may be placed with our distributing partner:

Ingram Book Company
One Ingram Blvd.
La Vergne, TN 37086

Toll-Free Phone: (800) 937-8200
E-mail: customer.service@ingrambook.com

CPSIA information can be obtained at www.ICGtesting.com
Printed in the USA
BVOW032002210512

290733BV00006B/5/P